EX LIBRIS

SHOPGIRLS

THE TRUE STORY OF LIFE BEHIND THE COUNTER

Pamela Cox and Annabel Hobley

HUTCHINSON
LONDON

Published by Hutchinson 2014

2 4 6 8 10 9 7 5 3 1

Copyright © Pamela Cox and Annabel Hobley 2014
Copyright © Betty TV Ltd 2014

Pamela Cox and Annabel Hobley and Betty TV Ltd have asserted their right under the
Copyright, Designs and Patents Act 1988 to be identified as the authors of this work.

 This book is based on the television series *Shopgirls: The True Story of
Life Behind the Counter* produced by betty for BBC Two.

BBC and the BBC logo are trade marks of the BBC Broadcasting Corporation and are
used under licence. Logo © BBC 1996.

First published in Great Britain in 2014 by
Hutchinson
Random House, 20 Vauxhall Bridge Road,
London SW1V 2SA

www.randomhouse.co.uk

Addresses for companies within The Random House Group Limited can be found at:
www.randomhouse.co.uk/offices.htm

The Random House Group Limited Reg. No. 954009

A CIP catalogue record for this book is available from the British Library

ISBN 9780091954468

The Random House Group Limited supports the Forest Stewardship
Council® (FSC®), the leading international forest-certification
organisation. Our books carrying the FSC label are printed on FSC®-
certified paper. FSC is the only forest-certification scheme supported
by the leading environmental organisations, including Greenpeace.
Our paper procurement policy can be found at:
www.randomhouse.co.uk/environment

MIX
Paper from
responsible sources
FSC
www.fsc.org   FSC® C016897

Typeset by SX Composing DTP, Rayleigh Essex
Printed and bound in Great Britain by Clays, St Ives PLC

Dedicated to
Leonore Davidoff
and
Alice and Dominic O'Malley

CONTENTS

LIST OF ILLUSTRATIONS

Chapter Illustrations

1. Shopgirls at Marks and Spencer Ltd, 1890s. The Marks & Spencer Company Archive.
2. 'A Portable Shop Seat', *The Girl's Own Paper*, 1880. Public Domain.
3. Fashionably dressed shopgirl. Courtesy 18 Stafford Terrace, Royal Borough of Kensington and Chelsea.
4. Suffragettes with smashed shop windows, 1912. Heritage Images/Getty Images.
5. Selfridges shopgirls on duty, 1922. Reproduced by kind permission: Selfridges Archive.
6. 'West End Shop Girls' Strike', 1920. Courtesy *Daily Mail*.
7. Bombed-blasted shop, *c.*1940. Popperfoto/Getty Images.
8. Shop assistant Valerie Allen, 1969. Mirrorpix.

Plate Section Illustrations

1. Wisbech, 1854. Courtesy of the Wisbech & Fenland Museum.
2. Jenner's department store, 1895. © RCAHMS (Harry Bedford Lemere Collection) Licensor: www.rcahms.gov.uk.
3. The Burlington Arcade, *c.*1910. Getty Images.
4. Anderson and McAuley's, early 1900s. National Museums Northern Ireland.
5. *The Shop Girl* musical comedy, 1895. Courtesy Betty TV.
6. 'Miss Bondfield On Tour', *The Shop Assistant*, July 1898

PROLOGUE

'And there is a girl behind the counter too – I would as soon
have her true history as the hundred and fiftieth life of
Napoleon or seventieth study of Keats.'

Virginia Woolf, *A Room of One's Own*, 1929

In 1900, a quarter of a million women worked in shops. By the
mid 1960s, the number was over a million, nearly one fifth of
the country's female workforce. Today, women are such familiar
figures behind the till, the counter and in the boardrooms of retail
chains that it's hard to imagine shoplife without them. Yet there
was a time, not so long ago, when they were rare. This is the story
of shopgirls and the part they have played, from the Victorian age
through to the present day, in Britain's retail revolution.

Napoleon's famous line – often quoted in the many biographies
of him bemoaned by Virginia Woolf – that Britain was 'a nation
of shopkeepers' was meant as an insult. To him, we were a country
powered by nothing more than shallow commerce, not grand designs.

But British shopkeeping went hand in hand with growth in trade and empire. By the early nineteenth century, British commerce was booming and the country was indeed experiencing a huge growth in shops of every kind. And, as Woolf may have guessed, in becoming a 'nation of shopkeepers', we had come to rely on a growing, but unsung, army of shopgirls.

Coined in the 1820s, the very word 'shopgirl' was new: a new term to describe a very new kind of employee, and a term that would be used for the next 150 years. The Industrial Revolution had created jobs for legions of additional workers but they only had jobs if people bought the things they made. Britain's prosperity depended on consumers just as much as on manufacturers. As people left the countryside and crowded into towns and cities, wages rose and even the most meagre income had to buy basic provisions. More demand meant more shops, and more shops meant a different kind of shop assistant. From small local outlets to large drapery stores, proprietors started to see selling as a job for the girls and no longer just for the boys.

The story of British shopgirls is one woven deep into the fabric of our country's history and yet, until now, historians have allowed them to fall through the cracks. They have remained 'behind the counter' of history − playing a vital part in the stories of work, consumer culture, living standards and politics but rarely mentioned. We hope this book changes that.

In contrast, the writers of Victorian music hall songs, newspaper columns, plays and novels were obsessed with shopgirls. The label itself was always double-edged, quickly becoming a shorthand for both the lowering effects of mass consumer culture and, at the same time, its guilty pleasures and attractions. Certain kinds of shopgirls became the stuff of fantasy: who were these girls behind the counter in their demure black silk dresses and what were they really selling? Émile Zola's classic 1883 novel, *The Ladies' Paradise*, is a torrid tale of the temptations posed by Paris's new and decadent department stores. His lead shopgirl is ingénue Denise Baudu, a provincial draper's assistant. The story sees her battling through the store's moral maze to find her eventual reward, not only in a promotion, but also in a socially mobile marriage to the boss, Octave Mouret, having steadfastly resisted his earlier efforts to seduce her.

Zola based his novel on the Bon Marché, one of Europe's first and finest department stores. As we shall discover, by the time the book was published, Britain also boasted several stores of a similar scale, from Whiteley's and Harrods in London, to Kendals in Manchester and Jenners in Edinburgh. These large stores, with their opulent designs, seductive displays and luxury goods, seemed to be far removed from the two other worlds that the Victorians held most dear: home and work. Shops like these were places for spending, distinct from the more 'noble' arts of homemaking or manufacturing. Spending was the antithesis of 'working', however much thought, skill, planning and budgeting went into it. It was an activity of leisure and in particular of women's leisure, regardless of whether the items bought on a given excursion were 'essential' provisions from the grocer's or butcher's or more 'frivolous' purchases from the milliner's, confectioner's or draper's.

Shopgirls' lives have also been played out on screen in several period dramas. In the early 1990s, the television series *The House of Eliott*, told the story of the Eliott sisters as they evolved from humble dressmakers into owners of an haute-couture house in Edwardian London. The more recent *Mr Selfridge* depicts the same era and locale, presenting Harry Gordon Selfridge as a man who understands not only what his female customers want, but also how his many female staff can help give them just that. One of its storylines follows young Agnes Towler as she overcomes her deprived background and works her way up from junior assistant to head of displays.

Another television drama, *The Paradise* – based on Zola's novel but set in the 1870s in a northern English town – takes young Denise Lovett on a similar journey, moving from her uncle's dowdy draper's to the new department store down the road, eventually rising to become a head of department. These romanticised 'rags to riches' storylines were ripped apart by comedians French and Saunders in their own *House of Eliott* sketches, with the couture house mercilessly parodied as the 'House of Idiot'. The sketches were harsh but fair. In reality, although some shopgirls lived the dream and rose to the top, many others did not. An earlier 1970s sitcom was closer to the mark: one of the running jokes in *Are You Being Served?* was that poor Miss Brahms would never get ahead in ladieswear at Grace Brothers so long as the gorgon Mrs Slocombe lived and breathed.

All this has made it hard for us to think of shops, whatever their size, as serious workplaces. Shops were distinct from the workshops, sweatshops, mills, factories, farms, mines and docks, where 'real workers' spent their working day. They were the places where the goods that those workers had produced were 'merely' displayed and sold. This helps to explain why shopworkers themselves, both male and female, from the very beginning struggled to gain status, despite taking pride in their jobs. It also helps explain why the real, rather than the fictional, history of their working lives has been overlooked, despite their huge numbers. Theirs doesn't seem – at first glance – to be a courageous history.

Yet shops have always been about more than shopping. They are sociable places where, for generations, customers have come not just to buy but also to see and be seen, to catch up with friends, gossip and watch the world go by. They are places where creativity sparks and passions fly. Because they trade on trust, assistants have continually to find new and inventive ways to attract, keep and reward their customers. At the same time, of course, they are always ready to squeeze a profit from those same customers. Shopgirls have long been at the heart of these everyday dramas. Their work has always been about more than just selling. As Virginia Woolf suspected, shopgirls and their stories are a powerful part of our shared – sometimes heroic, sometimes shameful – social history.

Shopgirls in the 1890s at Marks and Spencer Ltd. Shopgirls had to provide their own black dresses as uniform, leading to a variation in dress and collar styles.

CHAPTER 1

THE GIRLING OF SHOPWORK

'Romantic Freak of a Glasgow Girl of Sixteen' – so read the head-line on an extraordinary newspaper story about one young person who was desperate to break into shopwork. In July 1861, the *Glasgow Daily Herald* reported that a young man had answered a provision dealer's advertisement, displayed in the shop window, and was duly hired as a shop assistant. All went well for the first few days, 'the lad giving rather extra satisfaction'. Then the landlady of the lad's lodging house visited the provision dealer and 'lo and behold! He was told that his young, active shopman, instead of being of the *masculine* was of the *feminine* gender.' The supposed shopman tried to deny it, but finally confessed to being a young girl of sixteen. Her employer promptly sacked her; he only employed men and wasn't about to give jobs to women, let alone a cross-dressing 'romantic freak'. The unnamed sixteen-year-old was clearly a girl with spirit, desperate to earn her own living, so much so that she pulled off the trick a second time, landing a situation in another shop, again disguised as a man. On being discovered yet again, she was sent back to live with her parents. The *Herald* reporter hoped she would never abandon her parental home again, except when married and in 'her proper position as a daughter of Mother Eve'.[1]

That same year, farmer's daughter Eliza Close was a little more successful than our courageous sixteen-year-old: she found work as a shopgirl in London. In Arthur Munby's account of meeting her in Hyde Park one June evening, Eliza comes across as a cheerful, though perhaps naive, young woman. Munby is a notorious figure today: a Victorian civil servant and writer whose fetishistic interest in working women was partly, though not solely, sexual. He took a forensic, anthropological approach to understanding the minutiae of working-class women's lives, collecting photographs of servant maids, pit lasses, acrobats and fishergirls. He sketched these objects of his fascination, wrote a book on the tombstone epitaphs of servants and kept diaries cataloguing his hundreds of encounters with these women, sexual and social. The fragile manuscripts, with page after page of closely written entries, record his evening conversation with Eliza as they sheltered from a shower together, under a tree: 'I found she was ready to tell me all I wanted to know about the life of the shop.'

Eliza enjoyed her shopwork, preferring it to living in the country – 'so solitary' was her complaint. Munby found her black silk gown and pretty green and white bonnet tasteful 'but beyond her class, as times go'. He implied that Eliza was dressing above her station, her colourful bonnet a little fanciful for a shopgirl, who would normally be dressed completely in black with a white collar. Munby was always obsessively alert to the gradations of status and class. She painted him a picture of life in the shop, ruled by the employer she called 'the master' and 'our old gentleman', and of sharing work and living quarters with seven other assistants, four men and three women. Their lives were shop-bound, with working hours from eight in the morning until nine at night and Eliza exclaiming, 'You don't go out of the shop all day except downstairs for meals.'[2]

Munby didn't quite understand why Eliza Close preferred working in this closed, restricted world to 'the freshness and freedom of a farm'; he dismissed her preference nonchalantly as 'the foolishness of half-educated girls'. Among other poorly educated girls Munby wouldn't have understood are Henrietta Woodward, aged seventeen in 1861, Georgina Bathurst, aged sixteen, and Sarah Lord, aged just fifteen, all three serving their apprenticeships at Stoddart's drapery store in the centre of the little town of Witney in Oxfordshire. We know from the census of 1861 that Sarah came from a village just three miles away, while the other two came from further afield, Wiltshire and Staffordshire. Sarah's father ran a small farm of 106 acres with his large family, and Sarah was the only one of her siblings to leave farming. But otherwise we know little about these teenagers, for Stoddart's drapery has not survived, let alone the girls' apprenticeship papers. They are likely to have been indentured to Stoddart's for three to seven years, receiving no wages.

Why were young women such as these drawn to shopwork? The attractions are not immediately obvious: shop hours were longer than those for factory work, which by the mid 1900s had been curtailed to ten hours a day for women, and the conditions were challenging. What world did these young women hope to enter and what kind of women did they hope to become as shopgirls?

The advertisements in the local newspapers of the day certainly made clear what kind of women the shopkeepers themselves were searching for:

Leeds Mercury, 22 March 1866:

WANTED, a Young Lady as SALESWOMAN, who understands mantles; one with a knowledge of Millinery; also a
good Second Milliner. Apply, stating terms and reference,
to M'Kenzie and Wilson, Sunderland.

Birmingham Daily Post, 29 October 1863:

WANTED, a Respectable FEMALE SHOP ASSISTANT,
must Write a good Hand and be quick at Accounts. One
who has been accustomed to Business preferred. – Address,
254, Post Office, Stourbridge, stating age and salary.

Liverpool Mercury, 15 July 1869:

WANTED, as Milliner and Saleswoman, a Young Lady
of good character and abilities. Enclose carte. – Booth
Brothers, Southport.

'Respectable', 'young', 'good character', 'knowledge', 'abilities'.
The spin is clear: shopwork was being advertised as suitable for
young women, a proper profession, a job with status. It sounded
attractive; no wonder women were rushing to apply.

Moreover, the number of jobs for women in shopwork was
increasing exponentially; this was something new. The young
women answering these ads in Sunderland, Stourbridge and
Southport in the 1860s were unknowing pioneers. They were the
first generation of women to enter into shopwork en masse, part of a
new wave of female workers breaking into a world that just a decade
earlier had been dominated by men. As our Glaswegian shopgirl in
disguise recognised, high-street shops in mid-century Britain were
largely owned, run and staffed by men, so that the experience of
going shopping was quite different from what we know today.

Take a small market town like Wisbech in the Fens, a decade
earlier. According to the Post Office directory of 1853, Wisbech
was 'one of the most considerable and thriving towns in the Isle of
Ely and Cambridgeshire'; it was 'lighted with gas' and boasted 'an
exchange hall and council rooms … a savings bank, a newspaper,
cemetery for Churchmen, and another for Dissenters'. It was also

home to a dedicated amateur photographer called Samuel Smith. He experimented with the new calotype photographic process, cheaper and more flexible than earlier techniques. This enabled him to photograph his home town with comparative ease and it is through his meticulous documenting of the streets and river that we can catch an accurate glimpse of what a market townscape looked like in the mid 1800s.

Standing in the middle of the cobbled street on Cornhill in his three-piece suit, looking across into the Old Market, Smith recorded the scene.[3] Since medieval times, towns across the country had been full of shops, most of them centred on the all-important marketplace that was the main source of fresh food. Some medieval shops had been simply stalls, but there had also been open-fronted townhouses and craftsmen's workshops, each dedicated to a particular trade. Smith's photographs reveal that in Wisbech in the 1850s the specialist trader still dominated, though by now most shops had bow-windowed fronts to show off their wares. He persuaded a handful of shopkeepers to stand still for the fifteen long minutes it took to expose his calotype; so we see figures we presume to be Mr McNeil the confectioner, Mr Foster the draper and grocer and Mr Goward the postmaster standing proud, while Mr Goode the saddler, Mr Barley the chemist, Mr Ford the ironmonger, and draper Mr Bellars are out of this particular shot.

The terraced brick houses of the Wisbech shopkeepers conformed to the traditional 'shop-and-house' layout, with the shop window taking up the whole ground floor, and the upper floors and cellar serving as storerooms and family living quarters. Theirs were small, family-run businesses dealing in specialised, narrow lines of goods.

Nelson Foster was both draper and grocer. He was a skilled professional, intimately involved in each stage of the shopkeeping process. He knew his suppliers well, he understood quality, he handled the purchasing and storing of his wares, and he monitored the accounts. Like his Wisbech neighbours the confectioner and the chemist, Nelson Foster was also involved in the actual processing of his goods; as a grocer he mixed his own spices, pickled his own chutneys, made sauces, bottled fruit, potted meats, patted butter and above all blended his own tea, tea being very profitable.

All the shopkeepers took a close personal interest in their local customers. Intimate knowledge of customers was vital, for these were the days of credit. The retail world functioned on a flow of credit, with customers buying goods on account, shopkeepers in turn buying off the wholesalers on credit, and finally wholesalers buying off the manufacturers on credit. The whole system relied on a chain of credit. Any break in the flow, any significant non-payment of accounts, spelt danger for the whole chain. Therefore it was of vital importance to Foster to know whether his customers were in work, expecting a child, arranging their father's funeral or travelling. Shops were centres of local gossip, but seemingly idle chit-chat was vitally important intelligence for these family businesses, for the information fed directly into the shopkeepers' assessments of their customers' ability to pay.[4]

A few hazardous coaching-hours east of Wisbech, in Norwich, Copeman's grocery was one of the city's most important stores. It kept meticulous records, in beautifully handwritten Correspondence Books, of the courteous letters between the grocer and his creditors. Even customers who failed to pay promptly were dealt with politely, with Copeman's apologetically writing that they 'must request a remittance of the balance by return of post … waiting which we are, Yours respectfully'. After waiting six months for payment, Copeman's was less respectful: 'if not paid soon the balance must be *pressed*'. One customer clearly was never going to pay up: 'Your word has so often been forfeited that we can place no dependence on it whatever.'[5]

Traders were multi-skilled and most took on a male apprentice for three to seven years. Apprentices were taught their craft and many of these young men nursed dreams of setting up a business of their own one day. They were unpaid but given board and lodging, usually living above the shop alongside the rest of the family.[6]

Wives and daughters often helped out too; these women were the original 'shopgirls', though their work usually went unrecorded and unpaid. In Wisbech the census of 1851 documented the following family living in Nelson Foster's store, 26 Old Market:

> Nelson Foster, aged 28, Draper & Grocer
>
> Eliza Foster, aged 21 [no occupation listed]
>
> John Batterman, aged 25, Draper's assistant
>
> John Skippon, aged 21, Grocer's assistant
>
> Ellen Allen, aged 21, General servant

The census doesn't record whether, in between running the household of five adults and managing the maid-of-all-work, Eliza Foster had any hand in the thousands of tasks it took to run the store, from displaying the broad cloths, doeskins and caps to accounting, sewing the ready-made clothing and stock-taking – let alone serving the customers and gathering the all-important gossip. Nor does it record whether any of the neighbouring shopwives helped out, Susannah McNeil at the family confectionery business, Caroline Barley and Ann Elizabeth Baxter at the two chemists', and Lucy Bellars at the second draper's. The Fosters' children, Nelson junior and Eliza junior, weren't born for another few years.

But what Wisbech had to offer in the 1850s paled in comparison to the exotic, extravagant variety of specialist traders in the larger towns and cities. London, the great metropolis, boasted pianoforte makers, French corset- and stay-makers, porkmen, eye-snuff manufacturers, turtle and venison dealers, emporia of novelty, gunmakers, theatrical booksellers, paper stainers and decorators to Her Majesty, slop sellers and a muffin and crumpet baker.[7] In London, awnings were rolled out above shopfronts during the day, protecting passers-by and shoppers from showers, some emblazoned with the shop's name: 'Sibley from Oxford Street' and the like. In the evening the streets were lit by gaslights and the shops' own external gas lamps, tempting shoppers in even after dark. Then, at night, shutters were pulled tightly down, securing each precious glass window.

Nevertheless, despite this cornucopia of wares, and the dedicated, professional service, many customers found the actual shopping experience unpleasant. French writer Francis Wey travelled around Britain in 1856, gathering material for his book *Les Anglais Chez Eux* ('The British at Home'), and was astonished at the detached, indifferent attitude of London shopkeepers, who seemed – to him – to have no interest in making a sale. 'I had the greatest difficulty in getting the assistant to show me more than two fingers of each glove as though displaying the entire article was beneath his dignity.'[8] It was not just the sales assistants: the cashier and the shopman himself both treated Francis Wey as if *he* should be grateful to *them*, rather than thanking him as a valued customer.

And it wasn't just foreign visitors who were put out. Writing in 1895, high-society hostess and journalist Lady Jeune remembered what a conservative business shopping had been in her youth, where each shop had its own speciality and each trader seemed an unrivalled, eternal fixture on the shopping circuit. 'Jones sold the best silks, Smith the best gloves, Brown the best bonnets, Madame X. was far and away the only good milliner and dressmaker, and no one had the temerity or boldness to contradict the fact or infringe on their monopoly.'[9]

Lady Jeune had been brought up in Brahan Castle in the Scottish Highlands and had gone on to marry first an army colonel and then a barrister; her dinner parties were legendary, with guests including writer Thomas Hardy and scientist Mary Ward, Scottish poet Robert Browning and even the politician Joseph Chamberlain. This was a woman with few social hang-ups. Yet even Lady Jeune had found having to interact with truculent shopmen hiding their wares beneath their counter a 'dreary affair'. She remembered being received by a solemn gentleman in black, who handed her over to a second gentleman, who handed her over to a third, who seated her and 'in a sepulchral tone of voice uttered some magic words, such as "Silk, Mr Smith", or "Velvet, Mr A."', before leaving to seek another 'victim'. She described buying only what was needed, not being shown or offered anything extra, and leaving in a sombre mood, so that 'with a great sense of relief the large doors closed behind one'.[10]

Lady Jeune left the shop relieved; other customers in less high-class establishments, who were doubtless not as well dressed as Lady Jeune, had far worse experiences. Some shopmen were rude, haranguing or insulting customers if they bought too little or had not dared to buy anything at all after having crossed their threshold. Prices were unmarked, so assistants quoted different prices to different customers and only they knew the lowest figure that the store would accept. Haggling, known as 'cheapening', was still the norm in many smaller shops. And as Lady Jeune pointed out, once the purchase had been made, the customer was expected to leave immediately: no browsing allowed.

William Ablett, in his *Reminiscences of an Old Draper*, confessed to having witnessed the effects such intimidating behaviour had on young customers. 'Many a half-frightened girl have I seen go out of the shop, her purchase in her hands, the tears welling up in her eyes.' Not only were the young ladies upset by the shopmen's attitude, they were often also pressured into buying the wrong item. The poor shopper would leave, 'shaking her head and saying, "I am sure

I shall never like it" – some shawl or dress having been forced upon her contrary to her taste or judgement'.[11]

Yet, by the early 1860s, such brusque, even bullying shopmen were out of touch with the times. The new wave of young women answering the ads for shopgirls in Southport and Stourbridge, let alone London, were poised to change the experience of shopping for ever. For mid-century Britain was a country in upheaval. The first phase of the Industrial Revolution was past, and city life and concomitantly country life were in the midst of a radical transformation. Riches from the British Empire and the Industrial Revolution flooded into cities like Liverpool, Manchester and London, bringing an enormous increase in both the amount and the variety of goods sold in the shops. Not only were exotic wares like ostrich feathers and tea, mahogany and pineapples on sale in the big cities, but mass production in British factories meant that a bewildering range of linens and wools, clocks and glassware, china and paper became readily available. The demand for these new products was undeniable: the customers themselves were getting richer, as the whole country, even poorer workers, experienced a rapid rise in real income per capita.

Traditional shopkeepers like our Wisbech draper Nelson Foster had to keep up with these changing times. They were faced with new wholesalers, new large-scale manufacturers, new goods of differing qualities, new customer demands. To top it all, it seemed that there was now a pressing problem to worsen their headache: half a million 'spare women'.

On the night of 30 March 1851, the head of each household had to fill in a form, recording who exactly was sleeping in his (sometimes her) house that night. Illiterate householders were helped by the thousands of 'census enumerators', who roved every district. It was the second census to record all individuals in each household, but compared to the one a decade earlier, this year's recorded people's exact occupations in far more detail – as well as their relationships to one another. One intention was to help the government get a handle on different 'classes' and 'sub-classes' of employment, particularly as masters of a trade were asked to state how many men they employed.

The results of this census were pored over by journalists, economists, government officials and intellectuals, all of them trying to understand better the society in which they were living. There was one extraordinary figure among them: Harriet Martineau. Martineau, who used an ear trumpet to battle the deafness she had suffered from since childhood, had supported herself as a journalist and writer for decades, ever since her father's cloth business had failed. She had come to fame with *Illustrations of Political Economy*, a series of twenty-three fictional stories that explored the negative effects of industrialisation on the lives of individuals and society; typical examples included 'The Manchester Strike' and 'The Loom and the Lugger'. She was described as having a masculine intellect for dealing with such subjects as politics, economics and industry. Martineau was a radical in the spirit of the Reform Movement, which had been inspired by the French Revolution and dominated public debate around the Reform Act of 1832, addressing issues of working-class autonomy and economic independence, issues that were to become profoundly relevant to our new wave of shopgirls. Now in her fifties, Martineau was focused on the controversial theme of the day, namely the Woman Question.

What exactly the Woman Question was is difficult to pin down; it was never just one question. Early feminists both in Britain and in the United States, which Martineau visited, were debating the status of women on all fronts: legal, economic, educational, domestic. Chewing over the results of the 1851 census, Martineau wrote an article in the *Edinburgh Review* which she titled 'Female Industry'. The warning it contained was stark, and immediately resonated with her readers.

The census had revealed an unbalanced ratio of men to women, with half a million more women, specifically single women, than men. They were the 'spare women', who either could not hope to 'marry and be taken care of', or who, as widows, might not have been left provided for by their late husbands. 'We go on talking as if it were still true that every woman is, or ought to be, supported by father, brother or husband,' wrote Martineau, arguing that this way of thinking was outdated and the country now needed to face the facts: 'A very large proportion of the women of England earn their own bread … more than two million are independent in their industry, are self-supporting, like men.'

Martineau warned that ignoring these facts would lead to 'an encroachment of pauperism at one end of the scale, and the most poisonous of vices at the other'. In other words, if society didn't help these two million women by providing them with sufficient job opportunities, they would face poverty and prostitution, ending up in either the workhouse or the brothel. It was a call for action and it prompted journalists and social critics to suggest all manner of solutions, from shipping these 'superfluous' women out to the colonies, to increasing the numbers of domestic servants.[12] But the person who answered Martineau's call directly was a younger woman called Jessie Boucherett, an action which was to change completely the direction of Boucherett's life.

Boucherett grew up in rural Lincolnshire and as a girl had been a keen rider to hounds. She was later described as 'delicate, highly bred, with a considerable sense of humour and great courtesy'.[13] Just five months after having read Martineau's 'Female Industry' article, Boucherett founded the Society for Promoting the Employment of Women, which suggested replacing men with women in one trade in particular: that of the shop assistant. She asked pointedly, 'Why should bearded men be employed to sell ribbon, lace, gloves, neck-kerchiefs, and the dozen other trifles to be found in a silkmercer's or haberdasher's shop?'[14]

Boucherett chose the headquarters of her new Society strategically. The address was 19 Langham Place, just north of Oxford Circus in London. These Langham Place offices already housed the *English Woman's Journal*, run by a small circle of female activists who came to be known as the Ladies of Langham Place. Boucherett was in good company.

She focused on the difficulties faced by unmarried women of limited means in finding the right work, wanting to free them up from being 'useless burdens on society, as inmates of our prisons, workhouses and charitable institutions'.[15] She felt that the choice of employment open to women was inadequate. The 'three great professions' of teaching, domestic service and needlework were so oversubscribed, Boucherett argued, that wages had been driven down 'to a point at which it is difficult to live'.[16]

So she set up the Society with two clear aims: to open up new areas of employment to women and to improve their poor standards of education, for the average length of school attendance for girls across the country was still a shockingly low two years. The Society set up the first register of employment for women, ran the first book-keeping class for women, and gave classes in shorthand, law copying and photography. And Boucherett herself superintended a commercial school 'for girls and young women, where they may be specially trained to wait in shops'. She had them taught accounts, the practicalities of how to tie a parcel, and that elusive skill of service, namely a shoppish manner, politeness towards customers 'and a constant self-control'.

Of course Boucherett's Society could not train up the whole country; nor did it set out to. The aim instead was to act as a pioneer, to stimulate public debate with their high-profile activities, and to influence 'people in high places'. Though it may not seem so today, the Society's suggestion that women spread their wings into other types of employment – particularly into shopwork – was truly radical.

The great tide of public opinion was against them. Not only was the Society suggesting that young women enter a profession in a man's world, it was also challenging the very notions of respectability and gentility that had become so central to mid-Victorian society. The title of an article addressing just this issue, published at 19 Langham Place, says it all: 'On the Obstacles to the Employment of Women'. The main obstacle was seen to be a false notion of respectability: according to middle-class standards, it was deemed unrespectable to work in a shop. It was not the done thing. The writers brushed this notion aside dismissively: 'Small account should be made of this however; for prejudices will never long withstand the money test.' The writers felt that in the face of economic hardship, women 'would soon abandon their fanciful gentility' and no longer worry about being ungenteel or 'losing caste' in a working environment.[17]

'Caste' is a strong word to use; to our modern ears it is associated more with Indian social hierarchies than British ones. However, this particular concern over losing caste was very real, and specific to the middle classes of Victorian Britain. What is actually meant by 'middle class' is hotly debated even today; but by the 1850s a named and identified category of people had emerged, of manufacturers, merchants and professionals, distinct from the aristocracy on the one hand and the working classes on the other. The term 'middle class' had come into use in the first half of the nineteenth century, taking over from 'middle ranks' or 'the middling sort'. By mid century the middle classes were defined politically, religiously and culturally; they were typically moderate reformers, Nonconformists, and with a belief in the importance of cosy domesticity, hearth and home.[18] And they were the most direct beneficiaries of the wealth of the Industrial Revolution.

One result of this increasing wealth was a complete redefinition of the role and duties of the middle-class lady of the house. Daily work such as spinning, weaving, preparing food and even childcare fell away. The new money paid for servants to take up the chores and childcare inside the home; and it paid for dressmaking and goods to be purchased outside the home. Indeed, for women in this category, work came to be seen as demeaning. 'Respectability' was central to the social codes governing middle-class life in the mid century, and respectability for middle-class women, married or unmarried, meant a life of leisure. The phrase 'working lady' had rapidly become a contradiction in terms. One woman observed acutely, 'A lady, to be sure, must be a mere lady and nothing else. She must not work for profit or engage in any occupation that money can command.'[19]

'A mere lady' had her world strictly defined: her place was inside the home, the private realm, with her vocation being marriage, motherhood and managing her household, including her servants. Large parts of public life were closed off to her; she was not to go out without a suitable chaperone, including for social visits or shopping. Under such social strictures, it was no wonder that gentlewomen forced by circumstance to 'work for profit' were seen to be lower caste. They were pitied: women who worked as governesses or teachers were often described as 'distressed' or 'decayed' and a great deal of charitable effort went into helping them. Harriet Martineau herself, who lived from her writings, had been expressly forbidden as a girl by her mother ever to be seen in public holding a pen. Needlework yes, penwork no.

Martineau and Boucherett's exhortation that middle-class women discard such social anxieties was heard by the political and cultural elite. The engine of change that broke down prejudice, however, came from elsewhere. Surprisingly maybe, the shift was generated by shopkeepers themselves. For in this economic boom time, they were in dire need of more staff. Not only was the number of shops on the increase, but new types of shops were emerging, including co-operative retail societies, 'multiples', which were later called by the American term of 'chain store', and the first department stores

– though they were never known as such in the nineteenth century. Nelson Foster in Wisbech in 1851 had been reading the runes – his store was already a draper's and grocer's combined – but many other small-scale traders lost out in this new era, forced to close down or simply engulfed by the new, larger-scale stores.

The visionaries, those entrepreneurs who grasped the new opportunities, were men like Messrs Kendal, Milne and Faulkner in Manchester and the flamboyant chancer Mr Whiteley in London. All four had served apprenticeships and all four went on to fulfil the apprentice's dream by setting up their own businesses.

Manchester then was not simply a hothouse of production, the world's first and greatest industrial city – 'Cottonopolis' and 'Warehouse City' as it was dubbed in newspapers and novels. It was also a centre of consumption: with its intercity railway and horse-drawn omnibuses criss-crossing the city from its heart to its suburbs, half a million people could now easily access Manchester's city centre. Deansgate was a crowded shopping street, catering both to its poorer working-class residents, with pubs and raucous food markets, as well as to a richer clientele who patronised the specialist traders. Kendal, Milne and Faulkner, all trained up in textiles, had worked together in Watts Bazaar when they decided to set up shop together as a drapery on Deansgate in the 1830s. By the middle of the century, they were calling themselves 'General drapers, silk mercers, &c., the Bazaar'. Then the expansion began: first they absorbed the two shops next door, an eating house and a hosiery business, under their banner. Then they took on more lines of goods, including upholstery, furniture, carpets and mourning outfits. Then *Bradshaw's Descriptive Guide to Manchester & Surrounding Districts* in 1857 recorded the effect of a new extension, admiringly describing its elegant Italian-style architecture as 'no inconsiderable addition to the street embellishment of the city'. *Bradshaw's* lists the four entrances giving access to this vast block. 'We believe it is one of the largest drapery establishments in England. It is, indeed, of leviathan dimensions.'[20]

Leviathan indeed. *Bradshaw's Guide* even provided a lovely little illustration of the enlarged store, showing horses, carts and busy shoppers outside. Not only was Kendal, Milne & Faulkner now one of the most extensive emporia in Manchester, it was one of the most expensive too. It easily equalled the largest stores in London in terms of its size and the quality and range of goods on offer. What it did not offer, however, was notoriety. This was being provided in spades by fellow draper William Whiteley in Bayswater, west London.

William Whiteley started out quite humbly in Wakefield, serving seven years as an apprentice draper, but he had no plans to stick around the Yorkshire market town. Aged nineteen, he went down to London to visit the Great Exhibition of 1851 in the specially built Crystal Palace, and later claimed that the *Works of Industry of All Nations*, particularly the trophy displays of arts, raw materials from the colonies and working machinery, inspired in him a vision of a truly modern department store. Released from his indenture in 1855, he returned to the capital, landing jobs in London's drapers' and haberdashers' and managing to save the £700 needed for his first premises.

1863 was an auspicious year to open up in Bayswater. This area of west London had been a lower-class residential neighbourhood until the aristocracy built mansions overlooking Hyde Park; in mid century, developers began to construct middle-class terraces and squares nearby. Then, on 10 January 1863, the Metropolitan Underground Railway was opened – the Tube, the world's first underground railway. It directly linked the area with the City, using steam locomotives to haul its gaslit wooden carriages from Paddington Junction to Farringdon, and was a significant incentive for prosperous middle-class families. As were the puff pieces in *The Landlord's and Tenant's Guide*, describing the area's 'detached family mansions, stately gentlemen's residences, and villas, with large gardens and lawns in front and at the rear'.[21]

For shopkeepers, it was risky to trust this seeming gentrification. Bayswater was still bordered by slums and working-class neighbourhoods and the main thoroughfare, Westbourne Grove, was dubbed 'Bankruptcy Avenue' because shops came and went so frequently. Many had been set up by assistants who dreamt of having their own businesses – and those dreams were dashed more often than not. Whiteley even described it as 'the worst business street in London'.[22] Nevertheless, attracted by the low rent, the adventurous still tried their luck and soon the Grove was lined with milliners' shops, drapers', grocers', tobacconists', ironmongers' and house agents. Bayswater was on the brink of a social and commercial face-lift, and Whiteley's Haberdasher's at 31 Westbourne Grove was to be the driving force behind this.

'What an ordeal it was for a young girl!' exclaimed Harriet Sarah Hill years later, describing the very first exhausting years as one of Whiteley's first two shopgirls when the business was still young. 'We lived at the top of the house ... and how well I can remember times without number sitting on the bottom stair holding a candle while he put up the shutters at night. Sometimes I could barely keep my eyes open, I was so tired.'[23]

Still, those first years can't have been completely joyless, for Whiteley had his eye on this particular assistant from the start: Harriet and William were married four years later with Harriet giving birth two months after their wedding. 'I was a good wife to him. How I worked for the man, slaved for him,' Harriet Whiteley recalled. 'My husband was always fond of a special custard which I would make for him with my own hands. If anyone else made it he wouldn't eat it.' Yet their marriage was not to be a happy one: its dramas hit the headlines again and again over the next thirty years, and its end would be both tragic and obscure.

In the early years of their marriage, Whiteley was very much focused on building his business. Some years later he wrote a bombastic article in the *London Magazine*, entitled 'How to Succeed as a Shopkeeper', with practical tips for 'earnest young fellows' going into business, typed up in handy boxes.[24]

> **Don't disappoint your customers.**
> **Supply the best goods at the lowest possible prices.**
> **Keep cool and don't lose your temper.**

He stated that within a year of opening, he had increased his staff from two to sixteen young women, plus two errand boys. The article was accompanied by a photograph that showed the exterior of the store filling an entire block, with an arrow pointing to one particular shop window. 'The small blank window represents Mr Whiteley's first shop, from which his great business has grown.' They were heady early days.

His article also explained how he came to be known as the U.P., the Universal Provider, who could and did answer his customers' every need, from the most mundane to the most curious, from birth to the grave – literally, as Whiteley's had a mourning department selling the most subtle gradations of mourning attire, from faintest mauve-coloured ribbons merely hinting at sorrow, to deepest black cloaks denoting inconsolable grief.

Of course, it was the absurd requests from Whiteley's customers, loudly advertised by the proprietor, that stuck in the public's imagination: elephants, second-hand coffins, even wives. 'Execute it, of course!' was Whiteley's response when his staff told him of an order for a pint of live fleas – or so Whiteley claimed. His story goes that he contacted the superintendent of London Zoo and a certain Mr Jamrach, wild beast dealer, requesting them to comb through their monkeys' fur and send through the proceeds. By the evening a pint jar of live fleas was safely delivered to the troublesome customer.

The store grew at a prodigious rate, swallowing up nos. 31, 33, 35, 37, 39, 41, 43, 45, 47, 49, 51, 53 and 14A Westbourne Grove, as well as nos. 147 and 149 Queen's Road (now Queensway) over the next decade. The *Essex Weekly News* reported admiringly on the colossus, calling the store 'this busy hive' and noting it took fifty people simply to open each morning's post, which averaged a couple of thousand communications and requests – home deliveries of course being de rigeur in this period.[25] Where Harriet Hill and her fellow shopgirl had once been the only staff, there was now an army of two thousand living on the premises, with thousands more living off site. 'There is a good deal of fun to be got out of business,' Whiteley admitted.

However, Whiteley's rapacious acquisitions had destroyed, or at least threatened, the livelihoods of his neighbouring shopkeepers on Westbourne Grove. On Guy Fawkes Day 1876, just two days after the sycophantic article in the *Essex Weekly News* was published, they were out to get him. At lunchtime an angry, raucous parade of shopkeepers marched along Westbourne Grove in a traditional Guy Fawkes procession, making a hideous racket by banging cleavers against marrow bones. At the head of the parade was a gigantic effigy, kitted out as a draper in a conventional frock coat. It was modelled on Mr Whiteley, as was clear to all passers-by. He held a handkerchief in one hand and – here lies the controversy – a piece of beef in the other. The paraders marched Whiteley's effigy into Portobello Road, then ceremoniously burnt it on a bonfire.[26]

It was not unusual in Victorian Britain to be so direct and public about a hated local figure: female scolds, wife-beaters and unscrupulous tradesmen were often targeted.[27] The next day the local paper shed light on the reasons for the retailers' anger, under the headline 'Wholescale Butchery in Bayswater – the Victims'. One victim complained he had witnessed 'a startling succession of feats in the art of shutting up your neighbour's shop and driving him elsewhere, but this last daring and audacious feat – this vending of meat and greens as well as silk and satins – overtops them all'.[28]

It was this combination of handkerchiefs and beef, of selling drapery and foodstuffs, that was beyond the pale for the other shopkeepers in the vicinity. The Guy Fawkes protest was the culmination of four years of pitched battles that had begun when Whiteley had tried to get a liquor licence for a small refreshment room; he had since gone on to open an estate agency and a cleaning and dyeing service, all on the premises.

Whiteley was a complex figure, a man of vision and chutzpah, self-belief and arrogance. He was pushing the boundaries of traditional retail, challenging the conventions of specialist trading – and with great success. Customers poured into his store, eager to open their purses, dismissive of other retailers' opposition to the Universal Provider. Whiteley was in the process of fundamentally reshaping the shopping experience for British men and women – as well as for the shopgirls that served them.

His own shopgirl, Harriet, however, suffered. The police had warned the whole family – they had four young children by now – not to go out at night, and Harriet frequently received threatening letters warning her to expect her husband's sudden death. That November was indeed a pivotal moment for the Whiteley family, and not just in reputational terms. The store's profits for 1876 were an astonishing £66,000; yet for the next decade they would only decrease. Britain had hit a recession, caused by over-production at home and decreasing exports and protectionism abroad. In order to weather it, stores all around the country had to sharpen up their act, or go down.

By the spring of 1877, the outcry against the Universal Provider had, according to the *Bayswater Chronicle*, died away, partly because 'Mr Whiteley's "Cheap meat" sensation' had 'drawn more people to Westbourne Grove, and made the place a better mart than ever'.[29] However, it was not simply the whiff of a scandal that had lured customers into the area. The shopkeepers that had not been driven out by Whiteley had upped their own games, offering bargains, sprucing up their interiors and focusing more on enticing window displays. One of them was quoted as saying that Whiteley was 'better for all of us. He makes Bayswater a grand market for all of us except the old-fashioned.'[30] And this was not simply a local phenomenon. One of the principal national responses to the recession was to try to enlarge the home market for consumer goods: shopkeepers were looking for new customers and bigger sales. In the decade that followed, Whiteley's multi-department store no longer looked so unusual. All over the country, shops and co-operatives were expanding into larger emporia. The iconic stores that we know and love today were taking a recognisable shape: Jenners of Edinburgh and Bennetts of Derby, Austins in Derry and Allders in Croydon, Debenhams, and Fraser Sons & Co., later renamed House of Fraser.

It was a change felt not only in the commercial and industrial hubs, but in rural market towns and seaside resorts, in northern industrial suburbs and provincial capitals. And there was a certain grocer's in central London that was fast growing into what would, in time, become the most famous department store in the world: Harrods. At this point Harrods was but a minnow in comparison to great factory-style stores like Whiteley's. Unlike most of the department-store proprietors, with their backgrounds in the drapery trade, Henry Charles Harrod had started off running a handful of groceries. He first opened his grocer's at the famous location in Knightsbridge, west London, in 1851, with just one room, two assistants and a messenger boy. The area was dominated by the Knightsbridge Barracks and had

had a notorious reputation, but after the Great Exhibition of 1851 across the road in Hyde Park, it started to improve rapidly. Harrods rode the wave of gentrification, so that by the late 1870s it was a smart store with food, perfumery, stationery and flower departments, employing around one hundred shop assistants.[31]

The need for staff was great. Even though the vast majority of shops in Britain were still single traders or smaller establishments employing just a handful of assistants – the emerging department stores still represented less than 1 per cent of retail trade[32] – the actual number of shops was increasing exponentially all over the country. In 1875 there were just under 300,000 shops; it is estimated that over the next thirty years this number doubled.[33]

No wonder the local papers were full of advertisements for shopworkers. And the main reason why proprietors were recruiting 'Young Female Shop Assistants'? Not only were there thousands of 'superfluous women' in need of work, as highlighted by the census and the Langham Ladies, but these women came cheap – they were significantly less expensive to employ than the men. A shopgirl in the 1870s received two thirds or even just half of the salary of a young male assistant. Typically in this period a shopgirl might receive £25 a year, while her male counterpart would take home £40. It was this single factor that galvanised the shopocracy into fighting against all the other bars to employing women in shops. The concerns about respectability and gentility; the worries that women weren't physically strong enough or professional enough to work on the shopfloor, these all went out the window as soon as the monetary benefits became clear. In this regard, these male shopkeepers had become the unlikely allies of the early feminists.

However, it is difficult to get a clear picture of shop salaries, even among women workers, because of the large number of factors involved. Shopgirls' pay depended on the status and location of the shop – a London Regent Street store offered substantially more than

Nelson Foster's in Wisbech. Wages also reflected each shop assistant's exact role within the store, from apprentice to junior assistant, from senior assistant to floorwalker. In addition, shop assistants often received commissions on sales, but employers usually deducted fines at source. For example, Eliza Close, the young woman interviewed by Arthur Munby in Hyde Park, received less than £20 a year, plus board and lodging. Munby, with his eagle eye for detail, noted in his diary the effect the differing salary grades had on women and the clothes they wore when walking through London on a Saturday afternoon: 'They seem to be of two classes, generally, elegant milliners and shopwomen, earning good wages and affecting the dress and style of ladies, and needlewomen and prentice girls, whose clothes are of fashionable cut but worn and poor.'[34] Typically for Munby, he admires them all: 'The number of fair faces and tall good figures in both of these classes is remarkable.'

Eliza Close was quite aware that her fellow shopmen earned better salaries than her – 'the men get a deal more than us' – but she also recognised that she earned more as a shopgirl than as a servant, saying, 'It's much better than service.'[35]

Despite the commercial imperative and the desire of women like Eliza to move into shopwork, the shopkeepers still had quite a job on their hands to break down the social barriers to employing this plentiful cheap source of labour. While Jessie Boucherett and the early feminists felt that the main social concern about shopwork – its supposed lack of respectability – should simply be dismissed, the wilier members of the shopocracy across the country had more concrete tactics. The original model for apprenticeships, which saw apprentices living as part of the family above the shop, was based on an ideal of benevolent paternalism. Young apprentices like Nelson Foster's assistant in Wisbech, John Batterman, were regarded as members of the household, sleeping, eating and socialising in a domestic setting. Shop proprietors now adapted this paternalistic model to their growing businesses, increasing the number of live-in staff. The message they were sending was clear: we are in charge of the welfare of our young shop assistants, we can protect your sons and daughters from physical and moral harm, we will keep them respectable. 'Eliza, what 'ud your father and mother say to me if I didn't keep an eye on you?' asked Eliza Close's master, who lived alongside his seven assistants in rooms above his drapery.[36] The old gentleman, who came from Harborough in Leicestershire just like Eliza, refused to let her go to dancing rooms, made sure she went to church and frowned on any joking with young men.

Like this old gentleman, many proprietors were genuinely motivated to play the role of benevolent paterfamilias – often because of their own Christian beliefs. Emerson Muschamp Bainbridge, founder of Bainbridge's in Newcastle, was a force of nature, his activities 'volcanic' according to his fellow Tyneside store-keeper J.J. Fenwick.[37] Bainbridge led from the front and demanded a willing subservience from his employees. Both Bainbridge and Fenwick were staunch Wesleyan Methodists; Bainbridge preferred to recruit Methodist assistants and, despite his authoritarianism, he was comparatively generous. At a time when working hours were still extremely long, Bainbridge allowed his staff time off as follows: 'one evening a week for courting purposes and two if they go to prayer meetings regularly'. James Howell was the founder of Howells department store in Cardiff (now rebranded as House of Fraser); he too was a devout Methodist, instituting evening hymn sessions in the men's dormitory.[38] Other proprietors recruited directly from religious institutions, such as Roman Catholic schools, hiring school-leavers as apprentices and keeping the local priest on hand to communicate with and monitor the welfare of his former pupils. One large draper with thirty apprentices took them all from local Sunday schools; he knew the family background of each and felt he could mould his apprentices, being 'of the opinion that an employer can make his hands what he likes'.[39]

Religion and concepts of morality imbued all aspects of Victorian life – private and also public – in ways difficult for many of us to fathom today. These store proprietors in Manchester and Newcastle, in Derry and Southend, were shaping a public role for themselves as embodiments of civic pride. Religiously and politically active, they emerged as influential figures in the growing Victorian cities. As well as a shopman, Joshua Allder in Croydon was a Nonconformist, elected onto the local Board of Health and Croydon County Council. Charles Jenner not only founded and expanded the oldest department store in Scotland but also became the first director of the Royal Hospital for Sick Children in Edinburgh – perhaps galvanised by the deaths of his own children – and was a philanthropist, patron of the arts and man of science, investigating plants and giving his name to a grey-felted thistle and an alpine moss.[40] The Brown family fundamentally reshaped Chester by organising, together with other traders, a policing rota to rid the Chester Rows of 'rowdies and dissolute women'. The Rows, as the streets around the cathedral are known, have architecturally unique medieval first-floor covered walkways, which in the early part of the nineteenth century were seen as a centre of vice. William Brown's plan worked: by the 1870s central Chester had blossomed into a middle-class resort, its medieval and neoclassical architecture tempting shoppers to town.[41] William and his brother Charles became town councillors; Charles Brown was elected Mayor of Chester six times and his portrait, in oils, in which he sits almost regal in fur-trimmed robes and gold chain, still hangs in Committee Room 1 of Chester Town Hall.

For some, however, the claim to respectability and benevolent paternalism by many of the shop-owners was nothing but a useful ploy, motivated less by Christian and philanthropic values and more by the need to win over the new cheap labour.[42] William Whiteley, as always, took the most flamboyant approach, wholeheartedly embracing his public role of genial father figure to his employees and incorporating his actual family into his performance. He was not alone in setting up a range of activities to occupy his shop assistants in their precious leisure hours, such as a brass band, quoits, reading rooms and a rifle volunteer club, all of which were designed to promote a sense of loyalty to the family firm. But he explicitly took the concept one stage further, linking his real family with the wider corporate family, and making Harriet and the children attend performances of the shop's Amateur Dramatic Club.[43] All the while, however, his behaviour in private belied this public image: as we shall see, he started sampling other shopgirls after Harriet.

Still, a Leicestershire farmer's family such as Eliza's, or tradesmen's families in Newcastle, keen to ensure a respectable position for their daughters, must have been reassured by the high civic status of many store proprietors, and by the fact that 'living-in' was a form of chaperonage, supposedly a surrogate family. On top of this, the actual work appeared genteel, professional and highly enjoyable. Dealing in ribbons, bonnets, kid gloves and silk scarves in an attractive-looking shop trumped shift-work in Haslam's cotton mill in Colne or parlour maid duties in Southport. 'To be aside those huge plate-glass windows, with beautiful new things on every side, and well-dressed people coming in and out all day, what a delightful life a London shop-girl must lead!' Or so the dream of glamorous shoplife was described in a young woman's journal.[44]

It was also cleaner and less obviously physically demanding than factory work or service – a young woman's hands remained white and soft, not rough and calloused, and there were fewer industrial accidents. Shop assistants had to be cleanly and neatly dressed, usually in plain black with no jewellery or adornment, so as to remain in the background and not distract from the merchandise. Most assistants had to buy their own clothes, as Eliza Close explained to Munby: 'We have to dress nicely for the shop, of course, but he doesn't like us to be too smart.'[45]

This public veneer of gentility was further built up by the way shop assistants spoke. Addressing the customers was an art, an exercise in polite, soft-spoken deference, however tricky or rude the customer might be. There were hours of 'standing and smiling and serving' as one London shopgirl put it.[46] Munby commented from the point of view of a gentleman obsessed with speech and dialects that shopgirls' 'habits of speech come midway between the dignified reserve and fastidious delicacy of a lady and the honest bluntness and crude vulgarity of a servant'.[47] In stores located in upmarket areas, the shop itself – the actual interior – was a space where lower-class shop assistants came into contact with higher-class clientele; working women and men with ladies. It was a space where different classes met, talked, interacted – even touched. For many middle-class and upper-class ladies, the only other such cross-class interactions they had was with their servants at home. Nevertheless, the counter still acted to separate shopkeepers and shop assistants from their customers. It was a physical barrier between those serving and those being served.

By the 1870s, the new wave of shopgirls were not only daughters of farmers and clerks, like Eliza Close, but also middle-class women who had to support themselves and whose fears about ungenteel shopwork the Ladies of Langham Place had sought to dispel. They even advertised their services in the local papers:

> Wanted by a young lady, an engagement in any light
> business as Saleswoman. Good reference. Address B.
> 16 Brunswick St., Barnsbury N.[48]

The number of shop assistants spiralled upwards from mid century onwards, with the number of women shopworkers increasing at an astonishing three times the rate of men.[49]

Society hostess Lady Jeune welcomed them with joy, feeling that no shopman could ever fully understand a female shopper's dilemmas or desires. In her experience female assistants were much quicker than men at grasping the shopper's many conflicting pressures and vanities. 'They can fathom the agony of despair as to the arrangement of colours, the alternative trimmings, the duration of a fashion, the depths of a woman's purse, and more important than all, the question of the becomingness of a dress, or a combination of material, to the would-be wearer.[50]

Like Lady Jeune and Jessie Boucherett, many customers and proprietors now agreed that women were 'naturally' better suited to selling goods to women – but some still believed them incapable of heavy work or professional processing. This meant that shopgirls were generally welcomed in haberdashers', drapers' and milliners', as well as fancy goods shops, tobacconists', confectioners', stationers' and the new multiple stores, but they continued to be excluded from many other trades, raising the hackles of the Langham Circle. Women's education was poor, so any job that required long and expensive training, such as at a chemist's or a druggist's, was unlikely to be open to women. 'Rough' trades like butchery, fishmongery and ironmongery were excluded on physical grounds. Shops catering only to gentlemen, their outfitters, hatters and bootmakers, did not hire women. And shops with expensive stock, like jewellers and booksellers, stuck to hiring shopmen, perhaps for fear of loose-fingered women.[51]

Some individual proprietors in the more 'genteel' trades were also still set against hiring women. Charles Digby Harrod had taken over the running of Harrods from his father and throughout the 1870s he refused to recruit women, claiming that shopmen were more efficient and more loyal to the family firm. In 1885, much later than his competitors, he finally cracked, hiring Ida Annie Fowle and two other women as clerks in the counting house. She theatrically described her male colleagues' reactions on her first day: 'Several of the junior members of the staff peered round showcases to see the "beauty chorus" arrive.'[52] Miss Fowle proved to be resilient, tactful and considerate and was soon put in charge of the Sales Ledger Section. Harrods' profits at £12,500 in 1890 were a mere fifth of what Whiteley had earned fifteen years earlier. But all this was set to change. As Harrods boomed, Miss Fowle's band of female clerks grew ever larger and became known as 'Fowle's Chicks'.[53] She was to preside over her brood for a record-breaking thirty-six years' service, helping a flood of women pursue their dream of entering the 'lighter' areas of shopwork. And she witnessed what happened to these young women's dreams when they were confronted with the harsh realities of life around the shopfloor.

'A Portable Shop Seat': this was the suggested solution of *The Girl's Own Paper* to the problem of standing upright for long hours with no rest, known as 'The Standing Evil', 1880.

CHAPTER 2

SERVANTS OF THE COUNTER

Margaret Bondfield was one of Britain's feistiest shopgirls and the story of her extraordinary life, from rural beginnings in Somerset to becoming Britain's first female Cabinet minister, is deeply revealing. At the start of her career, she too was part of this new wave of pioneering young women who saw shopwork as the chance to chase a dream of independence and glamour, or simply a straight income.

Bondfield loved her apprenticeship at Mrs White's exclusive drapery establishment in Hove, Sussex. She was just fourteen when she started there in 1887, and didn't return home for five years, though in her autobiography she declared that she had 'no regrets': she relished the opportunity to earn her own living. At Mrs White's, Margaret was treated as a member of the family, learning the detailed needlework skills needed for brides' trousseaux and babies' layettes. 'It was a period when "liberty" frocks became the rage, and I spent hours at a window, around which a passion flower mysteriously bloomed, smocking lovely silks for babies' frocks.'[1]

But Mrs White's was the only place she was ever happy. When she moved on to take up junior roles in big Brighton drapery houses, the teenage Margaret was shocked to the core. She found the living conditions appalling, the hours exhausting, the rigid hierarchy difficult to deal with. And the moral challenges confronting a young woman in a busy town were frightening.

Margaret was not alone. The thousands of young women now flocking into shopwork were discovering a reality far harsher than they had imagined. By the 1890s, there were a quarter of a million shopgirls in Britain. Though they were still outnumbered by over half a million female textile workers and well over a million female domestic servants, their numbers were growing fast.[2] There was no stopping the 'girling' of shopwork.

Girls like Margaret had been called in as a new type of worker for a new kind of shopwork. The old art of shopkeeping was undergoing a total transformation. In the past, a skilled shopkeeper had presided over all aspects of his business, from buying in goods to selling on to customers. Nelson Foster had been king of his own small castle – his family grocer's and draper's in Wisbech. But the new world of late Victorian shopwork demanded that a series of ever more specific tasks be undertaken by a growing army of ever more task-specific employees. By the 1880s, even small stores like Foster's were employing cashiers or book-keepers alongside their regular assistants. William Ablett recalled in his *Reminiscences of an Old Draper* that his store had traditionally employed just two buyers – a 'drapery buyer' for furnishing fabrics and heavier goods and a 'fancy buyer' for smaller, lighter goods. By the time he finished his memoir in 1876, the store had expanded and so had its specialist staff, which now included 'glove buyers', 'lace buyers' and 'hosiery buyers' among others.[3] Choosing suppliers, selecting and storing goods, preparing them for display, promoting them, pricing them and, most important of all, persuading customers to actually purchase them were becoming distinct activities as commerce of all kinds became more complex.

This new division of labour was taken to a whole new level by the first generation of department stores. The shop owned by Methodist draper Faithful Cape in Oxford was a prime example. Mr Cape had set up his small store in the 1860s in the St Ebbe's district of Oxford, a mixed area catering to both working-class and professional sections of Oxford society, and having little to do with the famous university. By the end of the century, F. Cape & Co. had expanded to nos. 28 to 32 St Ebbe's Street, and also had branches in Little Clarendon Street, Cowley Road and Church Street. It now sold everything from ladies' corsets and children's hats to hosiery, haberdashery, lace, baby linen, sheeting, blankets, quilts, shoes and furnishings.

When Cape retired in the early 1890s, a new owner – fellow Methodist Henry Lewis – took over with his three sons, who were employed as buyers. Tom bought gloves, scarves and lingerie, Russell bought cotton goods and menswear, and Edmund bought mantles, the outer cloaks favoured by the well-to-do. Together, they were known as 'The Firm' and they ran a staff of nearly a hundred workers within the stores, in addition to providing employment to many more messengers, delivery men and suppliers beyond the shop walls. Henry, Edmund, Tom and Russell had their desks on the shopfloor, in order to keep a beady eye on all activity both behind and in front of the long, mahogany sales counters. The hierarchy at Cape's was strict. Directly below 'The Firm' in seniority were the floorwalkers (also known as shopwalkers), who acted rather like sergeant majors, patrolling departments and imposing discipline and fines; they were often obsequious to customers while simultaneously bullying junior staff. Next came the senior assistants, then their juniors, who were also known as 'improvers'. At the bottom were the apprentices, porters and messengers.

Where Cape & Co. employed around a hundred people within its shops, some of Britain's biggest department stores employed nearly ten times as many. Within fifty years of opening, Harrods in

London, Bainbridge's in Newcastle, and Kendal, Milne & Faulkner in Manchester each employed over a thousand workers.[4] Large workforces like these were divided and ruled through even stricter hierarchies. Here, the new service sector had much in common with the world of domestic service. Servants in large country houses were organised into very particular ranks, with the butler and housekeeper at the top, the cook, lady's maid and valet in the middle, parlour maids, kitchen maids and footmen further down and tweenies, or 'between-stairs maids', scullery maids and hall boys at the very bottom. Department stores organised their 'servants of the counter' in a similar fashion. Escaping domestic service did not necessarily mean an escape from 'knowing your place'.

In these large flagship stores, men still ruled the show as managers, floorwalkers, buyers and supervisors. The top shopfloor position that could be held by a woman was that of head of a department, usually ladieswear, and she was responsible for her senior and junior assistants. Behind the scenes in the increasingly specialised back offices, however, new opportunities were being created. When Ida Fowle was hired by Charles Harrod in 1885, she was taken on as 'second ledger clerk', working in a small team of just six. Within five years, her world and the whole of Harrods' back office operation had been transformed. She was promoted to chief ledger clerk and placed in charge of a staff of more than four hundred. She remembered this period as 'sensational', with the business expanding 'by leaps and bounds' and its Brompton Road buildings 'growing up around us year by year'.[5]

Two decades after Ida's appointment, a large percentage of Harrods' colossal staff of five thousand were women. They not only worked on the shopfloor and in Ida's ledger department but also in its bank and estate agency, its hair and manicure salon, chiropody court, writing room and ladies' club room.[6] The store's Grand Restaurant employed cooks, pastry chefs and waitresses to service the first generation of ladies that lunched. Tucked away out of sight and far behind Harrods' many counters, still more shopgirls beavered away in back-room roles as clerks, sewing hands and packers. In many ways, the singular term 'shopgirl' hardly does justice to the range of jobs – from the glittering to the gritty – on offer at retail's top end.

As in the country house, a store's hierarchy served more than one purpose. For those young women who worked hard and upon whom their seniors smiled, a graded pecking order held the promise of promotion. It provided a pay scale stretching from most junior and least skilled to the most senior and highest skilled. And it also kept staff at all levels in line by dispensing discipline down a chain of command across the entire store. Apprentices answered to junior assistants who answered to senior assistants who answered to floorwalkers, and so on. Many stores – large and small – also had extremely strict rules and imposed harsh penalties upon those who breached them, ranging from warnings to fines and even to instant dismissal. Fines, for example, could be imposed for being late, giving the wrong change, sitting down on the job, returning late from a break, dropping or breaking something, talking or laughing with fellow workers, conversing in staff corridors, and even allowing a customer simply to leave without making a purchase, or 'taking the swop' as it was known.[7]

William Whiteley, typically, operated one of the most notorious disciplinary systems. By the 1880s, the Universal Provider's store employed nearly five thousand staff, who he apparently patrolled 'like a rearing lion'.[8] His revised staff rulebook, issued in 1886, contained no less than 176 separate rules and potential offences. There was to be no gossiping, no loitering, no noise, no leaving early, no insolence to superiors, no bad language, no fighting, no liquor, no standing on chairs, no toiletries in shop, no leaving without a superior's permission. For good measure, rule 176 covered 'any mistake not before mentioned'. Anyone breaking these rules could expect to pay a hefty fine, from sixpence – the cost of a week's supply of tobacco – for insolence towards a shopwalker or failing to obtain permission from the counting house before placing an order, to one shilling for bringing matches onto the premises and a staggering two shillings and sixpence – around a quarter of a week's wages for a female assistant on £20 per year – for charging up the same goods twice. Whiteley was rumoured to keep monies forfeited in fines for his own personal extravagances, but he more likely ploughed them back into the business once they had been processed by his separate 'fines department', which itself required seven clerks to handle the volume of work.[9] The most unfortunate or recalcitrant workers found that they had no wages to collect at all at the end of the week or month, because they had all been lost in advance. For some this degree of discipline was too much, and they left for other jobs as soon as they were able.

Whiteley had good reason to ban matches. His store suffered a series of damaging fires in the 1880s. The London press speculated that disgruntled assistants were exacting very direct revenge. *The Pall Mall Gazette* ran a large feature in 1887 asking, 'Why is Whiteley's so often burned down?' It included an anonymous letter from a former employee hinting at staff collusion. He or she had left Whiteley's five years previously when the 'number of fines was only 99' but was aware that this had since increased dramatically. Being fined was bad enough but being publicly shamed was worse: 'Not content with fining you, your name and department are posted on a large green baize board in the dining-hall, like you see convictions posted at the Metropolitan and other railway stations.'[10] Other correspondents defended the Universal Provider and suggested that competitors could be to blame. The real culprits were never identified.

For shopworkers, the discipline didn't end with the working day because many were required to live in, usually above the shop or close by. This suited shopkeepers for two reasons: it allowed them both to keep wages low and to ensure that staff stayed on the straight and narrow. The living-in system was reinvented on an industrial scale to accommodate retail's growing army of young workers. In 1891, 450,000 shopworkers lived in – well over 60 per cent of the total number of shopworkers listed in the census taken that year. Over the previous decades, many shopkeepers had expanded their businesses by employing the daughters of respectable families. As a result, they were under pressure to provide respectable lodgings because where a girl slept at night was crucial to her good character.

Luckily for shopkeepers, 'respectable' was a very elastic term. And they certainly stretched it. Some provided decent lodgings that may well have been a vast improvement on the more humble family homes some girls had left behind. Staff at F. Cape & Co. lived above the Oxford store, where their accommodation was made up of shared bedrooms, a day room with piano and a dining room where all staff took their meals. Lodgings like these were modelled on servants' quarters in large private houses. While the lower floors of the St Ebbe's Street store were ruled by The Firm, the upper floor was ruled by the housekeeper, complete with a set of jangling keys. It was she who kept a sharp eye on the assistants and the maids: Henry Lewis brought his Methodist morals into all corners of his workplace.

Many other lodgings, however, were far less homely. They were dank, overcrowded and horribly unhygienic. One young shopgirl left her job in a Baker Street store in 1898 after just two days, having found that twenty-three assistants were sharing three rooms and that she was expected to share a bed with two others.[11] Draper's boy Philip Hoffman had an even worse experience. He remembered his first horrendous night living-in, at the age of fourteen, at Samuel Lewis's Holborn Silk Market:

> I found myself along with half-a-dozen other young shavers in a small dirty room. The ceiling was very low. Walls and ceilings were bare, grimy and splotched. The boys hunted for bugs on the wall, cracking

them with slipper heels. They lifted up their nightshirts and asked will this pass? Will this pass? I thought my sensitive heart would break. I sobbed through that dismal night.[12]

The young Margaret Bondfield faced conditions that were equally testing. After leaving the lovely Mrs White's drapery establishment and her stitching of baby frocks, she lived in at several of the big drapery houses in Brighton and London. She remembered the struggle she faced just to keep clean, with some housekeepers allowing a jug of hot water and foot-bath only once a week. Margaret recalled in her memoir that she and some of her friends 'made up our minds that we would have at least one hot bath a week'. This meant sprinting straight from the shop to the public baths on the one night when they stayed open late. They used to 'make a dash the moment the shutters were down and run at full speed for about half a mile', reaching the baths 'in time to have exactly quarter of an hour to undress, bath and dress again before the attendant had to turn us out'.

Margaret was also horrified by routine harassment. During Brighton's Race Week, her lodgings became a magnet for local lads trying to pay late-night visits. She remembers that they 'knocked at our ground-floor windows and tried to pull them down'. Not being 'that kind of girl', she and the other occupants managed, often after a struggle, to slam and bolt the windows. The experience frightened Margaret deeply. All she knew of sex 'was the shaming gossip of school girls'. She may have known how to make beautifully ornate baby clothes, but the making of actual babies was a completely different matter: 'I felt hot all over if I saw a pregnant woman, because one was not supposed to know anything about a baby until or unless it appeared – and as a result of marriage.'[13] Occasionally, similar stories made it into the newspapers. Under the headline 'Disgraceful Affair at Cardiff', *The Drapers Record* revelled in the tale of 'two gentlemen of good position' who broke into the female lodgings of Howells department store late one night, where thirty women were asleep. Some shopgirls were so frightened that they locked themselves into their bedrooms, while others alerted the authorities. On being arrested, the men claimed that they thought the lodging house a brothel.

Some of the larger department stores seemed to offer a better deal. Indeed, many of them took living-in to new heights. Nestled in their roof lines were dormitories, with rows of small, ornate windows, where many of their staff spent their nights. As payrolls expanded, proprietors bought up local premises and converted them. Many of Whiteley's female assistants lived in two cul-de-sacs close by, in a modicum of comfort. Bedrooms were shared by up to three girls and furnished with feather beds, a washstand and a chest of drawers. Every morning they dashed to the store, some wrapped in shawls, to be sure to be there for breakfast, served at eight o'clock sharp.[15]

Living-in conditions may have been more comfortable in the larger stores, but workers certainly paid for the privilege. Fines, not unique to Whiteley's, resulted in yet more 'deductions' being made for transgressions at their lodgings — for being untidy, leaving the gaslight on, or entertaining visitors, especially of the opposite sex.[16]

It was no wonder that the living-in system was a major source of grievance for shopworkers. Staff that lived above or near the shop were, of course, on hand around the clock. Store owners took full advantage of this, with many opening early in the morning and closing late in the evening, leading to notoriously long hours. By the mid nineteenth century gas lighting had spread to streets and to stores. Henry Mayhew lyrically chronicled the metropolis at night, calling the sight a delightful 'fairy charm': 'Far as the eye can see, stretch the jets of gas, brilliant as gems, in long and charmed vista. Within the shops, innumerable gas-jets light up the wares of the merchant, or the products of the manufacturer, with the lustrous shimmer almost of sunshine.'[17] Late-night shopping, made possible by gas lighting, long hours and customer demand, was a Victorian invention.

In fact, there were no fixed closing times. Store owners often refused to pull down their own shutters until they were certain that their rivals had done the same. Many lived above the shop themselves and saw little distinction between home and work. When she was working at a small shop on Commercial Road in London's East End, the young Margaret Bondfield was sent out by her employer late in the evening 'to scout around and see if the shops over the way showed any sign of closing; if they did, we too would hastily and gladly put down the shutters'.[18] This meant that shopworkers could frequently work as many as eighty to a hundred hours each week, for up to fifty-one weeks of the year.

One shopgirl described her punishing daily routine to *Cassell's Magazine*. She worked in 'a large shop' employing nearly a hundred other women. Her long shift started at eight in the morning with a half-hour dinner break at noon after which 'the standing and smiling and serving' began again for a further eight hours with only a short tea break in the middle.[19] The 'standing and smiling' might have looked effortless – indeed, this was part of the vital illusion that shopping was a 'pleasure' and never a chore – but in reality it could be a daily endurance test.

The first organised campaigns to counter this gruelling timetable had already begun in the 1840s with the Early Closing Association. Led by Victorian philanthropists – a steely mix of prominent charity workers, churchgoers, professionals and politicians – the association campaigned to shorten shop opening hours and, in particular, to put an end to Sunday trading. With the growth of towns and cities, the number of small traders had mushroomed and many were opening all hours, to cater for working-class customers whose own jobs demanded very long hours, including on Saturdays. It was these traders that the association had in its sights. Their campaign was successful in establishing some voluntary early closing agreements between shopkeepers, and half-holidays for assistants. But these improvements were limited. Local agreements like these quickly fell apart when just one shopkeeper opted out and they were no substitute for government legislation, which had begun to regulate other industries. Since the early 1800s, at least ten Factory Acts had famously limited working hours in selected industries and workshops; however, this legislation only benefited a fraction of the country's total workforce and mostly applied to women and children in textiles. Millions remained outside its scope, including shop assistants.

In 1873, things looked like they might be about to change. Liberal MP, banker and amateur naturalist Sir John Lubbock proposed that the Factory Acts be extended to shops. His Shop Hours Regulation Bill, sponsored by a new campaign group, the National Early Closing League, proposed that the working hours of women, apprentices and children be cut to ten and a half per day. Lubbock was already a household name: it was thanks to him that bank holidays had been introduced two years previously, referred to by many as 'St Lubbock's days'. He had been a strong supporter of the Factory Acts but thought it very unfair that shopworkers were not covered. He noted the absurdity of factory inspectors sometimes having to walk through a shop, right past assistants working eighteen-hour days, in order to climb the stairs to enforce legislation protecting those producing the goods on sale.[20] Lubbock also seemed impressed by his more personal dealings with the shopworker class. He was a passionate public speaker, giving regular lectures on the natural sciences to literary and scientific societies as well as to working men's associations. Shop assistants, ever eager to better themselves, were often in his audience.

Many middle-class commentators agreed with his message – that workers should seek self-improvement – but not with his methods. One vociferous opponent was Jessie Boucherett, now a veteran member of the Society for Promoting the Employment of Women.

In a letter to *The Spectator*, she argued that Lubbock's bill would 'throw women out of work' because shopkeepers, particularly those in poor areas who wanted to stay open for long hours, would have to hire male assistants. If they were to close early, as Lubbock advised, they would lose vital custom and, just as troubling for Boucherett, deprive other working women of their only chance to shop. As she put it, 'The servant-girl goes out in the evening, after the late dinner or supper of her master and mistress, to make her purchases; the charwoman goes out after her day's work is done, and she has put her children to bed and given her husband his supper; the woman or girl employed all day in handicraft or in manufactory goes out after she has had her supper and changed her dress.' It followed that 'at nine o'clock the shops are still busy, busier indeed than in the middle of the day'.[21]

Others shared her concerns. Another *Spectator* correspondent feared that enforcing Lubbock's bill would require the creation of 'a number of new offences', 'a crowd of fresh officials' and a new inspection regime 'of an exceptionally inquisitorial and offensive kind'. He invited readers to 'imagine every shopkeeper in the kingdom who employs a woman being liable to the domiciliary visits of an inspector at any hour of the day or night!'[22] In the event, most MPs agreed and the bill was shelved. Nevertheless, it marked an important staging post in a national debate about shopwork and trading hours that would run and run to the present day.

The question of whether women's bodies were physically suited to the demands of shopwork, or indeed any kind of paid work, would also run and run. In rejecting Lubbock's bill, MPs had decided that, compared with factory work, shopwork 'could hardly be considered fatiguing, much less unwholesome'.[23] Supporters of regulation now set out to prove them wrong, in print and in the lecture halls. In 1878, *The Times* ran a series of letters on 'the standing evil', exposing the 'suffering' of shop assistants and 'domestic slavery in the West End'.

Seats for customers had long been part of the furniture in the more fashionable stores, from mahogany high chairs at the ribbon counter to the occasional softer fauteuil in the dressmaking department. But for shopgirls themselves it was a different story. Shopkeepers demanded that their assistants stand eagerly at the ready, obligingly alert to a customer's every whim. Customers themselves felt affronted if ever they encountered a shopgirl sitting down. In one of the letters to *The Times*, Dr Arthur Edis, obstetrician and assistant physician at Soho's Hospital for Women, intervened on behalf of the ever-ready shopgirl. He wrote of 'a most cruel and pernicious custom that exists in nearly all ... large millinery and drapery establishments' and of young women unable to 'endure the fatigue and discomfort caused by this incessant standing'. He called on shopkeepers to do two simple things: provide their assistants with seats and, most importantly, allow them to use them. In the meantime, *The Girl's Own Paper* had its own suggestions. One ingenious but invidious one was that a dainty device rather like a shooting stick might be discreetly sewn onto the back of a shopgirl's bustle. A sketch portrays two smiling, perfectly attired shopgirls demonstrating the use of the device, apparently inspired by a similar one used by Alpine shepherds.[24] More of a perch than a proper seat, it was a perfect illustration of the shopgirls' social position as servants of the counter.

The following year the National Health Society held a lecture on 'London Shopwomen', highlighting 'the standing evil' and the many other strains of shopwork. Dr Edis was the main speaker and he quoted from a revealing letter written to him by a shop assistant who said she had 'stood until 1 p.m. without food', having missed breakfast in her lodgings. She and her fellow shopgirls had just twenty minutes for midday dinner and had to return to their duties as soon as the bell rang, 'whether we have finished or not', or face a 'fine of one shilling'. Supper was available 'from seven till seven thirty, and after that time, although detained in business, none was given us unless we had a written order from one of the firm, and if kept in to mark off goods, none was given us till we had finished, which was often as late as nine thirty'. Apart from mealtimes, shop staff were not allowed to sit down: 'Seats are not provided here, and if found sitting we should be fined and eventually dismissed.'[25]

Sir John Lubbock was among those who followed this debate keenly. Edis's evidence confirmed Lubbock's long-held belief that women needed to be protected from physical strain, and he may also have been influenced by his physician brother. Lubbock would eventually champion the wonderfully named Seats for Shop Workers Act in 1899. This required shop-owners to ensure that 'in all rooms of a shop … the employer carrying on business in such premises shall provide seats behind the counter … in the proportion of not less than one seat to every three female assistants'.[26]

Dr Edis's rallying cry was also taken up by other activists, including barrister Thomas Sutherst, working his way up to become chair of the reformist Shop Hours League. His book, *Death and Disease Behind the Counter*, was alarmist in tone but gave shopgirls a chance to tell their story, or at least one element of it. Kate M., an eighteen-year-old draper's assistant in south London, told a plaintive personal tale:

> I was quite well when I went into the business but after being behind the counter six months I began to feel the effects of the standing. I've been constantly unwell since. The long standing causes the most painful feelings in the feet, legs and back, and for the want of fresh air and outdoor exercise, an almost constant headache. Towards the end of the day the whole body aches, and a wretched low spiritedness accompanies it.[27]

And the problems she experienced wouldn't simply be remedied by being granted an occasional chance to sit down. Kate reported that she had heard all her workmates, 'six females and two males', aged from fourteen to eighteen, 'complain of the pains I have described as feeling myself'. She believed herself to be 'suffering from weak action of the heart, and often have fainting fits, especially when the shop is stuffy and no air about'. The experiences of 25-year-old Emily P., however, showed that shopwork could, in some cases, be life-threatening. She worked in drapery in Deptford and on London's Old Kent Road and her hours were brutal. Her shift began at 8 a.m. and ended at 10 p.m. in the week and midnight on Saturdays. Her breaks lasted just fifteen or twenty minutes and were cut even shorter as she was 'often called forward from a meal to the shop to attend to customers'. Meals were left 'half consumed' and then the food 'is either cold or we get no more'. Exercise and fresh air were rare. Emily couldn't 'get out for a walk except on Sunday, as no respectable girl cares to go out between ten and eleven at night'. She reported that 'when apprenticed to the drapery, my health was good, but it is gradually failing and the doctor says I am in a consumption'. As a result, she said she was 'obliged to leave at the end of the month'.[28] Sutherst did not record what became of Emily after she left her drapery job with little prospect of a full recovery.

Reformers like Sutherst and Edis succeeded in their efforts to keep political attention focused on shopgirls. In 1886, Sir John Lubbock proposed a further reform of shop hours, more than a decade after his first attempt. The Liberal government of the day, led by the ageing William Gladstone, appointed a select committee to examine the case again. The committee explored every element of shopwork, from working hours to wages to the class of assistants generally employed. They summoned expert witnesses, among them Sutherst and William Abbot MD, honorary physician to the Early Closing Association. Now, the medical case turned increasingly on the issue of shopgirls as future mothers. The committee was keen to know whether their work might 'injuriously affect them as childbearing women in after years'. There was no doubt in Dr Abbot's mind that it 'would do so' because 'according to all scientific facts, it leads to pelvic diseases and would affect them in after years when they became mothers'. The committee probed further. Would he 'in general way say that a domestic servant would be more likely to be a bearer of healthy children than a girl who stood in a shop for fifteen hours a day'? Dr Abbot was 'certain' that she would, because she 'has more frequent change of position, and a greater variety of occupation'. So, it was official. Unreformed shopwork was bad for young women and even threatened to undermine the British birth rate. Worse still, it followed that lower-class servants were now threatening to outbreed more respectable shopgirls – an idea guaranteed to strike fear into a generation still grappling with Darwin's terrifying idea that only the fittest of species would survive. The committee concluded that 'apart from the immediate injury to the person concerned' this was 'a very serious matter in the interests of a nation as a whole'. Dr Abbot again agreed. Shopwork was no less than a question of 'the physical condition of the future race'.[29]

The problem with these highly emotive arguments was that they were wheeled out whenever Victorian women made social progress of any kind. While the Society for the Promotion of Women's Employment was lobbying for the opening up of more trades to women and the changing of conditions to counter any resultant hardships, many other Victorian reformers were just as highly exercised about the damage that work – of all kinds – might do to women, rolling this out as another reason why they shouldn't be working at all. They had very mixed motives. Some wanted to establish and defend the rights of *all* workers. Others wanted to protect the pay and status of skilled male workers against the influx of 'unskilled' labour into all kinds of trades. For some, this meant excluding those unskilled workers altogether, especially cheaper female ones. There is more than a hint that this is what was going on when some campaigners insisted that shopwork was 'especially' harmful to young women's health.

As a consequence, men like Dr Edis, Dr Abbot, Thomas Sutherst and even Sir John Lubbock sometimes sounded all too similar to those who called for the exclusion of women from everything from factory work and farm work to politics and the professions. The 'problem' in each case was generally linked to women's apparently troublesome bodies. Earlier in the century naysayers had argued that women shouldn't be allowed to work in textile mills because their long hair would get caught in the machinery or that women were a hazard to others because, if they were breast-feeding, fellow workers might slip on errant breast milk. Outside the workplace, men with doctorates had warned that if women were admitted to universities they would be much weakened by the sudden rush of blood to their poor over-stimulated brains. Viewed in this light, arguments that shopgirls — rather than shopboys — should beware the pelvic perils of too much standing took on a dangerous logic. And after Darwin's evolutionary bombshell, motherhood assumed a whole new meaning. Many saw that well-bred women now had a duty not just to their husbands but also to their country to produce fit and healthy offspring. These new eugenic arguments became even more powerful when added to older economic ones that warned of dire consequences likely to follow if women were allowed to undercut male wages and dilute traditional male skills.

Yet powerful as these emotive arguments were, the parliamentary committee considering Lubbock's legislation was not minded, in the end, to restrict women shopworkers' hours. The 1886 Shop Hours Act was duly passed but it only protected children and apprentices, not adult women. And after all the debate, it decreed that young shopworkers aged between thirteen and eighteen could still work for a staggering seventy-four hours a week. Even then, sharp-minded employers found ways to push the legislation to its limits. Shortly after it came into force, sixteen-year-old Lizzie Cox accepted a two-year apprenticeship at F. Cape & Co. She was to learn 'the whole trade of Retail Drapery', to 'serve diligently and well', to be housed at Cape and to be paid nothing for her efforts. Cape was sticking to the letter of the law: Lizzie's one-page, handwritten indenture document shows that she had signed up for a seventy-hour week: 'her hours of business will be 9 o'clock a.m. to 8 o'clock p.m. and Saturday 9 a.m. to 9.50 p.m.' with 'any time lost by absency to be made up at the end of the apprenticeship'.[30] The spirit of the Shop Hours Act was arguably undermined by the apprenticeship system, which was still in force in many shops, including Cape; this meant that teenage recruits like Lizzie worked their long but legal hours for no pay at all.

Margaret Bondfield had eagerly taken up her own apprenticeship at Mrs White's in order to be independent; she had seized the chance to earn her own living. Money bought independence. So, even when disillusionment set in, when Margaret experienced first-hand the unhygienic conditions, endless hours and strict hierarchies in the stores and at her lodgings, she stuck with it. For shopwork held the promise of good pay. Broadly speaking, shopgirls' wages, at least at the upper end of the trade, compared quite favourably to women's wages in general – even after compulsory deductions for bed, board, work clothing and any fines were taken into account. According to a 1898 *Dictionary of Employments Open to Women*, female shop assistants could expect to earn £10 to £60 per year depending on their experience – a very wide pay range, equating to between approximately £4,000 and £22,000 in today's earnings. In the same era, a kitchen maid could expect to earn £24 per year, and a lady's maid £32. At the lower end of the female wage scale, those in tailoring and other sweated (or sweatshop) trades took home as little as five shillings a week or less than £20 per year, from which they had to pay for lodging and sometimes buy their own work materials. At the upper end, women in leading textile mills could earn up to nineteen shillings and sixpence per week, or just over £50 per year.

Among shopworkers of different grades, there were significant pay differences between the 'ordinary assistants' and the 'charge hands', who were responsible for groups of junior workers. Wages in London and leading provincial stores were much higher than in rural areas. Margaret Bondfield started on £15 a year and saw this rise over the years to £25, which included 'free' board and lodging worth around £20. The problem, however, was that few women – in any line of work – were ever paid what was considered 'a living wage'. At the time, living wages were for male breadwinners with mouths to feed. They were certainly not for young single women without family responsibilities or for older married women with husbands to support them. This logic, such as it was, was seriously undermined by two vital facts. First, husbands couldn't always find work or at least enough of the kind of work that would enable them to feed every member of their family. Second, there were at least two million 'surplus' women 'earning their own bread' in the late nineteenth century, some with families, as Harriet Martineau and the Langham Ladies had pointed out.

Low pay had other consequences. For one thing, it compromised shopgirls' all-important quest for respectability. A collection of essays, *Social Twitters*, put it this way: 'the pretty little milliner, with the bright hair and dove-coloured eyes, who shows off the Reubens hat to such perfection, cannot out of her salary afford pleasant airy lodgings or many home comforts'. Shopgirls like her and so many others were no princesses. After her 'hard day's work was over, she had to take off the fine clothes belonging to her employers, put on her own shabby ones and, like Cinderella, return tired and worn to a home in which neither peace nor pleasure is to be found'.[31]

Of course, not all shopgirls were content to spend what little leisure time they had stuck in their lodgings. But their options were limited, as explained rather balefully by Miss Corus, a 'young shopwoman in the Kingsland Road', in a letter to the journal *Social Notes* in 1878. She wrote in response to an earlier piece that had inquired, 'What do the young men and women do when the shop is shut?' Miss Corus said she was 'earnestly desirous of spending my leisure time both healthfully and improvingly' but surely spoke for many when she asked, 'But how am I to do so? Where am I to go? What am I to do? Where is there any place of easy access suited to my needs?' It was easier for young men. They could go to music halls or, if more serious minded, to evening classes. Miss Corus put it plainly: these pursuits were 'no use to us girls' because 'to walk there and back would consume all our time; to ride, we have no money'. The end result of this predicament was, in her view, that 'too many of us thoughtlessly engage ourselves to young men we do not respect, just to have someone to take us out, there being, as far as we know, no respectable place that we can go to alone!'[32]

However heartfelt, Miss Corus's dilemma could not compare to the situation faced by some others. For the story of Victorian shopgirls is inseparable from the story of Victorian sex work. Prostitution was one of the few female professions that could pay extremely well. It took many forms and, as with other kinds of work, had a distinct hierarchy defined by price, predilection and location. Male customers were certainly not short of choice. Those wanting to spend more could head for high-end arcades. London's Burlington Arcade was one of the first and most famous. Modelled on Parisian *galeries*, this covered passage of forty-seven luxury shops was built in 1819 by city landowner Lord Cavendish, who wanted it to offer 'gratification for the public' as well as 'employment for industrious females'.[33] The arcade was designed to draw in monied women customers who, as they browsed the glorious array of fabrics, jewels, millinery and confectionery, would be kept safe by liveried beadles guarding each entrance. Together with other Regency arcades around the country like the St James in Bristol and the Argyle in Glasgow, the Burlington was creating a new kind of female shopping experience. But it was an experience that carried a particular kind of scandal.

In the 1820s, the Burlington had advertised for 'professional beauties' to work in its shops and add to their allure. Those hired almost certainly sold discreet sexual services from lodgings above the premises as well, while the beadles turned a blind eye. Trade was brisk. Located on a block bounded by Piccadilly, Regent Street and Bond Street, the Burlington was at the centre of London's fashionable bachelor quarter, an area buzzing with gentlemen's clubs, chambers, chop houses, coffee shops and rented rooms.[34] West End prostitution had long been a part of this pleasure zone that took in Mayfair and Marylebone and served super-rich male clients including peers, politicians, professionals and dandies.

Young women became 'professional beauties' in the Burlington and elsewhere through a variety of routes. Some were doubtless attracted by the money and the lavish lifestyle and may even have seen it as their vocation. Others, however, had clearly been duped and even trafficked from the Continent, as court records reveal. In 1854, Frenchman Monsieur Germain Marmaysee appeared at the Court of Common Pleas in central London. The case against him had been brought by one of his employees, Miss Margaret Reginbal, who accused him of stealing her clothes and withholding £70 of her earnings from her – a high wage by any standard at the time but especially high for a young woman. She had been brought to London from France by Monsieur Marmaysee to work, or so she thought, as an assistant in a perfumier's but then found there was another, darker side to the deal. She was expected to become a prostitute. Whether or not she knew what she had signed up for, after around six months of it, she escaped, but was unable to retrieve her clothes or any payment. This must have happened innumerable times to innumerable 'shopgirls'. But this one, Miss Reginbal, took the unusual step of going to the police and shopping her pimp. Further investigation revealed that Miss Reginbal shared her lodgings with at least nine other young 'servants', eight of them from France, and that Monsieur Marmaysee himself made frequent trips back and forth across the Channel to procure fresh flesh. He was found guilty but avoided imprisonment and left the country.[35]

Court cases like these, and many others, show that prostitution was part and parcel of British urban life. But according to the official census reports, it didn't exist. The only women whose occupation is recorded as 'common prostitute' were those who spent census night under arrest in police cells. A 'professional beauty' residing in the Burlington Arcade would have appeared as 'milliner' or 'dressmaker' or 'shop assistant' or, like Miss Reginbal perhaps, 'perfumier's assistant'. The true scale of prostitution in Britain was thus concealed by self-censoring census entries. But self-censoring was only part of the story because the majority of women involved in sex work were indeed also respectably, if not gainfully, employed in precisely these kinds of female trades; trades that employed young women to make the goods destined for the shops as well as to sell them in those shops.

These connections have been made by using crime records to unlock a more secret census. Official census reports were edited from pages and pages of raw notes made by census enumerators who went from house to house and street to street. When the original enumerators' notes are read against local court records, however, the scale and true nature of Victorian sex work starts to slide into view. In 1841, another Frenchman, Timothe Cheval, was prosecuted for keeping a brothel. He lived at 15 Norton Street in the West End with his son and six young women, all French, all aged between fifteen and twenty years, and all listed in the census of that year as 'dressmakers'. In another case, Thomas Dorval was prosecuted soon after for the same offence. He gave his address as 67 Newman Street in Marylebone – a well-known red-light area and also home to Germain Marmaysee. The census shows that a few houses along, four milliners shared a house with three live-in servants. Given that four milliners were unlikely to be able to afford to pay three staff, it is highly likely that all seven women were sex workers.[36]

But this 'open secret' sex trade was not just a feature of the capital's consumer economy. In peaceful provincial Worcester, an anonymous whistleblower revealed the shocking truth behind the city's famous glove trade. At the time, the city still produced most of the country's gloves, famed for their quality and durability. The Glover's Needle remains one of the city's most well-known landmarks today. But in a letter in 1852 to *Reynolds's Newspaper* signed only 'Yours respectfully, Humanitas', the dire position of the gloveress was exposed. 'One of these poor girls informed me the other day that, after working all the week, at the average rate of sixteen hours per day ... she received 4s, out of which she has to pay 1s 2d for silk, the remaining 2s 10d being left to pay lodgings, coal, candle, and to *subsist* upon!' In these circumstances, many went out 'by owl-light to prostitute themselves to make up for the robbery they have sustained from the unprincipled, fiend-like employers'. Across the city, it was 'a common saying, "that gloving is only a cloak for something worse"'. Humanitas concluded that 'to be a gloveress is enough to stamp them with no enviable fame'.[37]

This whistleblower was unusual in linking sex work with women's low wages. While prostitution was certainly seen as the greatest vice of the Victorian age, it tended to be cast as a problem caused by immoral prostitutes themselves and the sexual temptations they posed. Men who succumbed were castigated by social commentators but their moral lapse was seen to be rooted in, and justified by, their natural physical urges. Only a small handful of reformers suggested women might be driven to prostitution because of 'cruel, biting poverty' and that the fault lay with mankind, not womankind.[38] Among these were a few doctors like William Acton and early feminists like Harriet Martineau. Others, like Scottish surgeon William Tait, made a similar link but took a harder line:

some women might be pushed into prostitution to make ends meet but others actively chose it as an indulgence, to pay for the fineries in life. In the 1840s, Tait authored *An Inquiry into the Extent, Causes and Consequences of Prostitution in Edinburgh*. He acknowledged that working-class women faced sharp unemployment and extremely low wages with 'sewers, dressmakers, milliners, bonnet-makers, stay-makers, colourers, book-stitchers, shoe-binders and hat-binders' earning an average of just six shillings per week. He was even moved to ask, 'How can a woman maintain herself if she is paid so little for her work?', citing the particularly reprehensible example of 'one shopkeeper in the Lawnmarket' who 'paid only 3d for a man's shirt'.[39] And yet, Tait still maintained that the 'natural causes' of prostitution were a young woman's licentious desires, pride, covetousness and love of dress. Some he labelled '*femmes galantes*', a reference to the sumptuously attired, feted and admired courtesans that he believed some young women tried to imitate.

Men like Tait saw a clear connection between consumerism, shopping and sex. Court cases like those involving the West End brothels had seemingly proved this connection beyond doubt. Now, newspapers like *The Morning Post* found further evidence. In January 1859, it calculated that one small network of the capital's streets had 'no less than 149 notorious houses of ill fame containing from six to ten fallen women each, which fearful array of prostitution was swelled by a large number of young women lodging in the districts who were known to be gaining their livelihood nominally by working for shops, but principally by the wages of night prostitution'.[40]

In the decades that followed, reformers made huge efforts to tackle prostitution. Some campaigned for its total eradication through moral restraint. Others, however, started to take a more pragmatic line. They believed that prostitution could never be eradicated but that it could be contained and cleaned up. The year 1864 saw Parliament pass one of the most hotly debated pieces of legislation of the times: the first

Contagious Diseases Act. It did not outlaw prostitution. Instead it effectively set up zones around key military towns and naval ports where women would be allowed to practise prostitution provided that they were registered and submitted to regular gynaecological checks. The checks included vaginal examination with a speculum and were intended to curb the spread of venereal diseases, then rife across the country and rampant in the armed forces. If found to be infected, the woman had to agree to be admitted to a lock hospital where she would stay until cured, if a cure was indeed possible. Even if they could see the logic, most people were appalled at the prospect of what was effectively licensed prostitution, despite the fact that this was common on the Continent. To feminists like Harriet Martineau, it seemed to give men licence to treat women however they liked – to pay them low wages, to push them into prostitution and then to curtail their liberty in a lock ward. Like thousands of others, she was further appalled by another implication of the Act: that *any* woman going about her business in these zones, maybe returning home from visiting friends or from a late-night trip to town, and merely *suspected* of being a prostitute, could also be subjected to the speculum. In 1869, together with Josephine Butler, she set up the Ladies National Association for the Repeal of the Contagious Diseases Act. It quickly became one of the biggest lobby groups in a generation. Over the next decade and a half it would submit over seventeen thousand petitions to Parliament, bearing over two million signatures. In 1886, over twenty years later, Parliament listened and repealed the hated legislation.[41]

But the very next year, the case of a Lincolnshire seamstress would reignite the debate about women's freedom of movement. Elizabeth Cass, twenty-four years old, was a mantle cutter from Stockton. In the spring of 1887 she moved to London and had just started a new job with a Mrs Bowman in her dressmaking business on Southampton Row. All went smoothly until one evening in

June when she went window shopping on Regent Street and was roughly arrested on suspicion of common prostitution. The arresting officer, PC Endacott, claimed he had seen her 'soliciting gentlemen' both that evening and on previous occasions. Miss Cass strongly denied the charges and was backed by an outraged Mrs Bowman, who put up bail and later lodged an official complaint. She was let off and discharged with a warning but she wasn't satisfied as she felt her reputation had been destroyed. Her attempt to prosecute PC Endacott for perjury failed but hit the national news headlines, making her a cause célèbre.[42]

Many Regent Street tradesmen supported her. After all, her reputation was tied to theirs. In July 1887, over forty of them held a meeting in the banqueting hall of the St James's Restaurant to vent their anger at Robert Newton, the stipendiary magistrate at Marlborough Street police court who had presided over the case. Mr Newton had dismissed Miss Cass with a warning but the traders believed that this in itself sent out a woeful message to other women: that they browsed the capital's brightly lit shop windows after dark at their peril. That could only be bad for business. The traders complained that Newton had sent a similar message when he had previously fined a group of 'well-dressed females' and issued them a stern rebuke: 'You were in Regent Street after ten, and you should not be.' From the traders' perspective, such magisterial decrees meant that, in effect, 'at ten o'clock every night a Black Flag were hoisted at either end of one of the most magnificent thoroughfares in London', setting it apart 'as a happy hunting ground for the debauchees of the town'. As they saw it, 'if the police may arrest and a magistrate imprison every woman in Regent Street after ten − then, *a fortiori*, every woman, especially if she be young and pretty, is fair game for the fast man about town'.[43] In other words, Mr Newton's efforts to curb prostitution by enforcing his own personal female curfew would endanger perfectly respectable women – and shopkeepers' profits.

Yet no one could deny that prostitution *was* endemic around Regent Street. It may have been one of London's premier shopping parades, but it was also one of its premier pick-up joints. A few months before the Cass case, another former shopgirl who had started off in an Edinburgh store had written a startling letter to the Duke of Westminster, an influential member of the Vigilance Committee of London, an organisation dedicated to the suppression of prostitution. Her story countered that of Miss Cass: she *had* found herself headed towards prostitution:

> Before I was married I had to get my own living. I had some experience at a large house in Edinburgh; left there and came to London in order to be near my parents, and about two years ago applied for a situation at a fashionable milliner's in Regent Street. I saw the master, who examined my reference, found it satisfactory, and offered to engage me at so small a salary that I said, 'It is impossible, it would not buy my clothes.' To which he replied, 'Oh, a girl with a figure like yours can easily pick up a good deal more than that in London. All our young ladies have latch-keys, and we ask no questions.'

She had a question of her own, however, for the Duke: 'Don't you think if men like this can be dealt with it would do more good than trying to convert girls who have been forced on to the streets?' She ended the letter: 'I have often longed to make this, my own experience, public, but dared not so long as my living depended upon the shopkeepers.'[44]

Soon after this and the Cass case, the nation would be gripped by the gruesome murders of 'common prostitutes' by Jack the Ripper in the capital's destitute East End. At the same time, a high-class sex trade was thriving in its decadent West End, operating under the cover of 'respectable' feminine trades. It was a pattern that was likely repeated in other cities. The true scale of Victorian shopgirls' involvement in prostitution will remain a mystery. They themselves, as well as the shopkeepers and their suppliers, had a clear interest in covering their tracks. As a result, the small amount of documentary evidence that exists linking shops and the sex trade provides but a hint of the true scale of the issue. The relentless rumours on this topic raised continual questions about shopgirls' respectability and fuelled endless fantasies about what some might be prepared to sell.

A fashionably dressed shopgirl, reading while she walks, photographed by *Punch* cartoonist Linley Sambourne.

CHAPTER 3

SCANDALOUS SHOPGIRLS

The violets were the last straw. Years later Harriet Whiteley recalled how her husband had come home one summer's day carrying a small bunch of flowers. She had heard enough rumours about his predilection for his own shopgirls and had written him a pleading letter, asking him to avoid public scandal and think of their four children. In private Harriet and William were already leading rather separate lives and he often travelled to the coast for the weekend instead of joining his family in their country home, Manor Farm, in Finchley, then a rural parish to the north of London. But when he dared come home with violets and unashamedly explained that they were from one of his shopgirls – 'plucked by her own dear little fingers' – Harriet could take it no more: 'I couldn't have them in the place, and I threw them away.'[1]

From this point onwards, Harriet and William Whiteley's marriage of fourteen years unravelled still further. They rowed and Harriet packed up the younger children with their governess, Miss Tollputt, and left for Folkestone, where the eldest child was at school. As the outspoken newspapers helpfully reported, this sparked 'rumours with a thousand tongues'. The next month, in August 1881, Harriet filed for judicial separation, on the grounds of adultery and cruelty. [2]

'The Great Whiteley Divorce' screamed the headlines, and over the coming months the intensive coverage of the 'Whiteley vs. Whiteley' scandal sold thousands of extra newspapers. When Harriet appeared in court in order to retain custody of the children, she was veiled, with a blanched face and tearful eyes. What Harriet stated in her divorce petition was the stuff of clichéd romance. Shopgirl Alice Allen, known as Daisy, had caught Whiteley's roving eye. He had wooed her in the store, with Whiteley and Daisy often alone together in his private room – where Harriet claimed that adultery had taken place. With his family safe in the capital, Whiteley had whisked Daisy off for weekends in Tunbridge Wells and in Hastings – it was all rather blatant.

The ensuing collapse of the Whiteley marriage and the characters caught up in the saga fed the Bayswater rumour-mill. A year later the Whiteleys settled just before their divorce was to be heard in court, with Harriet receiving an alimony of £2,000 annually. A young woman – presumably Daisy – who had worked at Whiteley's for nine years and who had been subpoenaed to give evidence for Harriet, was sacked the moment she returned to work with a note saying she should apply to the cashier for her remaining wages.

Daisy's story chimed perfectly with the perspective of the times. The public image of the girl behind the counter was not of a demure and callow innocent. In the musical comedy *The Girl from Kay's*, staged a few years later, Nancy, Mary, Cora, Mabel and Hilda made up the shopgirl chorus. They sang of being 'goody, goody little girls' who nonetheless were going to be 'naughty, till we're getting on for forty … we like a bit of Life!'. Flirtatious and mischievous, yet wanting to become good wives – this was a difficult balancing act within the strictures of late Victorian society. Women were depicted on the one hand as virtuous and tender ministering saints, chaste before and even within marriage, where sex was for procreation only and not an activity to be enjoyed. On the other hand was the feared, notorious figure of the prostitute and her imitators, described as oversexed, luxurious and diseased. Angels or the devil's temptresses: the middle ground was difficult and dangerous to negotiate.

And it was onto these shifting sands that the newly independent, earning, attractively dressed young women serving behind the counter were set to tread.

As the real-life Nancys, Mabels and Hildas flooded into stores and behind the counters, they swelled the ranks of shopgirls to hundreds of thousands and formed a whole new category of working women. In the ever-growing Victorian cities, crowded and bustling, shopgirls were a highly visible new workforce. They were agents of change, both because there were so many of them and because they had working lives and leisure time unlike any who had come before.

Shopping itself was changing and the foundations of how we shop today were being laid. A monumental shift was occurring in the way retailers thought about shopping. Female customers had always been important; when shopping for their families, wives were usually the decision-makers in terms of provisioning the household and clothing their kin, even if it was the husband or at least the husband's wage packet that was ultimately used to pay off the credit weeks or months later. But now the shopping entrepreneurs decided to elevate the female customer to new heights: she should take centre stage, for the key to commercial success lay with her.

In 1892 a large fire destroyed Jenners in Edinburgh, the oldest department store in Scotland. Founder Charles Jenner was by now an old man, but his entrepreneurial zeal remained undiminished. He chose the architect for the redesign and oversaw the project, fire-proofing the building with an iron and steel frame and introducing modern electric lights, hydraulic lifts and even air-conditioning. Britain's leading architectural photographer, Henry Bedford Lemere, took a stunning series of photos of the still-empty new interior, capturing this masterpiece of Victorian Art Nouveau.[3] Diffuse sunlight from the central lightwell softly lit up ornate balustrades, Corinthian columns and swirling milk-glass electric chandeliers. The delicate high chairs in the haberdashery department were waiting for the first customers, standing tall at counters displaying lace, handkerchiefs and shawls.

The redesign was an unmitigated success. On the day of the store's reopening, 25,000 visitors flocked to the Princes Street and South St David's Street entrances. The façade that confronted them featured carved figures propping up columns and standing on balconies. Female figures. They were caryatids representing the countries Jenners serviced: Scotland, England, Ireland, France, Germany and America. The message was clear: women were at the core of his business. Without them, the edifice of Jenner's store, his enterprise employing hundreds of people and the high-quality service offered to shoppers across the world would crumble.

Jenner was absolutely correct. As the middle classes had become richer over the course of the century, shopping for them had developed into a female-orientated activity, even a leisure pursuit, a status symbol of wealth as well as a functional necessity. Writer Anthony Trollope observed this in his articles on London tradesmen, describing the great firms of his day, the Marshalls and Snellgroves, the Meekings and the Whiteleys, with their largely female clientele. 'Send a man alone out into the world to buy a pair of gloves,' wrote Trollope, 'and he will go to some discreet and modest glove shop from which when he has paid his 3s 6d over the counter he can walk away.' His wife, Trollope countered, preferred one of the big stores where, as well as buying gloves, she can 'lounge there, and talk, and be surrounded by pretty things'.[4] Jeanette Marshall was one such wife from a professional family and her diaries in the 1870s and 1880s show that her weekday walk combined both exercise and shopping, visiting Lewis's, one of the co-operatives or Liberty's most days. It was rare that she exclaimed, 'For a wonder, did not buy anything at Lewis's or elsewhere!'[5]

Cartoonist Osbert Lancaster painted an astutely funny portrait of his great-aunt Jenny in his memoirs, comparing her intimate relationship with Whiteley's Universal Stores to that of an abbess and her convent. She saw Whiteley's and others as part of her domestic domain. Each of Lancaster's female relatives had their favourites: for Great-Aunt Bessie the Army & Navy Stores 'fulfilled all the functions of her husband's club', while Lancaster's mother preferred Harvey Nichols. Lancaster wrote that it was hard to underestimate how personal the relationship was between these lady customers and the shopkeepers. Some of the shop assistants became the ladies' confessors, 'receiving endless confidences on the state of their health, the behaviour of their pets and the general iniquity of the Government'.

In the 1880s, Great-Aunt Jenny lived hard by Whiteley's on Inverness Terrace, and after reading most of *The Morning Post* in the drawing room, she would pay her daily visit to the store. She witnessed each successive stage of growth and innovation, deploring each development as spelling future disaster. Nothing was too trivial to escape her attention. 'The appearance of a new cashier in hardware or a change in the colour of the parcel tape was immediately noted and gave rise to fears for the firm's stability.' Great-Aunt Jenny then returned home just in time to read the Court Pages – and their daily gossip – before lunch.[6]

Public life was opening up for the mistresses of villas and upper-class ladies like Jeanette Marshall and Great-Aunt Jenny. Visiting and travelling around city centres had previously been a restricted, even dangerous activity for women like them. Until recently, city centres had been dominated by men's lives: at work in factories, banks, courts; at play in men's institutes, clubs, dining rooms and pubs, as sites of prostitution. The streets themselves were an assault on the senses. They were teeming with life and activity, with working-class men and women living, working, eating, buying and selling on the streets. Henry Mayhew was an astute social observer, journalist and co-founder of *Punch* magazine who catalogued London life in his writings on the shops of London and, most famously, in *London Labour and the London Poor*. His weighty volumes are an encyclopaedia of street sellers of all kinds, from the most elegant to the most depraved, from sellers of gelatine, ballads and china ornaments to 'crawlers' begging, pickpockets thieving and prostitutes soliciting.[7] Often selling and entertainment went hand in hand; early photographs from the late 1870s show Caney, an ex-clown, caning chairs out on the street, and capture a little Italian boy playing a harp to collect pennies.[8] Charles Dickens had it right.

This world had not disappeared when Jeanette Marshall headed out into the thronging streets; she still had to contend with street sellers, sexual harassers and beggars. But she was living through a heady period of social change and rules on being chaperoned in public places were relaxing. At the same time, increased public transport, such as the new two-horse trams, gave her greater freedom to move around the city, and better amenities allowed her to stay away from home for longer, with teashops, ladies' kiosks and public lavatories all playing a part. For out-of-towners, special excursion tickets on railways like the Great Western made day returns into the capital feasible, leading one older lady to complain that 'people think nothing of running up constantly to London and ladies travel alone and unattended for reasons which would, in the eyes of their grandmothers, hardly have justified a jaunt into the nearest market town'.[9]

There was much to run up to town for. Public spaces, attractions and entertainments were opening up everywhere. Queen Victoria's Golden Jubilee in 1887 was marked by the acquisition of hundreds of plots of land for public parks, such as Victoria Park in Partick,

Glasgow.[10] City councils and philanthropists believed that providing green space in crowded areas would improve the physical and even moral health of the working classes. But park promenading was by no means restricted to working people; parks were conceived as places where all members of society could mingle freely, enjoying the flower displays, musical entertainment on the bandstands, sports, neighbouring art galleries – and each other. After all, it was promenading in Hyde Park on Saturday afternoons that allowed Arthur Munby to observe the tall good figures of elegant milliners and shopwomen and to strike up a conversation with shopgirl Eliza Close while sheltering from poor weather. And if it was pouring with rain, then middle-class ladies only had to run indoors, where a wealth of new entertainments were on offer. Spectacle was the byword; more so than ever before, the Victorian public was being treated to a wealth of visual delights and theatrical trickery. Liverpool, London, Edinburgh and Manchester all boasted exhibitions, panoramas and dioramas where, in a small theatre, winter snow might be magically transformed into a summer meadow and rainbows would glow after thunderstorms.

Shopping entrepreneurs fed off and fed into this new hyper-visual culture, both in Britain and across the water. *The Drapers Record* trade magazine for retailers faithfully monitored advances in Paris and the United States, where pioneers like Marshall Field in Chicago and husband-and-wife team Aristide and Marguerite Boucicaut in Paris were trailblazing a new consumer culture. Paris was at the forefront of modernity, 'the capital of the nineteenth century' as the German cultural critic Walter Benjamin later described it. From the French capital, an entirely new vision was filtering through, a revolution in display, marketing, consumption – and even ethics.

Monsieur Eiffel had helped design the most famous department store in the world in the 1870s, the Boucicauts' Bon Marché in Paris, creating a fantasy vision in glass and steel, openness and light. It was set out as a permanent fair, dazzling and sensuous. This was a new shopping experience, an international urban development as important as the twentieth-century out-of-town mall. For here it was all about browsing and show. It was a physical and social emporium of delights. Fixed prices were on display, you did not have to buy, and you could mingle with the other shoppers. You could be a strolling *flâneur*.

But, perhaps typically, the British didn't simply copy the French. Instead many British stores developed their own hybrid versions of the *grands magasins*.[11] Yes, Jenner designed sweeping staircases and galleries with long, flowing lines. And Harrods installed Britain's first moving staircase, at the top of which a shop assistant stood with smelling salts and cognac in case 'travellers' were upset by their new experience. And yes, Arthur Lasenby Liberty created the highly fashionable Eastern Bazaar in the basement of Liberty's, offering up a sumptuous display of decorative furnishings, fabrics and *objets d'art*, a feast for the eye that would not have looked out of place in Paris. But Liberty was set on challenging Parisian style and methods. He designed his in-house clothing range in defiance of Parisian haute couture and he built lasting relationships with English designers, many of whom were part of the Arts and Crafts and Art Nouveau movements. In this way Arthur Liberty personally fostered the decorative arts in Britain, so much so that Art Nouveau in Italy became known as the 'Stile Liberty'.

The resistance to overseas influence was, however, far more deep-seated than concerns over which chiffon to choose and how to design a walking dress. The concept of free browsing, of shoppers mingling and gazing with abandon, revelling in sensory delights in the middle of an urban crowd of mixed classes and mixed genders, was initially seen as dangerous, a threat to bourgeois society. And anything that allowed women to extend their shopping experience – new amenities such as rest rooms, luncheon rooms, writing rooms and lavatories, for example – might further threaten a respectable lady's morality. These innovations were challenging the fundamental purpose and ethics of shopping, posing the question as to whether shopping was a healthy, profitable activity, or an evil that was both socially dangerous and economically ruinous.

As ever, William Whiteley and his antics stood at the centre of this anxious, ongoing national debate. Whiteley had opened the first ever in-store Luncheon Room in London. Then in 1872 he applied for a licence to serve wine and beer alongside the buns and ices. He argued that this would be a convenience for the hundreds of country visitors who flocked to his store each day; he said he was simply responding to customer demand, being 'constantly asked for a glass of wine and biscuit'.[12]

His application unleashed a furore. At the general licensing meeting, the magistrates sat in the Vestry Hall, Paddington, and listened patiently to both sides of the argument. The opposing barrister, Mr W. Wright, rallied an eloquent attack on Mr Whiteley. Mr Wright contended that providing wine and beer to middle- and upper-class customers was dangerous; alcohol consumption among ladies was on the rise and Whiteley should not be encouraging them. Having advanced so far, he then tried to back away from his implied criticism, claiming he had no intention 'of questioning the respectability of Mr Whiteley or his customers'. But the aspersion had been cast; he had touched on the social assumption that virtuous ladies did not drink; alcoholic beverages were the preserve of racy, louche and immoral women.

Mr Wright then voiced his second concern. He feared that lower-class and 'fallen' women might dress up as respectable ladies and use Whiteley's as 'a place of assignation'. All in all, Mr Wright was suggesting that serving wine and beer would transform the Bayswater store into a brothel, where women would lose their grip on morality, and prostitutes, disguised as ladies, could meet their pimps and punters.

Whiteley's department store did, in fact, already have a louche reputation, partly as a consequence of Whiteley's own flamboyance and partly since it was located in a mixed area. With this in mind, Mr Wright's concerns were appreciated by the chairman of the bench, who felt that providing drink to Whiteley's customers was unnecessary; the magistrates promptly rejected the application.

But that was not the end of the story. A few months later the popular journal *The Graphic* labelled Whiteley's lunch room a dangerous 'importation from Paris' since it enabled customers, specifically female shoppers, to refuel during their supposed shopping marathons. Fortified by soups, cutlets, omelettes, macaroni and fritters, they would 'return once more to the slaughter' and spend, spend, spend. Namely their husband's money. 'The afternoon's excitement has all the attraction of a delightful dream, with a slight dash of an orgy.'[13]

Beneath his titillating tone, the *Graphic* journalist was articulating serious anxieties around female shoppers on several levels: reputational, sexual, moral, financial. His fears? Women's unrestrained desires, a looseness with their husband's purse and the seduction of a good bourgeois lady who might throw off all caution and even chastity.

The person who perfected this art of reader titillation, combining it with outraged moral condemnation – a literary tease – was Eliza Linton. She was a controversial, successful and widely read novelist and journalist. Earlier in her career she had defended women's rights; now she turned into a most ardent opponent of the same. She condemned the 'shrieking sisterhood' of women like Harriet Martineau and the early women's suffrage movement, who sought the right to vote, and she even criticised the 'modern mother'. Her most notorious article was called 'The Girl of the Period', an extraordinary meditation on English womanhood. She lamented the disappearance of the fair young English girl of old, with her innate purity and dignity, 'neither bold in bearing nor masculine in mind', whose aim in life was to be a good wife, a tender mother, an industrious housekeeper. She condemned 'the girl of the period', who 'dyes her hair and paints her face', her sole ambition being to indulge in the extravagance of fashion. For this she needed money; thus she sought a rich husband not for love but to allow her 'so much dash, so much luxury and pleasure'.

Linton's article was deeply conservative, harping on the eternal theme that the newest fashions were too immodest, too revealing, too impractical, too ugly. 'If a sensible fashion lifts the gown out of the mud, she raises it midway to the knee.' If bonnets were reduced in size, hers became a mere 'four straws and a rosebud'.[14] If hair ointment became outmoded, she went to the other extreme and let her hair wander dangerously down her back. But the article was also a critique on an increasingly polarised society, where Linton saw capital becoming king and money the dominant driver. In her mind, young, well-to-do women – potentially mothers of the nation's leaders – had set off on the wrong path.

Linton honed in on her targets in another article entitled 'The Philosophy of Shopping'. It is a poetic rumination on shopping, which she saw as a worshipping of false gods. Linton wrote that shoppers were flirtatious coquettes, tantalisingly delaying the moment of decision-making as they flitted between competing indulgences, between different gaily tinted silks. She wrote about assiduous shopmen servicing the ladies, and the power kick a lady received when she was 'suddenly transported to a position of supreme command, with a world of material luxury at her feet'.[15] Linton used language that was implicitly sexual, the language of desire, longing, enticement, control and fulfilment. She herself was coquetting with her readers, sensuously describing the charms of an afternoon's shopping before cruelly lambasting them, censoring both the act of shopping and women who shopped. A 'waste of time', 'wholly unnecessary', a 'very expensive kind of amusement', better expressed

Linton's attitude to shopping. As for the actual shoppers: 'they have no method in their domestic management and are always at sea as to the real condition alike of their wardrobes and of their purses.'

The everyday allure of the products behind the counter was bad enough for writers such as Linton, but at sales time shoppers would completely lose control of themselves and their purses, according to the drapers and shopkeepers who profited from these snatches of consumer frenzy. Sales were not, however, a new phenomenon in the late 1800s: in *Reminiscences of an Old Draper*, William Ablett recalled how, as a teenage assistant in the mid century, he helped his master prepare for a sale of excess and damaged stock, a 'selling off'. On the first morning a surging wave of eager customers waited outside the heavy doors while everything was unnaturally quiet within. '"Open the doors!" shouted my master upon entering the shop, and in poured a multitude that filled it from top to bottom in a twinkling.' They bought goods of every description and 'critical old women, that under ordinary circumstances would have spent a long time, in the usual course of business, examining a pair of stockings, bought the same goods, instantly, at full prices'. Even when the sale products got into a sad mess, people still bought them, 'right and left, using but little judgement'.[16] A draper writing later that century was even less complimentary, noting in his diary that 'there is something about the crowds of women that reminds me of a farmyard'. His diary was published under the title *Hades! The Ladies!*, which aptly sums up his attitude towards his precious customers.[17]

Animalistic behaviour and a loss of human dignity and self-control: this is what consumer frenzy was apparently driving women to. And for a small number of shoppers, the desire for possession pushed them one step further. They stole. Yet their actions were seen not as criminal but as diseased, the disease of kleptomania. Petty theft was one of the most common women's crimes, but now it was 'lady shop-lifters' who caught the public imagination. It was difficult for staff and early store detectives to challenge a well-to-do customer who looked as though she had pilfered some goods, difficult for them to switch from being deferential to being confrontational. Many stores simply sent the ladies away with a gentle ticking off.[18]

Nevertheless, a handful of thieving customers were not just caught red-handed but were actually taken to court, as was the case for Mary Ann Harvey. At Whiteley's in January 1885, general manager Richard Burbridge was touring the departments when he spotted a lady looking 'very bulky'. He followed her for a moment, then asked if she had been attended to, to which she replied yes. At this point, being the general manager and having strong suspicions, he decided to challenge the customer. What had she under her cloak? he asked. Surprisingly, she replied, 'Velvet,' and on further questioning, she claimed that she had lost her sales ticket. Burbridge requested her to accompany him to the office; on the way there she was seen by the attendant shop assistants to drop forty-two pocket handkerchiefs, two pairs of gloves and twenty-four and a half yards of velvet. The police were called. When Mrs Harvey appeared in court two weeks later, she was sentenced to one year and eight months' penal servitude.[19]

This swirling public anxiety around the moral dangers of con-sumerism, voiced so eloquently by Eliza Linton among others, was heightened by the fact that those on the other side of the counter looked so desirable themselves. Shopgirls looked good. The counter assistants were young and unmarried; they had to dress smartly, with spotless cuffs and collars and carefully arranged hair. Their dress, though not ostentatious, often nodded towards the latest fashions. They cultivated an air of professional chic. There is a certain element of theatre involved in shopwork: shopgirls were out on display, in the public gaze, behind the counter for all to notice, admire, even gawp at. Antoinette R. sold gloves in her father's shop. She was pretty and found that the gentlemen she served stared at her 'as if she were an unseen object'.[20]

Shopgirls, like barmaids, actresses, music hall singers and maid-servants, were objects of male fantasy. Female cloth workers had already featured in pornographic material in the eighteenth century; early nineteenth-century pornographic engravings of the lingerie trade showed women flirting with their male clients and offered voyeuristic peeks at groups of women together behind closed doors.[21]

Some young men pursued them with dogged zeal, gathering eagerly outside staff entrances at closing time. Other customers and hangers-on had a more direct approach. One worried woman wrote in to *Cassell's Magazine* about her shopgirl sister who attracted a lot of attention from shopmen and gentlemen customers alike. They invited her out to plays and evening entertainments, 'and it does seem hard to be always keeping her at home with me'.[22] The letter writer succinctly summed up the dilemma of the modern shopgirl: 'It's a difficult thing to keep respectable in a large shop.'

As peddlers of objects of desire, young women were often explicitly hired for their looks above all other considerations. Their height, figure, perceived beauty, class and all-round manner were examined – the higher class the establishment, the taller, fairer and higher class the shopgirls needed to be. It was now even becoming acceptable for 'young ladies of birth and education' to stand behind the counter, as long as they had the right position in the right shop.[23] In larger firms, the job specification differed not simply according to the hierarchy of the shopfloor, where saleswomen were more elegantly turned out than mere counter assistants;[24] there were also differing demands from one department to the next, some more befitting these 'professional men's daughters' than others. Nevertheless, if you didn't look good you had less chance of being hired in any position – or you lost your job, like the shopgirl with the 'awful, ugly scar on her face' who was given notice in spite of her quiet manner and diligence when her master realised that customers preferred not to be served by her.[25]

A young woman's looks were scrutinised intensely when she first applied for a job. 'Crib-hunting' was the term given to looking for work. A young woman in need of a new position would scour the advertising columns of the morning papers for details of the newest vacancies. Then she toured the firms, traipsing through town, appearing on time at the allotted hour only to wait in a long queue of similar-minded, similarly dressed young women. One applicant described what usually happened next:

'What department do you want?' demanded the engager.

'Lace,' I replied.

'Too short,' was the answer, 'good morning.'

'Am I too short for any department?' I inquired desperately.

'You are, I said good morning!'[26]

She held out a little more hope for the next place – at least she was more thoroughly examined.

'Just turn round will you? Let's look at your hair. That's all right; thought it was short. Now take off that jacket thing, and let's see how you look in your business dress. H'm! Not so bad.'

Only once the applicant had passed the looks test did the engager get down to business, quizzing her about what salary she expected. She dolefully explained the usual endgame: 'Very often I'm afraid we end by begging to be taken on in the mean little shops that only put a card in the window.'

As the century drew to a close, even more emphasis was placed on appearance when a new beauty queen emerged among the so-called shoppies: the house model. The trend had taken root in Paris, at the instigation of Charles Worth, the father of haute couture. A Lincolnshire man, Worth started out in the London drapery trade, working at Messrs Swan & Edgar's, a silkmercer's and costumier's emporium on Piccadilly. He moved to Paris in 1846, took a job at a French draper's and married draper's assistant Marie Vernet, a *demoiselle de magasin*, who modelled shawls, mantles and bonnets in store. He soon asked his wife to take her modelling one step further: he wanted her to model a dress. And so Marie Vernet became arguably the world's first professional model. But this was just the start: Worth established his own dressmaking business in Paris, at 7 rue de la Paix, which became the internationally famous House of Worth, and as his artistic genius began to get recognised, orders flew in from the royal houses of Europe. Worth introduced the concept of fashion shows four times a year, his collections modelled by his wife and other *demoiselles*. When Charles Worth died in 1895, the House of Worth was taken over by his two sons.

The House of Worth's every innovation was carefully noted across the Channel. British couture houses and dressmakers also took to showing dresses on house models, who wore stiff black undergarments and laced boots in order to preserve propriety. The buyers for Liverpool stores Bacon's, Cripps and De Jong's, all of them on Bold Street, which was known as 'the Bond Street of the north', would go to London several times a year and buy a selection of sample gowns. They would advertise their return in the *Liverpool Mercury* and place a discreet card in the window announcing that they were 'Showing at 2.30 p.m.' At the appointed hour one of the shopgirls would act as mannequin to model the latest London fashions. Liverpool customer Miss Stevenson Jones recalled, 'The lady assistant might say, "Would you like the bodice so-and-so", or "What kind of trimmings would you like?" And then you would choose your material; the young men would bring suitable materials for you.' After choosing her preferred fabric, Miss Stevenson Jones would attend three separate fittings and then receive her new dress a fortnight later.[27]

In London, Lucile – born Lucy Christiana Sutherland – was the capital's most notorious couturiere. In her autobiography she scoffed at 'the plainest of girls' chosen as mannequins by her more conservative competitors. 'Even the most nervous mamma could safely take her son with her to the dressmaker's when temptation appeared in such unalluring guise.'[28] Lucile firmly believed that dresses should be shown in motion, that the movement of fabric on a live person was far more appealing and comprehensible to clients than a dress displayed on a headless wooden dummy or stuffed with tissue paper.[29]

But fabric in motion wasn't enough for Lucile. She wanted to push the boundaries of modelling way beyond anything Charles Worth in Paris or old Mr Cripps in Liverpool would have considered acceptable. Lucile's plan: to ramp up the sex appeal. She recruited her own corps of 'glorious, goddess-like girls', choosing her first six young women, full-busted and with long limbs, from the working-class areas in south London. She sent them to her own hairdresser and taught them how to walk elegantly by balancing books on their heads. She changed their names: Susie became Gamela and the other girls from Bermondsey and Balham were transformed into Dolores, Phyllis, Florence and Hebe. The photograph in *Sketch* magazine of her 'Beautiful Mannequins' shows sensually draped young women more voluptuous than today's catwalk models.

In 1900 Lucile staged the very first catwalk parade. She invited Princess Alice, Lily Langtry and the Duchess of Westminster. 'I shall never forget the long-drawn breath of admiration that rippled round the room as the curtains parted slowly and the first of my glorious girls stepped out onto the stage,' Lucile recalled. Her show was a runaway success: she was showered with congratulations and – more importantly – dress orders. From then on, Lucile's shows were more theatrical, more distinct than those of any of her competitors. She used ramps, curtains, lights and music to create a distance between the spectators and the mannequins; she was signally offering up her Hebes and Gamelas to be gawped at. The models themselves became the talk of the town, with customers coming to Lucile's parades out of curiosity to see the models as well as the clothes.

Then Lucile encouraged men to attend as well as women, which was still highly unusual, and gave her gowns erotic names such as 'Elusive Joy', 'Incessant Soft Desire' and the sensational 'Red Mouth of a Venomous Flower', modelled by a young woman clad in bright scarlet. The *Bystander* magazine reported on a later show, recording the effect on the gentlemen in the audience, whom the journalist listed as 'certain flâneurs of Bond Street, various loafers familiar to the Carlton "lounge" and celebrated Piccadilly-trotters'. These gentlemen gazed on suggestively, with easy insolence. 'They were invited to stare and smile, and they did. But there was something remarkably offensive in their way of doing it.'[30]

The same year as her first catwalk parade, Lucile married Sir Cosmo Gordon Duff. As Lady Gordon Duff, Lucile became England's first titled modiste and could now approach American heiresses marrying into the British aristocracy, the so-called 'dollar princesses', on an equal footing – which did wonders for her sales. Not all the men attending the fashion parades can have been that offensive, for all of Lucile's original models married 'above their station': Dolores married millionaire art-collector Mr Tudor Wilkinson; Phyllis wed the American Mr Jesse Franks, also known as 'the Wall Street Wizard'; Florence married into Scottish aristocracy; and Hebe ended up as a chatelaine in a castle outside Paris.[31] What Lucile's memoir does not record is whether any of her later models stepped out with her gentlemen customers but were never proposed to, becoming mistresses rather than wives.

Lucile's 'glorious girls' were the goddesses in the showroom firmament but inevitably there were soon hundreds of demi-goddesses, as bigger establishments increasingly hired young women who could venture out from behind the counter to model as occasion required. This heightened the sense that the counter and the showroom provided a legitimate, at times highly sexualised, meeting place between men and women of different classes.

The line between what a shopgirl was actually selling – the goods or her own body – sometimes became blurred. This reputational twilight for shopgirls did not brighten for decades; even in the first years of the twentieth century the same anxieties and accusations were being aired. In 1909 the radical Nonconformist minister Reverend Reginald Campbell went public with his theory that fashionable London stores were a major source of vice. At a meeting of shop assistants at the Champion's Hotel, he didn't mince his words. 'In some West-End shops young women are paid such a miserable wage that they are expected, and, indeed, encouraged, to eke it out by the selling of their bodies.' In Reverend Campbell's eyes, it was the combination of low pay and glamorous surroundings that proved so insidious. 'It is no doubt true that love of fine clothes, luxury or pleasure, has been the ruin of many girls, shop assistants, as well as clerks or domestic servants.'[32]

Reverend Campbell had thrown down a gauntlet at the shopocracy; he offered to give evidence in court against any establishment where immoral activity could be found. The shopkeepers responded to Campbell's challenge with alacrity. A reporter from *The Drapers Record* had been present at the hotel meeting, and he duly reported Campbell's speech. The following months saw a war of words between Reverend Campbell and the Drapers' Chamber of Trade, which accused Campbell of libel, slander and sensationalism. The Bishop of London sided with Campbell. Lloyd George, by then chancellor of the exchequer, had major political backers among Welsh department-store owners, so he sided with the proprietors.[33] Campbell and the Bishop never came up with the necessary hard evidence, so, in this particular skirmish, the shopocracy won.

Such public discussions about shopgirls' reputations hardly helped their cause. On top of this, conservative thinkers were worried that shopgirls' morals might be under attack from a wholly different foe. They were concerned about the dangers of loose reading. One of the leading suppliers of what they saw as unedifying reading material was Alfred Harmsworth. Harmsworth was to become a giant of the newspaper world, founder and proprietor of such famous titles as the *Daily Mail*, *Daily Mirror*, *Observer* and even *The Times*, dominating public opinion through his editorials in a way that no one else managed before or since. He started less illustriously, making his fortune selling cheap weekly papers to the hordes of newly literate boys and girls. School attendance was now compulsory for boys and girls until the age of thirteen, and literacy and numeracy levels across the nation were on the rise. The 1880s saw the first significant wave of Board School-leavers entering the job market and Harmsworth spotted a business opportunity, noting that these establishments were turning out 'hundreds and thousands of boys and girls annually who are anxious to read'. He saw that they were rejecting the ordinary newspapers; not for them *The Morning Post*: 'They have no interest in society, but they will read anything which is simple and sufficiently interesting.'[34]

Harmsworth was a publishing genius in many respects. He was one of only a handful of publishers who not only noticed this new category of readers but recognised them as a developing market and even helped shape their new identities. He published comics and popular magazines aimed at boys, such as *Comic Cuts*, *Union Jack* and *Halfpenny Marvel*. He also categorised and targeted the new 'girl market'. A 'girl' in his eyes was not simply a schoolgirl, but encompassed almost any young, unmarried and probably working woman. So his periodicals, such as *Forget-Me-Not* and *Girls' Friend*, addressed their madcap stories, advice columns, letters pages and advertisements to factory and mill girls, nurses and servant girls, lady guides and flower girls. And, of course, shopgirls.

Forget-Me-Not ran romanticised, serialised stories of shoplife over several weeks in 'The Adventures of a Shop Girl', 'That Pretty Shop Girl' and 'A Little White Slave'. The cast list of each tale often included a plucky shopgirl heroine, her virtuous but poor suitor, a tyrannical shopwalker, a villainous aristocrat and a millionaire's fortune. They were dramatic tales of mistaken identity and disguise, mysteries and false accusations. They contained lines like, '"Miss Raines!" cried Phoebe, "You had better come forward and confess the truth, and not bring dismissal on us all!"' In the end, wrongs were righted, identities were revealed, working conditions were set to improve and wedding bells rang.

Girls' Friend even featured 'Only a Shop Girl', which claimed to be the first published work of a real-life talented young shopgirl, portraying her surroundings and everyday struggles 'with a vividness and truthfulness which will hold the reader spellbound from start to finish'. Other articles in girls' magazines written by shop assistants described their working life, the hardships of the living-in system and the challenges of querulous customers.

One hot topic featured in *Forget-Me-Not* was 'The Shopgirl's Chance of Marriage'. The cheery column was quite positive on this issue, suggesting that shopwork provided 'special opportunities for meeting eligible members of the opposite sex'.[35] Another edition offered tips on 'How Shop Girls Win Rich Husbands', with supposedly first-hand accounts of businessmen from the Midlands and Scotland, country gentlemen and Irish colonials all being very pleased with their shopgirls-turned-wives.[36] Lucile's gorgeous girls could easily have featured here.

The reality for most shopgirl readers, however, was very different. Courtship, let alone marriage, was extremely difficult to negotiate. Late evening opening hours and the strict living-in regime set up countless logistical barriers to romance. On top of this, most stores had a – written or unwritten – marriage ban, for both male and female assistants. Permission from one's superior was needed in order to marry and after the wedding most assistants were dismissed. Consequently, a high proportion of shopworkers remained single and the store dormitories were referred to as 'monasteries and convents' where 'the celibate brothers and sisters of the counter' lived.[37]

Still, shopgirls' own accounts told eloquently of their longing for marriage as 'their one hope of release', with the anguished cry of 'marry anybody to get out of the drapery business'. It wasn't all anguished longing, however; the excitement of flirtation played its part too. In the back workrooms, chatter was 'chiefly concerning young men, love, courtship and marriage', with the most animated conversations dealing with 'Young Men's fancies'. And the reading material they were consuming often fuelled these excitable chats.[38]

Penny periodicals were cheap and could be bought on the street and at railway stations. Indeed, the railway newsstand, with its link to suburban commuter travelling, became an iconic site for popular reading material. A contemporary observer described the morning commute: 'The clerks and artisans, shopgirls, dressmakers, and milliners, who pour into London every morning by the early train have, each and every one, a choice specimen of penny fiction with which to beguile the short journey.' The observer pointed out a working man 'absorbed in some crumpled bit of pink-covered romance' and the girl in the carriage sitting opposite, sucking a lozenge, reading a story called 'Marriage a la Mode'.[39]

The stock plots of such pink-covered romances and penny fictions will be familiar to any Mills & Boon reader now – though more through today's historical series than the red-hot imprints. The very first book that Gerald Musgrove Mills and Charles Boon published in 1908 was a romance, and from the beginning they produced novels in a form and at a price that was within the reach of a wide readership. Nevertheless, some early Mills & Boon didn't fit the romance formula. Highly prolific romance writer Arthur Applin published his story *Shop Girls* under the Mills & Boon imprint, but his subtitle, 'A Novel with Purpose', hints at something less saccharine, less straightforward than we might expect. Indeed the central romance between respectable, business-minded Martha, a shopgirl in the hosiery department, and gentleman shopkeeper Horatio Brown is complicated, with Brown being exposed as a spy for a Whiteley-style shopping magnate and ending up in prison rather than in church. Applin describes shop conditions in the small town and in London as dystopian: shopworkers are characterised as industrial slaves, female friendships on the shopfloor are sacrificed to careerism and shopgirls have to have sex with proprietors to land a good job. Applin's *Shop Girls* ends not with wedding bells but with the Whiteley figure being alone in the world, without love or emotion, 'Just the man behind the counter who handed out the goods. Always that and nothing more.' Applin delivered on his promise of a novel with a purpose: the reader closes the book with a sense of the injustices of shopwork, and the dangers of life for vulnerable shopgirls.[40]

This explosion of popular reading material affordable to working people was welcomed by some feminist and socialist thinkers, who believed that any form of reading was better than none. But what is difficult to comprehend from a twenty-first-century perspective is the anxiety on the part of more conservative thinkers around cheap reading material, sentimental fiction and bitty magazine columns. From an educated Victorian perspective, reading was a fundamentally important activity, which had the power to shape the reader's body and soul, for good or evil. Reading was compared to eating, with Sir Francis Bacon often invoked: 'Some Bookes are to be Tasted, Others to be Swallowed, and Some Few to be Chewed and Digested.'[41] The importance of reading, its role in shaping the reader's moral and physical being, was discussed by church leaders and philanthropists, publishing magnates and parliamentarians, Charles Dickens and Anthony Trollope.

The argument followed that, just as eating bad food would lead to food-poisoning, so reading 'bad' literature would endanger the soul. 'The strawberry ices of literature glow on every railway bookstall,' warned an article called 'What Should Women Read?'. 'These are harmless occasional reading, but a mind glutted with them needs medicine as much as a greedy child after a surfeit of sugar plums.'[42] Others had far stronger fears and criticisms, for sentimental fiction with its pat romantic endings was rarely seen as mere escapism. Romantic fantasy might breed dissatisfaction in the reader when comparing her own life to a fictional life. It might give her ideas above her station, if all the stories she reads end with the girl like her walking up the aisle into the arms of a baronet. Another concerned writer criticised popular reading material as a false representation of real life. 'It heightens only imaginary and unattainable enjoyments, and transforms life itself into a dream, the realities of which are all made painful and disgusting.'[43]

But even worse than breeding internal dissatisfaction, the wrong kind of reading apparently had the power to spark an external questioning of the social order. There was fear that reading might stir up dangerous political instincts, leading directly to revolt. This was not as far-fetched as it seems: memories of the Peterloo Massacre of reformers in 1819, of Chartist uprisings and revolts against the Corn Laws of the 1830s and 1840s, all fuelled by political tracts written by pamphleteers, were still strong. There was an acute awareness of the power of the printed word.

Not just the body politic, but also the physical body was seen to be in danger. On the one hand, the distracted reading of short magazine pieces might destroy the mind's ability to focus on weightier, longer subjects: too much snacking, no substantial meat and potatoes. On the other, sentimental romances, with their 'imaginary and unattainable enjoyments', might inflame the reader's imagination, and thus her body parts, leading to early sexualisation or over-sexualisation in adolescent girls and young women.[44] For shopgirls, working in a sexualised environment of public display, it was feared that such reading might inflame them even further. American physician Dr Mary Wood-Allen certainly believed so. Her impressive title was World Superintendent of the Purity Department of the Women's Christian Temperance Union in the United States. Her work focused on women's health and sexual purity, and was read by similarly minded thinkers in Britain. In 1899, she published *What a Young Woman Ought to Know*, a most extraordinary how-to manual, with tips and views on countless aspects of a young woman's life, from dancing to fresh air, from the 'sex mania' sparked by over-passionate female friendships to the problems of 'tight clothing on the pelvic organs'.

Dr Wood-Allen warned, 'I would like to call your attention to the great evil of romance-reading, both in the production of premature development and in the creation of morbid mental states.' She felt that these negative mental states led directly to negative physical states, in particular to those afflictions classed as female. She listed 'nervousness, hysteria, and a host of maladies which largely depend on disturbed nerves'; such classic 'women's illnesses' were thought to stem from the female nervous and reproductive systems. Indeed, one of the most evil physical afflictions that Dr Wood-Allen identified was masturbation. Romance reading drew 'mental pictures which arouse the spasmodic feelings of sexual pleasure'.[45] Sexual pleasure was meant to be enjoyed not solo but with one's husband, and to remain firmly under covers in the marital bed.

Attending the music hall and the new musical comedies might not lead to a shopgirl pleasuring herself, but there was, it was believed, a real danger of her being pleasured by others in the excitable and unruly crowd, either during or after the show. By the turn of the century, music hall was at the height of its popularity; theatres up and down the country, from Glasgow's Britannia Music Hall to Leeds'

City Varieties, seated hundreds, sometimes thousands of people each evening. Variety was the name of the game: handbills advertised lions' 'comiques', escapologists such as 'the Daring Young Man on the Flying Trapeze' and, most famous of all, star singer Marie Lloyd. No wonder this entertainment seemed tempting to shopgirls who worked long hours and then returned to the strictness and drabness of shop lodgings at night.

A writer on domestic life, Mrs Jeannie Loftie, recognised the temptation: 'There are many steps between the shop and home. The pretty work-girl need not go alone.' She might be wooed by a 're-spectable young man' of her own class. Or a man superior in social position might take her 'to some place of amusement where pleasure, and above all, excitement can be found!'[46] And this, Mrs Loftie felt, was dangerous. For music hall crowds were rowdy; audiences were allowed to smoke, drink and eat, unlike in traditional theatres, and there was ample opportunity for getting close to your lover. On top of this, the very nature of the entertainment was spectacular, sensational and risqué. The aim was to stimulate and electrify a mixed crowd. To polite society, both the behaviour of the audiences and the entertainment itself seemed indecent and vulgar, and music hall came under sustained attack. In 1897 the London County Council launched an investigation. There is an apocryphal story that the LCC Theatres and Music Hall Committee called up Marie Lloyd to respond to the accusations of indecency. She sang them a supposedly offensive song straight, with no accompanying gestures. Next she sang the respectable drawing-room song 'Come into the Garden, Maud', adding 'every possible lewd gesture, wink, and innuendo'.[47] 'It's all in the mind,' she is supposed to have concluded.

Towards the end of the nineteenth century a new form of theatre emerged: the musical comedy. Elements of farce, vaudeville and comic opera were mixed with a longer, sustained storyline and presented by theatre managers as a more respectable entertainment, aimed directly at this new class of urban working people. Scottish theatre critic William Archer described his fellow theatre-goers on a Saturday night as 'young men and women who worked hard for their living at the desk or behind the counter. We were simply good, honest, respectable, kindly lower middle class lads and lasses, enjoying an entertainment exactly suited to our taste and comprehension.'[48] Another theatre critic had a more nuanced take on the 'lower middle class lads and lasses'. He was perplexed at the way they conducted themselves, noticing both the pleasures and dangers associated with their urban nightlife, as they wandered 'alone at night from one end of London to the other, spending all their money in gadding about, on six-penny novels, on magazines, and, above all, on the theatre'.[49]

Shopgirls didn't just form a part of this new audience; as in fiction, they were the heroines of the stage too. Playwrights like H.J. Dam saw the potential – 'As many people do business at the large shops and stores, I realised the stores formed an excellent sphere to make the basis of a musical piece' – and came up with *The Shop Girl*, which was staged at the Gaiety. The famous Gaiety Theatre was on Aldwych just outside the City of London, first established as the Strand Musick Hall. When *The Shop Girl* opened there in 1895, the show heralded a new era in musical comedy. It was less raunchy than earlier musical farces, but its plot was still romantic, as London shopgirl Bessie Brent turns out to be a millionaire's daughter and ends up marrying her poor but respectable sweetheart Charles. And the acts and songs were still racy. It was the first show to feature the beautiful dancing corps of the Gaiety Girls and its most famous song was 'Her golden hair was hanging down her back'. The show was a hit, a very palpable hit, to use Shakespeare's phrase. It transferred to Broadway and was performed again and again in Britain, perpetuating a certain sexual knowingness, despite its supposed respectability, that infuriated its conservative critics.[50]

The outpouring of anxiety around the morality of shopgirls,

from such a wide range of interest groups – conservative thinkers and feminists, philanthropists and medics, religious writers and parliamentarians – testified to a society that was trying to come to terms with a new class, the 'kindly lower middle class lads and lasses' that the Scottish theatre critic described. For the awareness of class, of one's 'station' in life, had in no way diminished as the population grew and society changed. In the teeming cities, where servants and mistresses, grocers and clerks, lords and shopgirls now lived and worked cheek by jowl, class awareness, and particularly awareness of the fine gradations between classes, arguably increased. This in turn raised the question of where this new breed of working people would fit in, and whether they would accept the status quo, or try to change it to suit their own lives.

Some people fitted in nowhere; they fell through the cracks in society. Horace Rayner was one such man: a complex, pitiable figure, his dramatic end the byproduct of a shopgirl's love affair. His mother was the sister of Louisa Turner, another of William Whiteley's shopgirl mistresses. Who Horace Rayner's father was remains a mystery. It was his 'great secret ... the curse of his life'.[51] Horace Rayner claimed it was William Whiteley, suggesting that he had seduced the two Turner sisters and fathered sons by them both. Horace Rayner stated his mother had revealed the truth to him on her deathbed. By 1907, Horace Rayner was unemployed, unable to support his young family, susceptible to erratic mood swings and depression. He needed money desperately. On 24 January, after several glasses of brandy, Rayner gained entry to Whiteley's office on Westbourne Grove. A messenger to an umbrella-maker witnessed what happened next. He saw William Whiteley come out of his office and tell his staff to 'fetch me a policeman'. Whiteley was followed by Rayner, who apparently asked, 'Are you going to give in?' When Whiteley replied no, Rayner said, 'Then you are a dead man, Mr Whiteley.' Rayner then pulled out a revolver and shot

Whiteley twice. The messenger didn't see what happened next, for he 'was frightened and ran behind the counter'.[52] A third shot rang out and the messenger saw Mr Whiteley fall.

Horace Rayner had murdered William Whiteley. He then tried to commit suicide, shooting himself in the right eye. But he was still alive and was taken to St Mary's Hospital, where he told the casualty surgeon, 'I am the son of Mr William Whiteley. I have shot Mr Whiteley. I have shot myself and have made a mistake. Give me something to make me sleep away, there's a good boy.'[53]

Five suffragettes hold a broken window in its frame, with Adela Pankhurst on the far left, following the chaotic 'War on Windows' in 1912, when over 270 shop windows were smashed.

CHAPTER 4

GRACE DARE UNDERCOVER

Grace Dare lived up to her courageous nom de plume. Going undercover to expose shopworkers' scandalous conditions, she took the fight for their rights to the top. In fact, Grace Dare was none other than Miss Margaret Bondfield. In 1896, at the age of twenty-three, Margaret was already a seasoned shopgirl, having worked her way up from draper's apprentice in Hove to positions in a series of high-class shops in London. She had become a secret member of the National Union of Shop Assistants, which was founded in 1891, an affiliation forbidden by her employers. She missed church on Sundays, her only day off, to attend union meetings. But she was far more than simply a secret union member. She was a spy. In 1896, she began penning a series of bold articles with the aim of stirring up the world of shop-keeping, aimed at exposing the exploitative conditions of shopwork. Margaret recalled how she would wait until her room-mates were asleep and then 'stealthily, with the feeling of a conspirator, knowing I was committing an offence for which I could be heavily fined, I would light my half-penny dip, hiding its glare by means of a towel and set to work on my monthly article'.[1]

Bondfield's fierce sense of social justice had begun at home. She was born the eleventh child of Anne and William Bondfield, but in spite of the size of their brood, they hadn't neglected Margaret. A Somerset textile worker, William had instilled in his daughter a strong sense of the dignity of work and a belief in women's rights. When Margaret left home to work many miles away in Sussex, she struck up an unusual and powerful acquaintance with one of her well-heeled Hove customers, Louisa Martindale. Mrs Martindale was a prominent reformer with a passion for women's freedom. Always keen on finding practical steps forward, she held open house for local shopgirls every other Sunday. The event had in fact begun as an open house for isolated and often poorly paid governesses, offering them a chance to unwind and make friends. Martindale's daughter, Hilda, recalls that her mother had then extended the event on alternate weeks to 'another set of women whom she began to think were also oppressed – shop assistants'. She remembers that '[a]mong these came an eager, attractive and vividly alive girl of sixteen, Margaret Bondfield'. The girl was 'not happy' and 'needed sympathy' and was just as ready as the governesses 'to talk when she found her hostess really wanted to listen'. Margaret was spellbound by Mrs Martindale, whom she later described as 'a most vivid influence in my life, the first woman of broad culture I had met, she seemed to recognise me and make me recognise myself as a person of independent thought and action … she put me in the way of knowledge that has been of help to many score of my shop mates'.[2]

When Bondfield moved to London in search of better prospects, she was further primed for politics. Ever eager to improve herself, she signed up for an evening class studying the poet Robert Browning, little knowing that she would soon sign up for much more besides. One of the other members of the class belonged to the Women's Industrial Council, an organisation newly set up by Clementina Black in 1894 to improve the lives of working women.

Black was a socialist and the daughter of a Brighton solicitor. Like other members of the Council, she was critical of the philanthropy so beloved by other middle-class reformers, believing that lasting social change first required solid changes in the law. In the evening class, Margaret's new friend persuaded her to assist the Council as an undercover agent. How exactly their discussions segued from Browning's verse to covert operations will have to remain a mystery; Bondfield in her autobiography is simply matter-of-fact about this highly unusual conversation, one that was to change the course of her life and propel her into politics.

Mrs Gilchrist Thompson, a leading light of the Council, explained that a scheme was 'hammered out' whereby Margaret undertook to spend two years investigating shop conditions. At her 'own dis-cretion', she was 'to obtain engagements in various shops and to stay long enough to judge of the conditions'. She started in 'a high-class shop (but one of the worst, as we believed)', but 'as her references grew shorter, she descended the scale of the shopping world'. She was thus, quite knowingly, 'ruining her future in her own profession for the sake of the well-being and safety of girls unknown to her'.[3]

Margaret proved to be the perfect spy. As Grace Dare, she documented squalor and exploitation behind the counter, her assumed character reminiscent of the courageous heroines dashing across the pages of the new girls' magazines. As well as providing first-hand evidence for a 1898 Women's Industrial Council report, her revelations were published in the union journal, *The Shop Assistant*, and were also reworked by the popular *Daily Chronicle* newspaper in a series promising to reveal the true 'life of shops'. The series covered everything from hiring to firing. It showed that when young women went 'cribbing', or job hunting, they had to be prepared for some pretty probing scrutiny about their personal lives. In one large West End drapery house, 'Grace' was interviewed by two men – one of the owners and one of the buyers. They asked about her prior experience, as expected, but also interrogated her about her parents, her brother and her politics. Her height and figure clearly gave cause for concern: 'She's very short!' At the end of interview, 'Grace' was asked, 'What is the very lowest salary you will take?' and told to write this down on a piece of paper as those kinds of figures, unlike the applicant's physical attributes, were never openly discussed in store.[4]

Grace's notes also record how struck she was by the contrast between customers' attitudes in the East and West Ends. In the East End, 'although the hours were long, the relationship of server and customer was much more human ... We could help to make five shillings go as far as possible in value. We would hear all about the joys and sorrows of the family, and get glimpses of brave hearts under the most sordid exterior.' It was a different story in the West End, where 'very rarely were we regarded as other than the lackeys to wait upon the customers as did their domestic servants.' Sometimes these customers were charming, 'as only cultured people can be charming'. However, they were often blunt and imperious. Grace recalled one incident 'when a very fine lady was extremely rude to me. I was not in a position to answer back; I just looked at her. She went as far as the door, and then came back, and said with disarming frankness: "I am bad-tempered today. I will have those stockings."' Grace's astonishment was not at the woman's rudeness, which she and others routinely encountered, 'but at her recognition of it'.[5]

There was some light relief. Sale weeks were hard work for the staff but also afforded some amusement as well as sheer bemusement. Grace and her fellow shopgirls were astounded to watch their social superiors almost come to blows:

I remember once, two women were quarrelling over a certain article. One holding one end, and one the other. 'This is mine,' said No. 1, 'and this is mine,' said No. 2. 'No it isn't,' from No. 1. 'I found it first and I mean to have it,' from No. 2. At this point the article came in two parts and the two women staggered back. I said gravely, 'That settles the matter, you can now have a leg each.' They meekly took up their belongings and disappeared without even a smile.[6]

Bondfield's main objective, however, was to capture some of the dire working and living conditions and the flagrant abuses of 'paternalist' proprietors. One shocking *Daily Chronicle* report featured the owner of 'a certain shop in Bradford' who disposed of diseased meat from his farm by serving it up as supper for his hapless assistants. Worse still, he fined them 2s 6d if they failed to clear their plates. On this occasion, the shopkeeper was taken to court and convicted. Far more commonly, it was the shopworkers who came off worse, such as the assistant who was first fined and then sacked for daring to leave uneaten pork on his plate. Any shopgirl finding herself summarily dismissed like this could face additional dangers. The *Chronicle* asked its readers to put themselves in the shoes of a young woman 'cast adrift, you and your one corded box, on the streets of London with no friends within call, your home away at a Somersetshire farm or in a Welsh valley, and the few shillings in your pocket not enough to get you there'.[7] The fear was, of course, that such unfortunates would end up in prostitution.

Reformers had been documenting the raw deal forced upon many retail workers since the 1860s. Yet nearly four decades later, Grace Dare's revelations and the *Daily Chronicle* reports still described long hours, low pay, bad food and other horrors of living-in. Individual assistants might have been 'too timid' to speak up, but – in the *Chronicle*'s view – it was 'not slanderous to tell the truth about breakfasts of stale bread and rancid butterine, the watery tea, the pallid chicory decoction which serves for coffee, the crowded, dingy, and ill-ventilated dormitories'.[8]

Reformers faced an uphill struggle against the shopocracy. Shopkeepers had emerged as a powerful political lobby during the nineteenth century. The wealthier among them had had the right to vote since the 1832 Reform Act and were the first generation of middle-class men to do so. Their politics were complicated, however. On the one hand, many fiercely independent traders loathed outside interference in their private, often family, business affairs. On the other hand, some believed they needed to band together to strengthen their interests by, for example, agreeing standardised closing times. Shopkeepers were broadly united, though, in their suspicion of the emerging labour movement and its calls for the increased and far-reaching regulation of working conditions. The labour movement had been given huge momentum by subsequent electoral reform acts, which had finally begun to extend the vote to many working men. It also took on increasing significance in the face of the volatile economic situation of the late Victorian period: periodic downturns meant that everyday wages frequently struggled, or simply failed, to keep pace with everyday prices, leading workers to look for more radical ways to improve their lot.

The first trade unions had been established earlier in the nineteenth century by skilled workers anxious to defend their pay and traditional craft status in a rapidly industrialising nation. Above all, they wanted to protect their turf against unskilled workers. By the 1880s, however, all this started to change. Unskilled workers themselves began to organise and to flex their labour-market muscle. Indeed, one group of young women made history. On 5 July 1888, around two hundred East End matchgirls walked out of the Bryant and May matchworks in protest at the summary dismissal of one of their workmates. They headed for the Fleet Street offices of the radical newspaper *The Link* in search of its editor, Annie Besant. A few days before, and with the support of fellow activist Clementina Black, Besant had published a damning article on conditions at the firm, exposing its controversial use of poisonous white phosphorous and branding its bosses 'white slavers'. With Besant's support, the action escalated and soon another

1,400 women walked out. They surprised everyone by winning their case. Their victory opened a whole new chapter in working-class politics. Thousands of unskilled, casual and sweated workers followed their example. The 1889 dock strike, for example, involved up to eighty thousand dockers, stevedores, warehousemen and casual labourers and brought London ports and their vital global trade to a standstill. This strike, too, was successful and inspired the creation of many new unions.

Among them were the United Shop Assistants Union of London, founded in 1889, and the much larger National Union of Shop Assistants, which was formed in 1891 when eleven shop assistants' organisations from cities around the country decided to join forces.[9] For the first time, shop assistants had access, in theory at least, to trade organisations representing their specific interests. This was a privilege already enjoyed by many of their employers, who were free to join federations of grocers, master bakers, meat traders and shopkeepers, to name just a few.

The two shop assistant unions merged in 1898 to become the National Amalgamated Union of Shop Assistants, Warehousemen & Clerks (NAUSAW&C). It had clear aims: 'to reduce the hours of labour; to abolish unjust fines; to secure definite and adequate time for meals; to obtain proper supervision of the sanitary arrangements of shops, and the abolition of the living-in system'.[10] Shopkeepers were not impressed, however. Many made it clear to their staff that if they joined, they would be shown the door. And perhaps because of this, very few assistants did sign up. By the late 1890s, membership of the National Union of Shop Assistants, Warehousemen & Clerks stood at just 2,000, less than 1 per cent of Britain's 750,000 shopworkers.[11]

Margaret Bondfield was quickly enlisted by the union to help to swell its ranks. She faced an uphill battle. Where matchgirls had led, shopgirls were reluctant to follow. Their long hours left little time for anything else, let alone activism, and living-in usually put them out of unionists' reach. Bondfield recalled running the gauntlet in several shops. Trying to 'avoid the shopwalker, or anyone who looked managerial', she would seize her chance and distribute her union leaflets until she was 'ordered out'. One irate grocer 'read a leaflet, tore it up and stamped on the bits', shouting, '"Union indeed! Go home and mend your stockings!"' If she did succeed in sparking a shopworker's interest, Margaret faced further challenges in trying to arrange a follow-up conversation. Calling again during business hours was very risky as it 'might mean the sack for the assistant'. A meeting might instead be 'fixed up after the shop was closed, in a café, or even on the pavement'.[12]

But it wasn't only logistical difficulties that deterred shopworkers from joining their union. It was often their personal politics, or lack of them, and their apparent sense of superiority over other workers. This exasperated activists like Margaret beyond measure. She gave vent to her frustrations in her scathing report of a nationwide recruiting tour that she undertook in 1898. The Berkshire town of Reading was one of the worst offenders. There, 'most assistants have time to enjoy a little social life after business and they do not trouble themselves to think of the thousands who haven't'. They were neither aware of, nor concerned by, the precariousness of their own positions: 'they are satisfied with their present conditions; they do not realise that *they are not fixtures.*'

Still, Margaret was prepared to accept that some workers needed, as she herself had, to have their eyes opened to the union cause, which attracted 'much prejudice'. Though Gloucester was a more positive prospect – Margaret judged that 'in this compact little town it should not be difficult to organise every shop worker' – Bristol was another matter entirely. Her inside-sources told her that 'a lion' was 'in the way' in the shape of a twin tyranny: first, 'that employers would instantly dismiss anyone known to join the union' and second, 'that assistants will never be organised because they are snobs'. This was too much for Margaret. She poured scorn on workers who needed to be 'cajoled to meetings by sugarplums in the shape of a bishop or a garden party!'. Such people would 'be better outside our ranks' and the local branch should devote its energies to those who 'detest their pretences of gentility as much as I do'.[13] Shopworkers who thought themselves too good for a trade union had an over-inflated and misplaced sense of their own importance that belied the fact that they were, in her words, a 'forgotten and negligible class'. Those who thought they were anything more should wake up and realise that to the 'throng of thoughtless purchasers' they were 'often less than nothing'.[14] Harsh words indeed.

When it came to 'class psychology', Margaret thought that shop-girls were even more flawed than their male counterparts. They were especially snooty, not only towards other working girls but also to some of their female customers. The disdain she had complained of in customers could work both ways, it seemed: 'Gentility, elegance, and inflexible regard for appearances, mark the shop assistant. The woman who goes shopping in the West-end will be eyed with cold disdain by the young ladies if she is badly dressed. There is an air about the assistant which suggests a certain status and independence, a professional chic which is inherent to the calling.' She saw their chic as a sham and one cause of the 'gulf that yawned deep' between the shallow assistant and the more solid artisan.[15] Their 'false gentility' needed to be 'weeded out', felt Margaret. Only then could shop-workers take their place as 'self-respecting working class people'.[16]

Even if a shopgirl could overcome these flaws and muster the courage, inclination and time to sign up to a union, she faced further challenges. Most unions, even the new ones, were run by men for men. As a result, the relationship between women and unionism was never an easy one. The earliest organisations had been set up to fight for a family wage for male breadwinners – a worthy cause, but one which was to drive a lasting wedge between the longer-term interests of male and female employees. It was difficult for the unions to justify the promotion of female workers' rights when the majority of their membership feared that women would undercut men's wages. On top of this, they were increasingly concerned that women might muscle in on their skills. Indeed, the Trades Union Congress was itself set up in 1868 in part to ensure that working men could be saved the indignity of having to send their wives and daughters out to work to make ends meet. Over thirty years later, when Margaret Bondfield attended her first TUC conference in Plymouth in 1899 as assistant secretary to the shop assistants union, she was the only female delegate in the hall.

The National Amalgamated Union of Shop Assistants was unusual in that although women made up only around 10 per cent of its membership, they occupied many of its senior positions. A young woman named Agnes Pettigrew, a former Glasgow shopgirl, was appointed as its first full-time female organiser in the 1890s. She was already a veteran activist, having helped to organise Scottish shoemakers. A fellow Glaswegian, Mary Macarthur, would become another of the union's leading lights. She was just twenty-three and had worked as a book-keeper in her father's drapery business, one of the first generation of girls to have attended Glasgow High School for Girls. She admitted that she'd gone along to her first union meetings to scoff, but was unexpectedly impressed by what she heard.[17] Duly converted, she signed up and rapidly rose up the ranks, quickly becoming the first woman on the national executive in 1903. She was nurtured and supported in all this by Margaret Bondfield. When Mary first moved south, she lived at Margaret's London flat and stayed for three years, a kindred spirit who became a lasting soulmate. At the time it would have been very difficult for the two women to have had any kind of open relationship, should either have desired it, but one of Margaret's early biographers believed Mary to have been 'the romance of her life'.[18]

Women like Margaret, Mary and Agnes certainly helped to put shopgirls on the political map, but they remained the exception. The majority of Britain's female workers did not join the new unions. There was, however, an alternative organisation to which thousands of women were drawn: the co-operative movement. It had been born half a century earlier, in the 1840s, when a group of local flannel weavers formed the Rochdale Equitable Pioneers Society, clubbing together to open their own small shop in Toad Lane. Known simply as 'The Store', at first it sold a small range of essentials — butter, sugar, flour, oatmeal and candles — but its aims were anything but modest. In the past, the scales had been tipped in favour of shopkeepers, with unscrupulous traders overcharging customers, fiddling weights and adulterating drink. By setting up their own shop and dealing with their own suppliers, the Rochdale Pioneers took control of their living costs. The Society met weekly in the Weavers' Arms pub just down the road to go over the books. The monumental difference between this shop and others, however, was that its customers had to be members of the Society too. And as members they shared both profits and responsibility for decision-making. This was a new kind of business — one owned and operated by its members, for its members.

The idea took hold. The 'Rochdale principles' were quickly adopted by other working-class communities across Lancashire and Yorkshire — and eventually around the world. By the 1860s, the Co-operative Wholesale Society, as it was now known, had truly broken the mould of British shopping and shopkeeping. It bought in bulk from wholesalers, and therefore far more cheaply than individual shopkeepers were able to, and sold the goods in its own outlets. People who wanted to shop there had to become a member of the Society, just as the original Pioneers had done. Prices were fixed and the stores accepted cash payment only, never offering credit. These innovations alone meant that Co-ops came to be forever associated with the 'better sort' of working-class families, those who were paid regular wages and didn't need to put things on the slate to get by. Members were rewarded with a generous quarterly dividend: the more you bought, the bigger the divi. In some stores, this amounted to a real-terms price cut of nearly 20 per cent.[19]

But this was not just about discounts. Co-operatism as a whole aimed for nothing less than moral renewal through everyday shopping. George Holyoake, one of its most prominent supporters, painted a picture of an average Saturday evening in the Rochdale store:

> Toad Lane on Saturday night, while as gay as the Lowther Arcade in London, is ten times more moral. These crowds of humble working men, who never knew before when they put good food in their mouths, whose every dinner was adulterated, whose shoes let in the water a month too soon, whose waistcoats shone with devil's dust, and whose wives wore calico that would not wash now buy in the markets like millionaires, and, as far as pureness of food goes, live like lords. They are weaving their own stuffs, making their own shoes, sewing their own garments, and grinding their own corn. They buy the purest sugar, and the best tea, and grind their own coffee. They slaughter their own cattle, and the finest beasts of the land waddle down the streets of Rochdale for the consumption of flannel weavers and cobblers.[20]

In Holyoake's view, the free market would never match up. As he put it, 'When did competition give poor men these advantages? And will any man say that the moral character of these people is not improved under these influences?' The moral model at stake was perhaps best summed up through that well-known nineteenth-century soundbite: self-help. The idea was simple: even the poorest could make a better life for themselves and their families through self-discipline and self-improvement. Fortune would favour the prudent and the prudent would look for fair prices. Two years before Samuel

Smiles' best-selling book on the subject appeared in 1859, Holyoake published *Self-Help by the People*, his own account of the Rochdale experiment. This was picked up by leading social commentator John Stuart Mill in his *Principles of Political Economy*, seen by many as a new kind of manual for a new kind of industrial society.

Whether drawn by the divi and its discounts, or by loftier promises of moral renewal, or both, customers flocked to the new Co-ops. In some places in the north-west, like St Helens, more than half the town's population became members. Understandably, traditional local traders were rattled and they hit back hard. Traders' Defence leagues and associations sprang up around the country from the 1880s onwards. They tried everything to stem the proliferation of co-operatism, from urging their own customers and suppliers to boycott Co-op stores, to financing anti-co-op candidates in local elections. They campaigned for 'fair trade' and 'fair profit' and accused Co-ops of overcharging unsuspecting customers with prices that were fixed deliberately high. The St Helens Traders' Defence Association published a guide on 'How to fight the Co-op', which was promoted through the national *Tradesman and Shopkeeper* journal. One of its recommendations was not to employ any shop assistant with personal or family connections to the Co-ops. Holyoake was scornful. To him, these shopkeepers were the 'pigmies of commerce'.[21]

There was no stopping co-operatism. It was becoming a colossus of commerce. By 1881 over half a million people, largely in the north of England but increasingly beyond, had joined nearly one thousand local societies, which had a combined turnover of £15.4 million per year. Thousands of people were employed by the movement, in its dairies, bakeries and factories as well as in its new banks and insurance offices and, of course, in its stores. Here, product ranges were expanding dramatically too. You could now buy everything from your weekly groceries to 'Integrity' underwear and 'Holyoake' boots, and you could even fit out your home with Co-op furniture.

The better-off were also beginning to get a taste for co-operatism, through what would become a high-street fixture. The first Army & Navy Store on Victoria Street, London, was started by a group of former officers in 1871, initially specialising in imported wholesale port and sherry. It soon branched out into good-value golf clubs, guns, leather goods and cigars, alongside household staples. This was co-operatism with a conscious touch of class and it proved an instant and enduring hit.[22]

From the start, the co-op movement forged a particularly strong connection with female customers, who, across the social scale, kept a sharp eye on everyday costs. While female workers remained marginal in most trade unions, female consumers flocked to become co-op members. They also carved out their own distinctive niche within the movement: the Women's Co-operative Guild. By the turn of the century, the Guild was one of the largest women's organisations in the country. Its twelve thousand members debated everything from food prices and family planning to women's work and pay. A much more radical foremother of today's Mumsnet, its kitchen-table politics had a profound effect on wider social debate. Led by a charismatic duo, Margaret Llewelyn Davies and Lilian Harris, the Guild was invited to serve on many parliamentary panels and inquiries, on topics from maternal health to divorce reform. Some called it 'the trade union for wives and mothers'.[23] Margaret Bondfield, who later joined the Guild, admitted that she 'heard more sound common-sense from those women' than she had heard 'in much more learned assemblies'. They didn't 'beat about the bush' but went 'straight to the heart of the matter'.[24]

While Bondfield herself was lifting the lid on private retailing, the Women's Co-operative Guild began to investigate working conditions in their own Co-op stores, suspecting that they were exploiting their many female workers. In the late 1890s, Lilian Harris surveyed 104 outlets employing 1,662 shopgirls and her first impressions were favourable: 'The women and girls have an hour for dinner, half an hour for tea and, as a rule, they go out for meals.' Looked at in the round, however, Harris found that Co-op shopgirls seemed to face the same challenges as those behind the counter elsewhere, working long hours for low pay, albeit with a longer meal break.[25] The Guild began to lobby the leaders of the Co-operative Wholesale Society on the matter, but to little avail.

It also began an intriguing experiment in shop-based social work. In 1902, Margaret Llewelyn Davies moved to Sunderland to help set up a new Co-op store with a difference. As one of Cambridge University's first female students, Llewelyn Davies had no shopkeeping experience herself. Undeterred, she saw it as a way of bringing co-operatism to the very poorest.[26] The store was on Coronation Street in one of the city's most deprived wards. Llewelyn Davies turned it into a People's Store that not only sold 'cheap, nourishing food', including hot soup for a penny and hot pease pudding for a ha'penny, but also offered a savings bank, a library, a meeting hall and social events. In addition to the normal shop assistants, the People's Store employed two live-in social workers from the Women's Guild. Known as the 'store ladies', they visited local families in their homes and also kept a desk in the shop next to the grocery area, from where they managed the savings bank and dispensed advice on budgeting, debt and much besides. The experiment was inspired by 'settlement houses' that had been set up in east London and Manchester some years before as a practical way of promoting self-improvement through outreach work. The Sunderland initiative had a promising start. Four hundred people attended its opening tea and one visiting reporter later described it as a 'mission to help people to help themselves', starting from their 'homeliest needs'. There was 'no patronage, no church, no charity', but instead 'a real neighbourliness and absolute social equality'.[27] This rather rosy picture disguised growing tensions, however, between the Sunderland Co-op Society, which was funding the store ladies' activities, and the Women's Guild. After two years, the ladies resigned on the grounds that they were being 'unduly interfered with' and the project came to an end.

Meanwhile, outside the world of the co-op, two thirds of Britain's 750,000 shopworkers were still living in, and arguments for scrapping the system altogether were mounting. The first public protest on this issue was led by shop assistants at Whiteley's. Not for the first time, Whiteley's proved to be a game changer. In 1901, six years before the proprietor's murder, a group of its male assistants took the dramatic step of parading along Oxford Street with sandwich boards advertising a mass meeting against living-in. One of their main complaints was that living-in was 'unmanly'. While it gave them a roof, it deprived them of much else, including a social life, higher pay and the chance to marry; also, by preventing them from owning or renting property, it excluded many from the right to vote. The parade was a call to arms. Philip Hoffman was a former Whiteley's worker from a German migrant family who had become a leading activist in the shop assistants union. He remembered that 'It roused London all right, especially drapery London.' The protest meeting was held at Westbourne Park Chapel and was presided over by radical preacher Dr John Clifford. It was packed, with 'hundreds turned away', and, according to Hoffman, sparked a wave of 'protest meetings and demonstrations all over the country'.[28]

Although powerful, the wave broke, leaving little lasting change in its wake. Another started to swell in 1907, however, as MPs debated legislation seeking to address the scandalous fact that many workers in all kinds of industries were still losing a significant slice of their wages through fines and other deductions. Once again, shop assistants testified to the trials of living-in. This time, the protest meetings inspired by their accounts spilled over not just into demonstrations but into strike action, starting in south Wales and spreading to other areas. In July 1907, twenty-four workers walked out of Daniels and

Co., a draper's in Kentish Town in north London. For Hoffman, these events were turning points. By then he was a veteran shopwork reformer. He'd shared numerous platforms with Margaret Bondfield, including at a mass rally in Trafalgar Square attended by over five hundred assistants in support of the 1904 Shops Bill, which attempted to enforce more extensive early closing. Hoffman saw the 1907 protests as nothing less than 'a revolt ... the first open rebellion of shopworkers against the ancient thralldom'.[29]

After sixteen weeks and much supportive press coverage, a settlement was reached that began to dismantle Daniels' long tradition of living-in. Anxious not to lose their staff to more progressive competitors, leading stores, including Grose Brothers, Debenhams and Derry & Toms, followed suit and began to allow male assistants, at least, to live out. But shopgirls were still generally required to live in. Employers continued to argue that this protected their moral welfare. Margaret Bondfield cut through this old line: if they were 'to become useful, healthy women' and, in time, 'healthy wives and mothers', they needed, as a matter of urgency, to 'begin to live rational lives'.[30] Shopgirls didn't need cosseting; they needed independence, shorter hours and better pay. Bondfield's own campaigns literally took a dramatic turn in 1908, when she was asked by writer Cicely Hamilton to advise on a new play. In the first scene of *Diana of Dobson's*, five shopgirls undress for bed above a Clapham drapery store. The curtain rises on a dormitory 'in darkness except for the glimmer of a single gas jet turned very low'. As the jet is turned up, it reveals 'a bare room [with] very little furniture except five small beds ranged against the walls – everything plain and comfortless to the last degree'.[31] According to Bondfield, 'it was the real thing, with boxes under the bed, clothes hanging up on hooks, the general dinginess'.[32] Less real was stage heroine Diana's temporary escape from her life as low-paid shopgirl, courtesy of a surprise inheritance and a Swiss holiday adventure.

The fictional Dobson's didn't offer much in the way of staff entertainment. But many real stores were making conscious efforts to up their game in this respect, perhaps in recognition of the fact that their young assistants were starting to expect more from life. Staff clubs and social events became increasingly common from the late nineteenth century. For many shopworkers, they were probably more memorable – and a lot more fun – than union meetings.

In Oxford, Cape & Co. overhauled its entertainments, offering a sports club with swimming, football and cricket teams and becoming well known for its annual outings – bus trips to Windsor, steam-launch jaunts on the rural Thames. Every February, like many other stores, it held an annual stock-taking party, theirs in the Cadena Café in Cornmarket Street with games, dances and recitals performed by staff, including manager Henry Lewis and his sons. In Newcastle, Bainbridge's ran staff Bible groups but much besides, including concerts, a choral society and evening lectures on scientific and literary themes. Selected assistants at Owen Owen's large Liverpool drapery enjoyed weekend breaks at Welsh beauty spots Penmaenmawr and Plas Mariandir at the proprietor's expense. Many Co-op stores prided themselves on being 'more than a shop' and offered staff and customers 'food for the mind' in the form of clubs, classes, debates, dances and days out.[33]

The social side of store life meant a lot to shopworkers. Until the 1920s and 30s, paid holidays were rare. Union calls for their working week to be cut to sixty hours were discussed at length in parliamentary wrangles over the 1911 Shops Bill, but the relevant clause was itself cut in the end.[34] The only significant measure that made it through into law was compulsory half-day closing one day a week. Workers therefore had little time or money to get away for any length of time, making the day trips and annual outings all the more important.

The social side of their businesses was also beginning to take on a new significance for proprietors of the larger shops. London's flagship department stores competed with each other at all levels, including their expanding social package. Harrods' social programme had a long history that now comprised ladies' sports clubs with coaching in hockey, swimming and rifle shooting. Staff could write for the *Harrodian Gazette* and attend lively evening lectures.[35] But the store whose own confident motto was *Omnia Omnibus Ubique*, or 'Everything for Everyone Everywhere', found itself facing a tough new challenge in 1908 when Harry Gordon Selfridge, never short of confidence himself, arrived from Chicago to start work on his Oxford Street store. Selfridge's majestic building went up in record time. A staggering number of young shop assistants queued for jobs, submitting ten thousand applications in the six months before opening. Harrods fought back with a hastily organised Diamond Jubilee in the same week that Selfridges celebrated its Grand Opening in 1909, the first salvo in a rivalry that would run for decades. Selfridge promised a new deal for shop assistants and his elaborate social programme was very much part of this. On top of the usual outings and sports clubs, staff could join the Selfridge Players and Music Society and even have the chance to travel abroad. Selfridge himself saw this as a form of training, proclaiming, 'Travel is the greatest educator!' and promptly granting fifty staff an Easter trip to Paris to visit the city's legendary stores.[36]

Selfridge knew what he was doing. Times were clearly changing. Workers were starting to demand more for themselves and some employers were starting to invest more in them, not because they were heeding union complaints but because, like Selfridge, they hoped that this would lift performance and profits. They also invested more in their workers because they were required to do so by a new generation of interventionist politicians. In the same year that Selfridges opened, the new chancellor of the exchequer, firebrand

David Lloyd George, put his People's Budget before Parliament, promising a dramatic redistribution of wealth through new tax and social protection schemes. In the face of fierce opposition from the Conservatives and the House of Lords, which forced a general election in 1910, it took a full year for the budget to be passed.

For shopworkers, one of the most important pieces of legislation that Lloyd George's radical budget enabled was the National Insurance Act of 1911. Before this, if illness or injury prevented you from working, in most cases you simply didn't get paid. You also had to find the money for a doctor. Many just couldn't afford to be ill, on either score. The new Act offered a safety net. A shopgirl bought special stamps that she would lick and stick into her insurance book. Her shopkeeper, whether running a corner store or a department store, would also contribute, as would the government. In the event of illness, these could be cashed in. As a national safety net, it was certainly a significant step up from self-help.

The shop assistants' union was another beneficiary of the new system. It became one of the 'approved societies' empowered by the 1911 Act to give out benefits to shopworkers, boosting its profile and its numbers. That said, still only around 13 per cent of all shopworkers had signed up by 1914 and that figure included those working in Co-ops who had joined their own Amalgamated Union of Co-operative Employees.[37] Perhaps some of the 77 per cent who remained outside felt their immediate needs had now been taken care of – if not by Lloyd George then by modernising employers. Or perhaps the shopgirls among them simply took the view that as long as women earned so much less than men, they would always have to rely on a future husband to truly safeguard their own prospects.

For women's low pay remained a major problem. Thousands of women were still stuck in the casualised and sweated industries that supplied many shops – dressmaking, tailoring and blouse-making in particular. Clementina Black and the Women's Industrial Council stepped in again, this time demanding that they be paid a 'living wage'. The idea of a living wage, defined by future Labour chancellor Philip Snowden as a wage that would 'allow the poorest command of the things which keep a human being alive', was beginning to gather support across the political spectrum.[38] The sweated trades and the women working in them became powerful icons of the urgent need for change.

In 1906, Black worked with the *Daily News* to organise a shocking exhibition on London sweatshops. It featured real women at work, revealing the speed and skill with which they stitched and sewed, and exposing the pittance they were paid. Black went on to set up the National Anti-Sweating League and to co-write a book introducing well-heeled readers to the women who made their clothes. She and a small team of volunteer investigators tracked down the 'makers' – women living in poor areas of south and east London, working from home or in small workshops – and coaxed them into telling their stories. Black described how one woman had shown her an intricately stitched silk blouse 'composed entirely of small tucks and of insertions of lace', for which she had been paid just ten pence. The item would be sold in a shop, possibly a leading West End store, for anything between seventeen and twenty-five shillings.[39]

Some of those interviewed were teenagers, who did not need to live on these pitiful wages because they still boarded with their parents, but others were mothers and widows with dependants who most certainly did. As Black put it, 'Underpayment, borne gaily enough in girlhood … grows an intolerable burden upon the wife and mother.' Worse still, 'she hastens to send out her own girls that their earning may lighten the pressure, and the story begins over again for them'. She added, 'in a world of clamour the silent and long-suffering are exceedingly apt to be overlooked'.[40] But to overlook these women was not just immoral, it was impractical and inefficient, felt Black.

She quoted an east London clergyman, admiring the bluntness of his address to his congregation:

> When will the ladies with the cheap blouses and the gentlemen with the cheap shirts understand that 6s 11d and 3s 11d are not the prices they pay. They pay those prices plus the difference between the minimum subsistence rate, 12s 4d, and the 6s 4d, the average earnings of a home worker. That same 6s per week multiplied by the number of workers makes a considerable sum, which mark you, has to be met. We think we do not meet it. O! yes we do ... How do you pay? You keep a large staff of parsons to raise charitable funds and run clothing clubs and soup kitchens, you keep an army of Poor Law officials, and build costly workhouses and infirmaries, you spend millions on educating children who are too sleepy and overworked to learn when they get to school.[41]

Like the clergyman, Clementina Black believed that the answer lay in paying a living wage: 'Only by setting a barrier to the downward trend of wages can we hope to remedy that kind of poverty which is produced not by the vice, the drunkenness or the idleness of the sufferers but by their industry, patience and abstinence.' In her view, this barrier needed to 'take the shape, as in trade union action it does, of a minimum wage; but, for the unorganised, the minimum wage must be enforceable by law'.[42] She wanted the rates to be set by new 'trade boards', each serving a specific industry. These would be based on a successful Australian model, much debated by Edwardian politicians, where employers and workers' representatives would sit down together to agree fair wage scales and working conditions.

Trade boards duly took off. They were strongly promoted by a young Winston Churchill, then president of the Board of Trade and working alongside Chancellor Lloyd George in Asquith's radical Liberal government. Vociferous in most matters, Churchill held characteristically firm views on the minimum wage, declaring it a 'national evil that any class of Her Majesty's subjects should receive less than a living wage in return for their utmost exertions'. Without it, and especially in the sweated trades, he warned that 'the good employer is undercut by the bad and the bad by the worst' and that 'where these conditions prevail you have not a condition of progress, but a condition of progressive degeneration'.[43]

Unfortunately for shopworkers, it proved more difficult to set up trade boards for retailers because their shops were just so diverse, ranging from the tiny tobacconist's kiosk to the family corner shop to the huge department store. But all was not lost. The drive for a minimum wage for shop assistants – or, at least, male assistants – was first led by the co-op union. In 1907, the Amalgamated Union of Co-op Employees started a campaign on the issue and within three years, five hundred local co-op societies had agreed to implement minimum wage scales for men. But only eight had agreed to do so for women. The Women's Co-operative Guild was having none of it. They insisted that women's pay be placed on the table too. A new round of Guild investigations, building on those conducted by Lilian Harris in the 1890s, revealed a woeful picture which shamed an organisation that prided itself on its fairness. A manageress in one Co-op store that took £400 per week earned just thirteen shillings a week herself. A twenty-year-old female assistant with three years' experience was taking home just eight shillings a week, having started out on a paltry five shillings.

Led by Margaret Llewelyn Davies, the Guild kept up the pressure in one of the most important of its many projects. She put it to the men at the top of the co-op that an adult woman such as the store manageress simply couldn't survive on thirteen shillings a week. Another Guild member, Mrs Wimshurst from Lewes, put it another way at her local district conference in 1909. The co-op movement 'ought not to make it compulsory for girls to marry if they did not want to', she said, adding that girls 'were often compelled to marry because the wages they received were so low that they felt compelled to accept the first offer from a decent man'. The Lewes delegates, almost all of them wives themselves, laughed heartily at this while resolving to win greater independence for their daughters and granddaughters. Their efforts paid off. By 1911, sixty local societies had established new minimum wage rates for women, and two years on, 250 had done so.[44] This was a pivotal moment. Most trade unions were still unsettled by the very idea of self-supporting women and the threat they posed to the male breadwinner wage. The Women's Guild was helping to change their minds.

Inspired by the co-op's example, the shop assistants' union embarked on a new battle for a minimum wage while stepping up its old battle against living-in. The two issues were inseparable. As long as they were required to live in, assistants would never be paid a living wage. But at what level should that wage be set in the sprawling and diverse world of shops? Union official Philip Hoffman wrote that early investigations to establish who was being paid what revealed 'an utterly confused and anarchic state of affairs'.[45] The union's effort to cut through the confusion came in the form of a modest green booklet published in 1910, which set out a new list of suggested minimum rates, organised by trade and location. A London grocer would pay more than a provincial grocer but less than a London draper, for example. The rates would also vary according to age and experience, typically with pay rises when staff reached seventeen, twenty-one and twenty-eight years of age. Predictably, the proposed new system preserved an old tradition: men were still to earn more than women at every level, although women's rates would be raised.

Having agreed their preferred wage floors, the union now faced an uphill struggle to persuade shopkeepers to adopt them. Hoffman was in the front line. He criss-crossed the country, visiting store after store, persuading assistants to stand firm until their demands were met. His first victory was at Staffordshire draper's McIlroy's of Hanley in 1911. Its staff of eighty-four, mostly young women and almost all living in, were paid between two and eight shillings a week. With the new and momentous agreement in place, their pay more than doubled. Those under twenty-one now earned 7s 6d and those over twenty-one earned seventeen shillings. They now had to meet their own living costs, but most were all too happy to do so, much preferring to have their own money in their own pocket. News soon spread across town and a group of assistants at a rival Hanley draper's, Teeton's, walked out on strike in an effort to win a similar deal. The strike lasted two weeks and was described by Hoffman as 'very bitter' because some staff refused to join, claiming that they were 'perfectly satisfied with their wages'. The strikers prevailed. Teeton's matched McIlroy's minimum wages.[46]

Spurred by the gathering momentum, Hoffman sped down to south Wales, where dissent was growing, especially in drapery. In Llanelly, he worked with the assistants of David Evans to abolish living-in. Moving on to Merthyr Tydfil, he helped organise a strike at Roger Edwards and Co. It quickly snowballed, becoming the focal point of a much bigger debate and culminating in a 'huge procession through town, with bands and banners looking gay and splendid in the sunshine'. The procession was bound for the local football ground, where the crowd was addressed from the grandstand by the local MP. It helped, of course, that the MP was Keir Hardie, a giant of the Labour Party and its leader until 1908. Hardie also ran a radical newspaper, *The Pioneer*, which devoted generous column inches to the cause. The whole affair had mixed results for Hoffman himself, however. Vilified by the town's shopocracy as 'that bloody German', he was successfully sued for libel by incensed octogenarian Mr Edwards, who took issue with *The Pioneer's* reporting of the case. Financially ruined, but undeterred, Hoffman found love in Merthyr, marrying one of Edwards' striking young shopgirls, a Miss Morgan. Edwards stood his ground, but not for long. Within a few months, Hoffman was able to claim that living-in had now been 'almost swept away from south Wales'.[47]

Momentous as these events were, the reality was that a minimum wage was not an equal wage. It was still the norm for young female employees – across all industries – to leave paid work when they married and this was a significant factor behind the holding down of all women's wages. And although groups like the Women's Co-operative Guild and the Women's Industrial Council were remarkably effective, their members were still denied the vote and, with it, access to the kind of political power that would force further change. By the 1910s, suffrage campaigns to change all that had been running for nearly fifty years. From the late 1890s, the movement had been led by Millicent Garrett Fawcett's National Union of Women's Suffrage Societies (NUWSS), a group more commonly known as the 'suffragists', who favoured peaceful and patient lobbying. But in 1903 a more militant group – the Women's Social and Political Union (WSPU) – was formed by Emmeline Pankhurst and her daughters. Dubbed 'suffragettes', initially by a mocking *Daily Mail*, they believed that the time for talking was over and began taking direct action. They called their new campaign 'Deeds not Words'. By chaining themselves to railings, setting fire to pillar boxes and burning down public buildings and the empty homes of politicians, the suffragettes courted arrest and publicity. Many of those imprisoned as a result used hunger strikes to protest against their being classified as criminals rather than political prisoners.

Though their actions shocked many, public support for the principle of votes for women was strong, particularly from the middle classes, but also reaching across the social scale. Early documentary film shows local suffragist groups being cheered as they paraded through the streets, often as part of traditional fundraising, May Day and Whitsuntide processions. In Crewe, for example, they marched as part of a pageant to raise money for the local hospital, behind stilt-walkers, marching bands, a harlequin parade and a fencing display.[48]

Canny shopkeepers had long realised that they could cash in on this public support and an extremely beneficial two-way relationship between shopkeepers and suffrage activists had evolved, making them rather cosy, if unusual, bedfellows. Many store owners profited from selling suffragist fashions and merchandise but, more significantly, they also paid to advertise in the suffragist press, all too aware that this gave them access to affluent, influential middle-class consumers. Journals and magazines like *The Vote*, *The Suffragette* and *Votes for Women* regularly carried adverts from stores such as Swan & Edgar, Burberry's, Derry & Toms, Selfridges and many more. This generated vital revenue for suffrage campaigners, who repaid the favour in order to secure it. *The Vote* explicitly called out to its readers to 'support those advertisers who support us', and each journal published 'shopping guides', effectively lists of stores advertising with them, encouraging its readers to shop there. This in turn directly influenced the fashions of the time. *Votes for Women* proudly claimed that their suffragette colours were *en vogue* for the autumn season: 'Almost every shop window is showing purple hats and green hats, purple ties and green ties, purple cloth gowns and green cloth gowns in endless variety.'[49] Displays of shoes in the windows of Lilley and Skinner were intertwined with suffragette ribbons. At Peter Robinson's, you could buy white walking costumes designed especially for parades and demonstrations.

At the newly opened Selfridges on Oxford Street, support didn't stop at hats, ties and walking outfits. Indeed, Harry Gordon Selfridge paid for the publication of the *Suffrage Annual Who's Who*, which lambasted the traditional *Who's Who* for excluding scores of high-achieving women.[50] His in-store theatre group, the Selfridge Players, performed a play called *The Suffragette* in the West End. Selfridge also allowed his own shopgirls to declare their support for the cause, at a time when many felt they had to hide their political allegiances from their proprietors. It's not clear how many of Britain's 366,000 shopgirls – now constituting the third-largest group of female workers, after domestic servants and factory workers – were active suffrage supporters. Certainly, the movement tried to reach out to them. The Cambridge Women's Suffrage Association opened a committee room and shop in Benet Street, and organised a young people's suffrage society with drawing-room meetings and garden parties aimed at shop assistants and elementary-school teachers. The Bristol NUWSS held joint events with the Women's Co-operative Guild and the shop assistants union. The Birmingham WSPU appointed Nell Kenney as their organiser. Nell and her older sister Annie were among the most prominent working-class women in the movement. Both had worked in textile mills and Nell had also worked as a shop assistant. In a November 1907 report for *Votes for Women*, she wrote, 'I am visiting most of the influential people in Birmingham and surrounding districts'. Like other groups, hers was also holding frequent drawing-room, open-air and factory-gate meetings, as well as addressing different religious groups and women's co-operative guilds.[51]

Intriguingly, the Pankhurst family themselves had twenty years of personal experience of shopkeeping. Partly in order to finance their political activities, Emmeline Pankhurst had run fancy-goods shops selling enamelled photo frames, milking stools and art furniture on the Hampstead Road in London, and then at 30 King Street in Manchester. She had dragged in her sister and later her daughters Christabel and Sylvia to help her; none of them liked shopwork. As Christabel later wrote, 'Sylvia's artistic gift might adapt her better than me to some phases of the undertaking, especially as her task was mainly to design and paint in a studio, but she, too, was not born for business'.[52] In spite of this personal experience of the daily challenges of shopwork and running a small business, and efforts by the wider movement to attract their support, the Pankhursts showed little interest in fighting for shopgirls to be included in the vote. This was a tactical move. Both suffragettes and suffragists were arguing for women to be enfranchised on the same terms as men as set down by the 1884 Reform Act. The Act had extended the vote to adult men who were householders or renting lodgings to the value of £10 a year. This excluded an estimated 40 per cent of British men, including most male shop assistants. Women suffrage campaigners passionately believed that only by demanding that the existing law be extended to include women would they have any hope of smuggling their Bill through Parliament; they knew that thousands would be excluded as a consequence.

Since the vast majority of shopgirls were young and had no hope of meeting the property threshold, they would certainly be excluded. Margaret Bondfield was unimpressed and drove a characteristically hard bargain. She was neither a suffragist nor a suffragette – not because she didn't support the cause but because she believed it didn't go far enough. Having moved on from the shop assistants union, she was now chair of the Adult Suffrage Society. Ahead of its time, this Society demanded that the vote be extended to *all* adults regardless of wealth or property. She felt that the suffragettes were selling out the working classes – men and women alike – and went head-to-head with them in a public debate. Sylvia Pankhurst watched her in action, describing her lyrically if rather waspishly: 'Miss Bondfield appeared in pink, dark and dark-eyed with a deep, throaty voice which many found beautiful.' But she didn't engage, on that occasion at least, with Bondfield's broader argument that the women's vote should simply be part of a much more radical move towards universal suffrage for men and women of all ages and classes, including shopgirls. Instead, Pankhurst belittled her line, stating that 'Miss Bondfield deprecated votes for women as the hobby of disappointed old maids whom no one had wanted to marry'.[53]

On 1 March 1912 the WSPU ratcheted up their 'Deeds not Words' campaign by some margin. Hundreds of suffragette supporters launched the extraordinary, chaotic two day campaign nicknamed

121

the 'War of the Windows'. Dressed in their team colours of white, purple and green, they rushed through the streets of London, from the Strand to the West End, smashing and breaking shop windows of famous stores with stones and toffee hammers, while suffragettes in provincial centres followed suit.[54] Among them were Kate and Louise Lilley, daughters of the suffrage-supporting owner of Lilley and Skinner. The militants targeted famous names such as Burberry's, Barkers, Swan & Edgar, Harrods, D.H. Evans and Regal Corset, but also scores of smaller shops, causing damage to more than 270 premises. They distributed handbills printed by the Women's Press to the gathering crowds, justifying their violent actions; they accused store owners of passivity, of not using their political clout. 'You, a prosperous shopkeeper, have had your windows broken,' the handbill began, and then explained why: 'You as voters and businessmen have enormous influence'. The suffragettes called on the shopkeepers to use this leverage to encourage MPs to support women's right to vote. The suffragette leaflet also contained a threat, warning the proprietors that if they didn't get behind the proposed Conciliation Bill, they might lose their all-important female consumers: 'You can get on very well without Mr Asquith or Mr Lloyd George, but you can't get on without the women who are your good friends in business.'[55]

The fallout from the window attacks was dramatic for the suf-fragettes – and considerably less dramatic for the proprietors. Over two hundred suffragettes were arrested and many were charged with window smashing,[56] resulting in three months' imprisonment for some.[57] Store owners were left scratching their heads, for their windows had been smashed by the very women whose journals and political activities many were directly funding. In business terms, it didn't make sense to respond with equal ferocity. So the proprietors simply shrugged their shoulders, repaired their windows, paid a little more lip service to the political aims of the movement and went on advertising.

One proprietor had got off more lightly. Harry Gordon Selfridge's very public support for the WSPU meant that his expansive display windows were largely spared. He had literally tied his colours to the mast, one of the first to fly purple, white and green flags when Mrs Pankhurst was first released from prison in 1909. However, one of his former shopgirls would test his support to its limits.

Gladys Evans joined Selfridges in 1908, having worked in shops from the age of fifteen. Her father was a wealthy stockbroker and one of the proprietors of *Vanity Fair* magazine. She was a suffragette. While at Selfridges, she devoted all her spare time to the furtherance of the cause, selling the magazine *Votes for Women* in all weathers. In November 1910, she was among those beaten and arrested by police in the notorious Black Friday confrontation, when hundreds of WSPU members protested against the deliberate stalling tactics of Prime Minister Asquith and his Commons supporters. She emigrated to Canada in 1911 but returned the following year with a steely determination to step up the fight. When she heard about the imprisonment of her fellow suffragettes following the window-smashing attacks, she was radicalised further. In July 1912, she and three others followed Asquith to Dublin, where he was due to speak on Home Rule. The group lay in wait for his carriage as it crossed O'Connell Bridge and, as it drew near, threw through its window a hatchet wrapped in a message that read 'symbol of the extinction of the Liberal Party for evermore'. It missed Asquith but injured one of his travelling companions. Gladys and the others then headed for the Theatre Royal where Asquith was due to speak the next day. Determined to sabotage the event, they launched a burning chair from an interior balcony into the orchestra pit and also succeeded in setting fire to the cinematograph box and causing a minor explosion.

The women were detained at the scene and soon appeared at a Dublin court charged with 'having committed serious outrages at the time of the visit of the British Prime Minister'. Gladys was found guilty of conspiring to do bodily harm and damage property. She and another of the four were sentenced to five years' penal servitude, the first time any suffragette had received such a severe penalty. She went on hunger strike in protest and, in another first, became the first suffragette to be force-fed in Ireland.[58] Back at Selfridges, 253 employees signed an open letter addressed to the Lord Lieutenant of Ireland, 'respectfully' requesting 'a remission of the sentence' on the grounds that 'the offence for which the prisoner was convicted was her first offence against the law' and noting 'her high character, to which we can all testify'. Her offence was 'committed with no criminal intent, but from a political motive, namely as part of an agitation to obtain the enfranchisement of women'.[59] In the end, Gladys was released early from prison on health grounds by authorities anxious to prevent her from dying and thereby becoming a political martyr.

For all this, enfranchisement remained an elusive prize. In their fury, suffragettes ramped up their militancy. In the first seven months of 1914 there were 104 acts of arson carried out by suffragettes, including the burning down of Great Yarmouth's Britannia Pier and the destruction of the Bath House Hotel in Felixstowe. The most infamous attack on property came when Mary Richardson slashed the *Rokeby Venus* in the National Gallery.[60] Nonetheless, a few days after the declaration of war in August 1914, the suffragettes called a halt to their militant actions and set out to support the war effort. It was the social upheavals of war that finally brought about change. The 1918 Representation of the People Act gave the vote to all men over twenty-one and to all women over thirty who were householders, wives of householders, occupants of property worth £5 a year or graduates of British universities. Most shopgirls and thousands of other young women would have to wait another decade before Bondfield and the Adult Suffrage Society achieved their goal of universal suffrage – votes for all adults.

But in other respects, much had changed for shopgirls since Bondfield had scribbled her first secret reports by candlelight, under the bedcovers in the 1890s. Thanks to her daring exposés, and the efforts of ground-breaking unions and co-operative and women's movements, as well as the support of more enlightened shopkeepers, the harshness of shoplife was beginning to soften. This was a time when shopgirls – as young workers and young women – began to demand more for themselves. But it was also a time when shopkeepers and customers began, in turn, to demand more from the shopgirls as Britain's consumer culture became ever more sophisticated.

Selfridges shopgirls stand on duty in front of the store's modern lift system, 11 December 1922.

CHAPTER 5

THOROUGHLY MODERN MANAGEMENT

On 10 January 1906 the ocean liner *Carmania* pulled away from the Liverpool quayside with 3,244 people on board. The third-class berths were full of emigrants dreaming of a new life in America – Russians, Poles and East European Jews fleeing persecution. The first-class cabins were occupied by Englishmen and -women, Americans and Canadians – and a Welshman and his nephew. Owen Owen of Montgomeryshire was sixty-one, founder of one of the most successful Liverpool drapery stores, a significant investor in London property and other large stores, friend of David Lloyd George (now president of the Board of Trade) and chairman of the Twenty Club, a dining club of influential national retailers. He had money and investments, he was generous to his extensive family and staff, and he contributed regularly to his local Unitarian chapel.

It was a far cry from the insecurity he had experienced as a child. His father, Owen Owen senior, had been a tenant farmer near Machynlleth, moving farms often as his fortunes waned and his family grew. Owen the younger left Wales when he was still a boy and became an apprentice at his uncle's drapery business in Bath. He was in effect following in the footsteps of the tens of thousands of young men and women from the remoter parts of Wales who set off in search of steady work in England – particularly in London, Manchester and just across the Welsh border in Liverpool.

'Who can tell what I am now laying the foundation of?' Owen Owen wrote in his notebook the night he first arrived in Liverpool in 1868, aged twenty. He continued in a rather Shakespearean vein: 'Is this the time and tide that leads to fortune, or is it a ship sailing on the world-wide ocean, without a compass to guide?'[1] It was indeed the former, for Liverpool was where many of Britain's raw materials were handled and the gateway through which the products of its large hinterland were exported overseas.

Shortly after he arrived in Liverpool, Owen Owen set about establishing his own eponymous draper's store on 121 London Road, a noisy, busy neighbourhood with lots of pubs and lots of customers. His strategy was to sell goods cheap, survive on minimal profit margins and maintain a rapid turnover. The plan obviously worked: just five years later, in 1873, an advertisement for Owen Owen in a guidebook for north Wales stated that the business employed over 120 people, and that Owen Owen himself had 'the reputation of being the Proprietor of the Cheapest Shop in Liverpool'.[2] Over the next two decades, the store grew and grew, as Owen bought up neighbouring properties and built two staff hostels, watched over by two Welsh housekeepers. In 1899 Owen Owen, like many other retailers, ceased being a family partnership and became a limited company. Lloyd George bought one thousand shares, while local people from Liverpool and north Wales flocked to buy smaller bundles, Miss Elizabeth Morgan of Machynlleth buying a grand total of twenty-four.

Now he had set sail again. Writing to his wife Ellen while off the

Irish Coast, he said, 'I never could have believed it possible to travel at sea in such luxury. How graceful this wonder ship glides through.' Owen had considerable investments in sixteen North American railways, including Erie Railroad, Pennsylvania Railway and Illinois Central Railway. He was going to inspect them; but above all he was on his way to inspect the manner in which American and Canadian shops went about their business.

If Paris had been the capital of nineteenth-century retail, New York had all the makings of becoming the shopping capital of the twentieth. Around the elite shopping district nicknamed 'Ladies' Mile', famous department stores were swiftly gathering and making their names: Bergdorf Goodman, Lord & Taylor and the gigantic Arnold Constable & Co. among them. Owen was impressed with these vast enterprises, which employed thousands; he understood that 'the Americans worship size'. North of Ladies' Mile was Macy's, which had over one million square feet of floor space and more than three thousand employees, and this was the store that Owen studied in detail. He was fascinated by its physical workings, by the building's structure, the layout of departments, the refreshments on offer. He was concerned that these emporia had expanded too quickly and were at risk of fire or collapse but marvelled at the modern engineering he found inside: 'Electric Band elevators are common for 1, 2 or 3 floors and Macy's have revolving stairs. The revolving stairs are more used than lifts.'

Writing to Ellen from the Waldorf Astoria hotel, Owen confessed, 'It has been a revelation to me the way business is done on this side: many of the ideas are those I have nearly all my life been trying to put into force.' For it was not just the new mechanics that struck him but also the 'Elaborate Methods of Attracting Business' – so read the headline in *The Drapers Record*, reporting on Owen's fact-finding trip. Owen was impressed by the American stores' radically different attitude towards the customer, who was regarded as someone who had to be lured and tempted into buying, with shopping treated not so much as a functional necessity but as a luxury, albeit an everyday one. The stores he visited in New York, Buffalo, Montreal and Toronto spent significantly more on advertising than any comparable store in Britain; they each had an in-house advertising man and Owen felt that their advertisements were 'singularly convincing. You read – and believe. And then a purchase cannot be far off.'

The aspect of American shopwork that struck Owen most forcibly was 'System! System! System!' He explained: 'No deviation is allowed from it. Next to the dollar, it is their fetish.'³ Every aspect of store organisation was managed through elaborate and fixed methodology, from regular stock-taking to prompt payment of credit. This was part of the wider efficiency craze sweeping American industry, based on the work of Frederick Winslow Taylor. With a stopwatch in hand, Taylor had instituted studies in factories, subdividing manual tasks into different stages and timing each stage. His aim was to increase workers' efficiency and productivity by finding the 'one best way' of performing each task.

This systems management was also applied to American shopgirls. Owen noted how, in the spirit of Taylorist efficiency, the girls' individual weekly sales were recorded and tabulated by the counting house. If a shopgirl had a slack week, she might be in danger of dismissal, but more often, her buyer would be admonished by the in-house 'system man' for not doing his job properly. It was the buyer's responsibility to lay out the stock in such a way that each shopgirl had a fair chance of achieving good sales.

Out of hours, American shopgirls were managed differently too. There was little pretence of paternalism, of proprietors and family-firm members as benevolent employers, supposedly looking after the well-being of their employees. In fact, there was no living-in system and thus no sense that the shop employers were taking on a parental role. American shop assistants were treated as grown-ups in their time off, not as errant teenagers to be reined in.

In some ways, American shopgirls were similar to their British counterparts. They too were largely working class – some were recent immigrants, with Italian, Jewish or Russian backgrounds. And they too were saddled with a poor reputation, being labelled blowsy and coarse. But attempts by their proprietors to make them more genteel and more deferential – particularly in the huge department stores – seemed less successful in the States than in Britain. Many shared with millions of American workers a spiritedness: they wished to work but not to serve. Some shopgirls rebelled against internal hierarchies, disobeying house rules and segregation within the stores. Saleswomen at Filene's were forbidden to use certain elevators; they rode them anyway. Moreover, what made their behaviour worse from the management's point of view was that the women were boisterous in front of customers.[4]

Forthrightness and familiarity with middle-class customers was the hallmark of many American shopgirls. Customers often saw this as over-familiarity, as one observer explained, 'The salespeople have become so forward as to call customers "Dearie." The use of such terms is a liberty which the woman of finer sensibilities quickly resents.'[5] Owen too noted the difference in manners when being served. 'The civility that is expected by customers in England is not expected there. That is why one hardly ever hears the simple phrase, "Thank you!" One often hears the laconic remark, "That is your parcel."' Still, he recognised that this abrupt tone worked well, contributing to the sense of the American shopping experience where 'business always seems to be at high pressure. Everything is hustle! Hustle! Hustle!' In summing up all he had learnt in the States, Owen concluded rather mournfully in his letter to his wife that 'these ideas have come too late and sometimes I wish that I had not come to America at all'.[6]

American visitors to Britain agreed with Owen that the British shopping experience was fundamentally different; in fact, some American tourists complained that it was actually rather backward. 'Oh, the Despair of Shopping in London!' was the title of international shopper Elizabeth Huber Clark's article in an American magazine – and it wasn't tongue-in-cheek. She couldn't bear what Owen had termed British 'civility', complaining that customers were never left alone to walk around a British store and browse; instead they were immediately accosted by floorwalkers and shop assistants. She claimed that British shopworkers didn't simply offer to help; they were trained to sell hard, forcing customers to buy items that they didn't really want. She said that the senior floorwalkers pressurised junior shopgirls into selling, and if a girl failed to seal a sale then her floorwalker would scold her with the rebuke that 'any fool can sell them what they want; you are here to make them buy what we have'.[7]

Elizabeth Huber Clark landed a punch. Her article was taken up by *The Drapers Record* in Britain, and the trade paper conceded that she was right in some respects: there had indeed been complaints about overbearing shopworkers in British emporia. But the *Record* didn't give in that easily, hitting back patriotically with the claim that British customers were more refined than Americans. On entering a shop, an English lady expected attention and it was the duty of the shop assistants to fulfil her needs, they claimed. The magazine then launched an assault on American lady shoppers, insulting their femininity – stating that they were 'more masculine in temperament' – and implying that as a consequence they felt patronised by British male civilities (for which read floorwalker attention). Englishwomen apparently had no such hang-ups. It all got rather ludicrous.

As soon as American stores started opening on British soil, the debate about the merits of British versus American values turned into all-out war. Issues of national pride were at stake, it seemed, as well as questions of tradition and modernity, and a woman's place in Edwardian society. The trade press was no longer the right medium for such heated discourse; the conflict was upgraded to the national newspapers.

Harry Gordon Selfridge and G.K. Chesterton were the two opponents squaring off in what became known as the 'Big Shop Controversy'. Having opened Selfridges on Oxford Street in 1909, the American retailer presented himself as the crusading, dynamic moderniser with a mission to kick British retailing out of the Victorian era and into a shiny cosmopolitan future. Gilbert Keith Chesterton, on the other hand – prolific man of letters and acerbic public speaker – held extremely firm views on his own particular brand of patriotic Englishness. He was an anti-moderniser, set against big business, big cities and government bureaucracy. He was for the 'ordinary little man', the shopkeeper, producer and tradesman working in small country towns, whose livelihoods he felt were being swept away by the Industrial Revolution. There was little room for women in his vision of the 'English tradition', other than in the home.[8]

Chesterton was tapping into a deep-rooted national concern about the demise of small shops on the local high street. Termed the 'Passing of the Grocer' debate, there was a nostalgic harking back to a supposed golden age of shopkeeping. Owen Owen had noted how, in each town he visited in North America, business was concentrated in the hands of a few large firms, cutting out the medium-sized and small shops. 'The small man, in so far as he exists, keeps a general store in an outlying district, and even then he has to compete with the big mail order house.'[9] The concern was that Britain was moving in a similar direction.

It was true that bankruptcy figures in Britain were high in the early 1900s and many local grocers and other shopkeepers were losing out to competition from larger retail groups, particularly in the industrial cities. Over the next decade, co-operatives and multiples grew to account for a huge 30 per cent of the national market.[10] Department stores made up a mere 2 per cent, despite the amount of public attention they generated.[11] However, the vast majority of the retail market – nearly 70 per cent – still comprised traditional smaller shops, many of them family run. The picture in Britain was still significantly different from that in North America: despite the concerns of Chesterton and his fellow traditionalists, the doors of the town grocers remained open.

While many other parts of the retail trade were undergoing momentous upheavals in the early 1900s, working life inside small shops had not changed much over the previous half-century. Certainly, both grocers and their customers were now overwhelmed with a huge range of pre-processed, packaged and branded goods – 360 different types of biscuit were available from firms like Carr's, Huntley & Palmers and McVitie's; a wide variety of jams came from Hartley's and Crosse & Blackwell; and Sunlight soap, Bovril, and Cadbury's cocoa essence were all making an appearance. Yet 'shops in the little country town I inhabit', as Chesterton wrote with warmth, still operated in the highly skilled, professional manner established decades earlier. Every grocer still mixed his own blend of tea, some-times warning the customer that it might taste strange out of the local area, due to the difference in water quality. The grocer and his assistants monitored maturing Dutch cheeses, carefully ripened bananas in back rooms with adjustable gas jet heating, mixed snuff and brewed their own beer. Little was wasted: at Albert Headey's grocery in Tonbridge, Kent, his son remembered how broken biscuit was sold off cheap on a Saturday night and any salt left on the floor after the great salt blocks from the wholesalers were broken up was swept together and sold to big country houses for use on asparagus beds.[12]

The relationship between the favoured grocer and a country house was an important one. Grocers or their assistants would travel around the outlying villages to pick up orders. Mr Headey himself used to pay regular visits to the big house nearby, wearing his top hat and morning coat. With his pencil behind his ear, he would accompany the housekeeper on a tour through each storeroom and service area of the house, from the kitchen and butler's pantry to the coachman's stores, taking stock of the sugar and tapioca provisions, tapping the rice and semolina drums and checking the tins of Brasso. 'That one's down a bit. Seven pounds of that,' he would say. But it wasn't the housekeeper who settled the bill. The day the lady of the house came to town in her carriage to pay her grocery bill was an important one. She would enter the shop and be invited up to the office, sitting down with a little glass of sherry. She would pay by cheque or in gold sovereigns. 'Quite a ceremony it was,' remembered Headey's son.

This world of grocery – let alone the highly skilled trades of butchery, ironmongery and smithing – was still male-dominated. Although in cities and in the bigger stores young women were increasingly being employed, so that by the turn of the century the ratio of shopgirls to shopmen was roughly equal, in market towns and smaller shops this simply wasn't the case.[13] Mr Headey once hired a certain Miss Owen to work on accounts in the office, the only woman alongside twelve male assistants, but he quickly replaced her with a man. The woman most likely to be found in a small family-run shop was still the shopkeeper's wife or widow. Guest's draper's in Shrewsbury was probably run by the wife of the proprietor – a photo of the shopfront captures her as a young woman on the steps in a black dress and white apron, her three children standing next to her.[14] It is likely that Mrs Guest also managed an ironmongery and agricultural machinery warehouse further up the street, but she was in the minority.[15]

Back in the capital, in late January 1912, G.K. Chesterton stoked the fires of the 'Big Shop Controversy'. The *Daily News* published his regular column under the headline 'The Big Shop'. In his article,

Chesterton dreamt of hell, and hell was a large modern store, 'the awful interminable emporia, which have room after room, department after department'. First he questioned the masculinity of shopwalkers, who dominated this vision, 'surely the most unmanly of all the trades of men'. He then vented his spleen on shopgirls, claiming that they were poorly trained and looked identical to the headless wooden mannequins standing next to them, the only difference being that shopgirls still had their heads. In the most extraordinarily vitriolic flight of fancy, Chesterton imagined decapitating the shopgirls too: 'When you look at the dress-model you think that some shop-girl has had her head cut off; when you look back at the real shop-girl you feel inclined to do the same to her.'[16]

On one level, the article was flippant and absurd. On another, Chesterton was clearly articulating his fears and prejudices in a very personal, visceral manner. Selfridge, though not named, took the attack on modern stores to heart. He responded in print four days later, accusing the 'ignorant' Chesterton of having a 'suburban and narrow knowledge of the present-day department store'.[17] Unwilling to be silenced, Selfridges' female staff also took up the cudgels in self-defence. 'Angry London Shopgirls Reply to an Attack by Mr. G.K. Chesterton: "Entirely Ignorant"' read the headline in the rival *Daily Express*.[18] They had held a meeting and composed a letter, signed by 180 of them, rebutting Chesterton's condescending and belittling views, his 'stigma of contempt'. They described themselves as 'business women associated with the House of Selfridge' and wrote, 'We are proud to say that we feel as women workers we have in our ranks some of the brightest intelligences associated with commerce.' The letter also outlined the responsibilities they were called upon to undertake, describing the 'intelligent democratic administration', the 'modern business methods', the educational programme they attended, including a 'business refresher', and praised the 'Staff Parliament or Council where free speech, free thought and general initiative is expected to be shown on all occasions'. They signed themselves: 'Women Workers, 100, Oxford Street, W1., Feb 1st, 1912'.[19]

They certainly didn't sound like poorly trained, dumb, headless mannequins. But Chesterton's response? A resounding silence. While he did reply to Harry Gordon Selfridge in print, sardonically linking him to vulgarity and pomposity and suggesting that Selfridge did not understand business, he did not deign to reply to the Women Workers of 100 Oxford Street W1, Feb 1st, 1912.

Their boss Harry Gordon Selfridge had pitched up on British shores in the early years of the new century with a conviction that the shop world should be female. As part of his pre-launch publicity he had taken out full-page newspaper advertisements and plastered the walls of the Underground and London buses with his signs; in an era of discreet column advertising, this was written off by many as vulgar and brash. But the ads certainly made his stance clear from the off. One read: 'This House is dedicated to Women's Service first of all', clear testimony to his belief in the influence and economic power of his female customers.

Such sentiments had of course already been articulated in Britain by the early store entrepreneurs: William Whiteley had provided women with ladies' rooms and refreshment rooms in the 1870s, and when Charles Jenner rebuilt his beautiful Edinburgh emporium, he expressed in stone the important role played by his female customers. Selfridge, however, was to take this much further. While Jenners, Harrods and Browns in Chester were presenting themselves as stores for upper-class women, Selfridge tried to break free from British social strictures and appeal to a wider class spectrum. His advertisements made clear that his was indeed an unintimidating modern walk-around store, the type that Elizabeth Huber Clark so missed on British soil. As Edwardian shopper Olivia explained in her *Prejudiced Guide* to London shopping, in most shops smartly attired shopgirls and their frock-coated floorwalkers still tended to bully customers. When Olivia wished to view rather than buy a certain shade of ribbon, the shopgirls cried out for all to hear, 'The lady says she merely wanted to *look* at it.'[20] In contrast, Selfridges was warmly welcoming, suggesting, 'Why Not Spend the Day in Selfridges?', offering the public the 'freedom of the store' and inviting them in to luxuriate in its modern surroundings. Here customers had no obligation to buy; Selfridge wished them to 'make the store their headquarters'. If they were then inclined to make a purchase, the prices were low, and kept lower still through the introduction of American bargain-basement sales.

Selfridge felt he instinctively knew his female customers and what they wanted. And his instincts weren't wrong – though it would take a few years until he was proved right. After the grand opening, women flocked in, at first just to recce the new store. Shop assistant Nellie Elt recalled the first day: 'Thousands of people streamed past us, staring at us … Very few, it seemed to me, were buying anything.' Business at first was slower than expected, but within three years Selfridges was beginning to make serious money. Harry Gordon Selfridge's own flair for showmanship, the popularity of the Roof Garden and the cheap deals available in the Bargain Basement all served to boost earnings, so that by March 1912 trading profits were over £50,000.[21]

Selfridge believed that the key to unlocking such profits lay with his staff, who were overwhelmingly female. 'When an assistant is serving a customer the whole reputation of the store is in the hands of that single assistant,' he explained.[22] Consequently, it was worth his while to hire and train good employees. Selfridge brought with him from the United States management methods and motivational techniques that were in many ways more progressive than those prevalent in Britain at that time, and were in turn to influence staff relations throughout the department-store sector. For a start, he rejected the living-in system still very common all around Britain. Staff were allowed to lodge where they liked, and therefore incurred no deductions from their weekly wages. He paid them a little better than elsewhere in the capital[23] and introduced training programmes covering merchandise and selling techniques. The store also provided leisure facilities, staff discount schemes and in-house medical services. As we know, other stores had similar initiatives, but the critical difference with Selfridge was the manner in which his naive enthusiasm and showmanship infused both his store and his workers.

In his house rules, in an early mission statement called 'Spirit of the House', and in his widely syndicated daily press columns, Selfridge time and again peddled the line that staff job satisfaction was all important. The *Guide Book* read quite differently from, say, Whiteley's earlier list of 176 strict house rules and associated fines. Here there were no fines; instead staff were encouraged 'to look upon work during the working hours of the day as a privilege, as a game … to look upon the bright side of things: originality, loyalty'. His Christmas cards to staff had little mottos and homilies, such as 'To travel hopefully is better than to arrive' and 'True success is labour'.[24] Staff happiness, according to Selfridge, came from being given responsibilities and having a sense of inclusion in the enterprise. No one was to know their place; instead they were to be assisted in furthering their ambitions. A staff council was set up, probably the first in British retailing, where representatives of each of the 130 departments plus senior staff met to discuss store operations. Selfridge cultivated the idea that 'merit and merit only' was the route to advancement, and that any stockboy given the right training might rise high.

So central were his staff to the business – and, he believed, to customers – that Selfridge even published his store's 'Personality Tree' in the *London Magazine*, showing an assistant (a young woman), a head of department (older woman), the chief of staff (man), then Mr Selfridge at the top.[25] This is a deeply revealing diagram, showing that for all his progressive ideas and eloquent sayings, Selfridge was still a man of his time. Despite him repeatedly and vociferously praising his female assistants in public, touting their professional skills and intuitive knowledge of their customers' needs, even he saw gender as a bar to advancement, his maxim of 'merit and merit only' seeming to apply just to his male hires. He was explicit about what is nowadays called the glass ceiling, writing that while 'there is practically no limit to the heights to which a man of ability might succeed' in his store, the same could not be said for his female staff: 'Women, although they might go far, can never attain a commanding position.'[26]

For most young women, what happened at senior management level didn't much bother them when they first applied to Selfridges. Becoming head of department was challenging enough in the London shop world; Paquins, for instance, rarely promoted their womenfolk to this level. Miss Olive Fisher started at Selfridges aged sixteen as a junior cashier. Along with the other under-eighteens, she had to attend evening classes four nights a week. Each month a buyer would hold a lecture concerning his merchandise and Miss Olive then had to write an essay on the topic. Subjects on the training programmes ranged from 'The History and Manufacture of Pianos' to 'Self-Discipline as a Business Asset'. She and the other shopgirls received marks out of ten for their essays; one shopgirl received only four out of ten one week, another was told to write on one side of the paper only. Miss Olive, however, fared better, enjoying the learning opportunities. 'I still remember how interesting the lectures were about gloves, linen, glass and china.' When she received top marks she was invited with her parents and the other students to a strawberry and ice-cream garden party held on the Roof Garden and was presented with two books, both signed by Mr Selfridge.[27]

Shopgirls' view of themselves as professional modern business-women was clearly in the ascendant, but, as Edwardian cultural icon Olive Christian Malvery admitted, many in London were 'not exactly pining for Mr Selfridge' and his new ways. Malvery was an Indian singer and writer, and a lively defender of the 'new blood' that Selfridge was introducing:

'We don't want any of those horrible American ways here,' was the critique Malvery heard in high society.

'To what horrid American ways do you refer?' she innocently enquired.

'Oh, well you know what I mean.'

'No, not really. Do tell me what it is you object to, at Selfridge's for instance.'

'It is all that American bluff and getting up large things and making their women workers so independent.'

Malvery would not let this stand. 'I see; you do not like women workers to be paid well and courteously treated. Is that it?'[28]

Malvery's conversation partner would surely have been under-whelmed by other new American techniques Selfridge was intro-ducing to British retail, such as his innovative, dramatic approach to display and window dressing. The traditional British approach was to have 'massed' shop windows fully stocked from floor to ceiling, with goods hanging off rails, hooks and wires, taking up every inch of floor, wall and ceiling space. Such 'stocky' windows took hours to make up and remained unchanged for several weeks.[29] Instead, the windows of Selfridges were more 'open' and showed far fewer items, silhouetted against a stark background. At night Selfridge lit his win-dows up, rather than shuttering them like most stores.

Quickly, though, the pioneering American display methods spread to other stores, strengthening a growing awareness throughout retail of their importance. Good window dressing came to be regarded as 'as an educator of public taste', as *The Times* put it. This had its consequences. Many London traders increased their spend on window dressing to such an extent and so successfully that crowds regularly gathered around attractive displays. On one occasion, retailer Mr W.E. Catesby's windows proved such a draw that the police were called to control the crowd and Mr Catesby was summoned to appear at the Marlborough Street Police Court. Police began ticketing shops whose windows caused problems. In response, a deputation of shopkeepers and trade journalists met the commissioner of the Metropolitan Police, requesting that they be assigned a policeman to keep order, as happened with theatre crowds. The commissioner turned down their application, arguing that unlike stationary, patient theatre crowds, a shopping crowd might be 'obstinate and cantankerous and refuse to be moved'. On top of this, felt the commissioner, if he agreed, 'it would not be long before every trader in London would ask for the "walking advertisement" of a London policeman'.[30]

The early 1910s were the heyday of store opulence, with drapers around the country upgrading their shops to department stores and department stores themselves being given extensive makeovers. In Liverpool, Owen Owen had its entire frontage and interior rebuilt, as did Bainbridge's of Newcastle, Debenhams in London and smaller stores such as Mawer & Collingham of Lincoln. However, in spite of their beautiful new Edwardian display areas, most traditional shopkeepers still saw their customers very much in old class terms, with the new buildings reflecting this starkly by providing separate entrances for different sections of the community. At Mawer & Collingham the posher 'carriage trade' was welcomed at the main doors, while the servant trade had a separate entrance and shop which provided the cheaper Manchester cottons, Bradford wools and heavy-duty boots.[31] Bainbridge's operated in a similar way, as superintendent Walter Brittain recalled: 'There used to be quite a dividing line and grading of customers.' The upper and middles classes were served in the French Room, Brittain explained, while artisan types were in the

Back Shop. 'It was amazing how smoothly this segregation worked, each class was comfortable in its own surroundings.'[32]

The declaration of war in August 1914 put a stop to the shop-fitting and building boom. The nation had more important things to worry about than the style of its shop counters. As *The Drapers Record* pointed out, 'To keep calm, to preserve one's balance … is not only a patriotic duty; it is the policy dictated from the point of view of our business interests.'[33] Yet keep calm British customers clearly did not. There had been little planning for the effects of war on the home economy, by either government or business. *The Drapers Record* complained that 'panicmongers' and stupid 'poltroons' did not pursue their 'ordinary avocations'; instead, individuals, as well as big businesses, immediately withdrew cash, advertising and custom across the board. Sales of all items plummeted except for food. As 'little sums of money' no longer frequently passed across the counters, day-to-day business was paralysed – or so the president of the Advertising Consultants described: 'As soon as the circulation of money stopped the industry of the nation received a check.'[34] The key economic problem was not reduction of trade with Germany, it was lack of confidence in the home market, the advertisers felt. They called on the press, manufacturers and retailers to promote 'the restoration to the normal purchasing conditions'.

But there was little prospect of normality. By the beginning of September, *The Drapers Record* had published a list of hundreds of male workers from wholesale and retail businesses who had already volunteered for the armed forces, surmising that 'we have every reason to be proud of the small army of men who are temporarily leaving their business duties in order to take their part in defending their country'.[35] Recruiting sergeants targeted large stores, promising that men who enlisted together would serve together. Many stores, including grocery chain J. Sainsbury, committed to giving them their jobs back when they returned. *The Drapers Record* listed Harrods as releasing fifty-seven men, Eaden Lilley in Cambridge twenty, Rockhey in Torquay nine, W.H. Watts in Liverpool eighteen, Draffen & Jarvie in Dundee two, Dickins & Jones thirty-five. By 1915 half a million young men from all industries and all walks of life had enlisted.

With male staff numbers dropping dramatically and custom collapsing in the uncertainties of the first months, many proprietors were forced to dismiss the majority of their remaining staff. On top of this, the War Office demanded that clothiers help supply the army. Despite the patriotic tone of *The Drapers Record*, drapers themselves responded with reluctance, protesting that such emergency demands would further upset their work patterns. Many drapers' shops and larger stores, including even the Army & Navy Co-operative Society – known as 'The Stores' – point blank refused the War Office requests.[36]

The government was unimpressed. The Home Office summoned shopkeepers to a meeting, where everyone agreed that the sackings should cease, in order to restore morale. In 1915 with the initial panic over, customers started buying again, and retail profits quickly recovered. Thus in time drapery firms got behind the War Office initiative of supplying the army, with companies such as Mawer & Collingham of Lincoln producing five hundred pairs of khaki trousers a week. Stores now needed to hold on to their staff.

Extraordinarily enough, this challenging time was just the moment that another retailer chose to begin implementing one of the most radical experiments in shopwork. In 1864, Somerset draper John Lewis had opened a small store at 132 Oxford Street, selling silk, wool and haberdashery. A highly principled, irascible man, Lewis had built up his business through five decades of sheer hard work. Now an old man but still going strong, John Lewis had been unperturbed by the arrival of Selfridges, realising that the new kid on the block would bring extra custom to Oxford Street and confident that the John Lewis policy of good value for money and a wide assortment

(*Above*) Shops on Cornhill, Wisbech, Cambridgeshire, including Foster's drapery holding a 'selling out' sale, Bellar's grocery, Baxter's chemist and the Post Office. Nelson Foster is likely the man standing on the left and postmaster, Mr Goward, the man on the right. Photographed by Samuel Smith, 6 September 1854.

(*Right*) View of the magnificent three-storeyed fabrics hall in Jenner's department store, Princes Street, Edinburgh. Photographed by Henry Bedford Lemere at the store's re-opening in 1895.

(*Above*) Shoppers inside the Burlington Arcade, Mayfair, London, *c.*1910.

(*Above*) The staff of Anderson and McAuley's department store, Belfast, in the early 1900s.

(*Right*) The 'foundling' heroines of *The Shop Girl* musical comedy in costume, 1895.

(*Left*) A sketch of 'Miss Bondfield On Tour' – addressing a meeting of shop assistants in the St. George's Hall, Hull – from *The Shop Assistant Journal*, July 1898.

(*Left*) The notorious case of Miss Cass, a shopgirl arrested on Regent Street, London. As pictured in the *Illustrated Police News*, July 1887.

(*Above*) The lively goings-on at Whiteley's, as drawn in a comic penny paper from 1887.

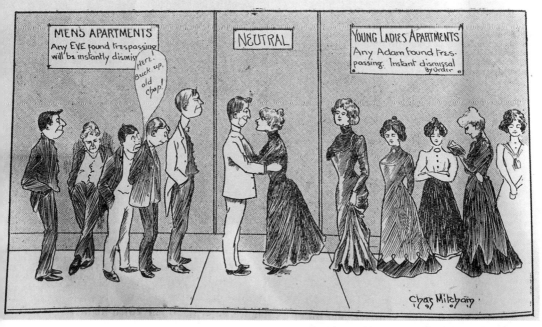

(*Above*) 'The Delights of "Living-In"', as depicted in *The Shop Assistant Journal*, March 1901.

(*Left*) On 16 November 1898, Harrods unveiled a technological marvel: Britain's first moving staircase.

(*Right*) A Marks and Spencer Ltd stall – 'Admission Free' – 133 Grainger Market, Newcastle, 1 December 1906.

(*Right*) Selfridges window display in its opening week, March 1909, showing just a few elegant mannequins rather than piles of stock as below.

(*Left*) A fine example of a 'stocky' or 'massed' window display at Marshall & Snelgrove's, with goods stacked or suspended from floor to ceiling. Photographed the same week that Selfridges opened.

(*Above*) 'London receiving her newest Institution': a Selfridges newspaper advertisement touting the new store's dedication 'to women's service', 1909.

(*Above right*) Lucile's fabulous shopgirl models in London, 1912.

Miss WALLER
Millinery, Dipton

Miss MULCASTE
Millinery, Langley Pk.

Mrs. SUDREN
Millinery, Medomsley

Miss JEWITT
Millinery, Central

Miss RICHARDSON
Millinery, Sacriston

Miss RAMSEY
Hosiery, Dipton

Miss PEEL
*Furnishing and Boot,
Langley Park*

Miss SIMPSON
*Furnishing and Boot,
Medomsley*

DEPARTMENTAL MANAGERESSES.

(*Above*) Over 200 suffragettes rush through the streets of London smashing shop windows with toffee hammers and other implements in protest, March 1912.

(*Right*) Departmental manageresses, Annfield Plain Industrial Co-operative Society Ltd, Durham, 1920.

(*Left*) One of Harrods' 'Green Ladies' summoning a cab during the First World War.

(*Below*) Women serving in a grocer's shop during the First World War, taking the place of men who have enlisted in the army, August 1915.

(*Left*) Shoppers outside the Co-operative Society Ltd in East Ham, *c.*1929.

(*Left*) Woolworths shopgirls struggling to keep up with the Christmas rush, as shoppers crowd to buy novelties and decorations, 14 December 1937.

(*Above*) Shopgirls from Marks and Spencer Ltd, enjoying their time at Dymchurch holiday camp, Kent in 1936.

(*Above*) Firefighters at work in front of John Lewis, Oxford Street, London, the morning after highly explosive and incendiary German bombs caused widespread damage, 18 September 1940.

(*Right*) A former Woolworths shopgirl working in a machine shop during the Second World War.

(*Right*) London's first self-service 'help yourself' store at Wood Green, September 1948. Note the wire baskets and a few shop assistants still on hand to help out.

(*Left*) Two sets of identical twins, (left to right) Michelle Hellier, Nicole Hellier, Susy Young and Rosie Young, who worked as shopgirls at Biba, Kensington, west London. Photographed in September 1966.

(*Right*) 'This is your Company', from the first pictorial style Annual Report produced by Woolworths, distributed to employees and shareholders, March 1958.

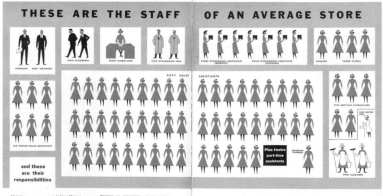

of stock would stand up to the new competition. Unlike other stores who were rattled by the American arriviste, Lewis did not increase his advertising budget and simply stuck to his tried-and-tested business methods. To keep prices down for his customers, he had always worked to a significantly smaller profit margin than his competitors, taking just 25 per cent profit on selling price, while most other drapers took 33 per cent. The policy worked; the store was profitable and if the enterprise came across as at all old-fashioned, so be it, felt the elderly John Lewis.

Unfortunately for his shop assistants, Lewis treated them with the same tenacious rigour. And Philip Hoffman, in his role as officer of the National Amalgamated Union of Shop Assistants, Warehousemen & Clerks, clashed with the proprietor time and again. In his autobiography Hoffman painted an eloquent picture of the man Lewis had become. This 'remarkable man' represented for Hoffman 'much of the worst type of employer in the rugged, rather shameless individualist past of the Victorian and Edwardian era'.[37] According to him, Lewis had grown tyrannical and eccentric, 'a fearless, obstinate man', who forced younger customers to use the stairs in his store rather than the lift if he felt they were fit enough, and was particularly fussy about his female employees' dress. Young women were to be all in black with high white collars kept up without wire supports. This was not only frightfully old-fashioned, but also an uncomfortable and impractical method of collar-management; he also particularly disliked seeing blonde curly hair – let alone redheads – on his shopfloor.[38] When prowling his store, he sometimes took instantly against a certain saleswoman or salesman, asking them a couple of questions about their length of service and then saying, 'You have been here too long. Go to the Counting House and get your money.'[39]

Some shop assistants actively avoided applying for jobs there, explaining, 'They're rotten payers.' Even Lewis's son Spedan described his father as 'the captain of a big ship much under-engined and with those engines much under-fuelled', whose staff were underpaid and undermotivated. They received but 'a bare living, with very little margin beyond absolute necessaries' and had none of the advantages that staff at enlightened stores were starting to enjoy: no sick pay, pension provision, staff amenities or playing fields. Spedan Lewis described the management system as 'ruthlessly close-fisted'.[40]

In May 1909 Spedan Lewis, then aged twenty-three, had been riding his horse on Rotten Row in Hyde Park. The horse had shied and Spedan had fallen off, seriously injuring himself, with one of his lungs severely punctured. For the next two years, he was effectively an invalid, undergoing a series of chest operations, struggling to recover and requiring long periods of rest. Spedan was a romantic, visionary young man, much influenced by his politically engaged mother, Eliza Baker, one of the few women to attend university in the 1870s, obtaining a pass degree from Girton College, Cambridge, in history and political economy.

Spedan owned a quarter share of John Lewis; his younger brother, Oswald, had sold his own quarter share back to his father, so that John Lewis senior at this point possessed three quarters of the business. The long months of recuperation gave Spedan ample time to reflect on his father's lifework and his own few years' experience of retail. He had been shocked to discover the enormous discrepancy between the annual profit of the John Lewis store and the annual pay sheet for staff, who were earning very low wages. Spedan, Oswald and their father enjoyed the income of about £26,000 a year; the staff wage bill for a workforce of just over 300 came to around £16,000 a year.[41] Even fifty years later, when the extremes of rich and poor in society were less polarised, Spedan Lewis said in a radio broadcast, 'It is all wrong to have millionaires before you have ceased to have slums.' He was not against capitalism, but in 1957, and probably even more so in 1909, Spedan felt that 'The present state of affairs is really a perversion of the proper working of capitalism.'[42]

From his sickbed, Spedan dreamt up a new model of business enterprise, 'the notion of the John Lewis Partnership', as he termed it, a notion that would ultimately prove so successful that it is still influencing business and government thinking today.[43] He wanted to overturn the quasi-feudal relationship between proprietor and staff, establishing instead a kind of professional partnership between all ranks of store workers, such as that enjoyed by lawyers and stockbrokers. In his autobiography he lyrically described his concept thus: 'Partnership is justice. Better than justice, it is kindness. It is harmony with what some people call the Nature of Things and some the Will of God.'[44] On his recovery, Spedan swapped his quarter share of John Lewis for total control of Peter Jones on London's Kings Road, which John Lewis senior had acquired a few years earlier. Peter Jones was to be Spedan's testing ground.

Things did not go well at first. Peter Jones had been performing badly before the outbreak of war and now, in spite of extraordinary trading conditions and reduced opening hours, Spedan chose this moment to launch the first stages of his new scheme. First on his agenda was to improve staff living conditions. The store had been constructed out of a number of dwelling houses on the Kings Road; while the shopfloor had been knocked open, the upstairs staff bedrooms were still dingy, dangerous, separate quarters. Spedan had the passages knocked through, got hot and cold running water installed and improved general hygiene. He expanded the living quarters for female staff and effectively ended the strict and obligatory living-in regime by removing all rules restricting personal freedoms for those over twenty-one.[45] For shopgirls under twenty-one, the hostel matron still played a parental role. Eating facilities were also renovated. Shopman Robert Bichan joyfully described the new-look dining room with 'interesting pictures on the walls, colourful curtains, black and red Tudor tile pattern linoleum'. The kitchen was modernised too, with piping hot food served by neatly uniformed waitresses.[46]

Secondly, and most importantly for the majority of staff, Spedan significantly improved pay, keeping pace with inflation. In 1915 he also started the 'Committees for Communication', what he termed his 'one really new idea', though it was not unlike Selfridges' Staff Parliament. His aim was to bridge the gulf between the managers and the managed; to this end, several times a year fifteen staff representatives in each committee met a senior manager – often Spedan himself – to discuss whatever was on their minds. Spedan discovered that at first they were shy and hadn't much to say. 'I used hastily to start a discussion upon something or other and keep it going for twenty minutes or so,' he said, but as the idea caught on he did not need to take the lead any more. Spedan knew his reforms would be dismissed as 'merely utopian, an unpractical lavishness that was hopelessly unsound business', but he stuck with them.[47]

Tudor patterned flooring, increased pay, refurbished living quarters, better food and giving staff a say in the business seemed like financial suicide to most other proprietors, who were battening down the hatches, including John Lewis senior. Indeed, Spedan's high spending was making staff costs spiral, with the pay sheet doubling in three years. But by the middle of the war, Peter Jones' finances had begun to pull through, with turnover growing year on year. Spedan was hopeful that his reforms would win out.

Peter Jones' shop assistants, provided with regular hot meals in the renovated dining room, were sheltered from many of the harsh realities of city life on the home front. Loss of supplies from continental Europe meant that food stocks were running low, and as a little girl, Dorothy Bouchier experienced first-hand what this meant. She would later work at Harrods, but in her autobiography some of her most enduring girlhood memories are of wartime hunger. 'We didn't seem to be getting enough to eat,' she wrote, describing how her family hardly managed to survive on her father's low wages as a corporal in the Royal Engineers, even when supplemented by her mother's dressmaking work. 'This undernourishment caused problems,' she felt, for when she cut or grazed herself, the wounds would fester. She recalled chaotic neighbourhood scenes as someone shouted down the road, 'There are some oxtails at the butchers!' or 'There's coal at the depot!' Everyone would rush outside, often arriving too late to get hold of the new supplies.[48]

In fact, the government's War Emergency Committee had attempted to control the distribution and pricing of food and necessities, but few of their regulations had been implemented. With food prices rising by 87 per cent in the first two years of the war, food riots soon broke out. Socialist campaigner Margaretta Hicks described them as 'mad raids' often carried out by women who were 'frenzied by the loss of relatives through the war' and by 'the gassing of soldiers, and the fearful fighting'. Hicks was sympathetic, but only to a degree: 'It is dreadful, but smashing a few shops only makes things worse.'[49]

Apart from highly erratic and often non-existent supplies, retailers had another urgent problem to worry about: staffing levels. With three million men on the front in 1915, the government had woken up to the fact that they needed to mobilise women. David Lloyd George said, 'Without women, victory will tarry,' and propaganda posters called out, 'Do your Bit, Replace a Man for the Front'. Women of all ages who had never before worked in shops entered retail in their thousands: for the first time ever there were more shopgirls than shopmen.[50] They started to take on jobs traditionally reserved for their male counterparts: at Peter Jones, Spedan Lewis began hiring women as the all-important buyers, while at Peter Robinson's, women drove the delivery vans, wearing smart grey uniforms. Harrods even retrained some of its female staff to become carriage attendants, the commissionaires who welcomed customers on the pavement in their distinctive uniforms, so that the famous 'Green Men' became 'Green Women'. Firms like Sainsbury's went on a recruitment drive, preparing a blank letter to be filled in by each branch manager, which read: 'Madam, If your parents reside within half a mile of our _____ Branch, and you are not less than five feet six ins. in height; and not under 19 years of age, please call here between _____ and _____ tomorrow presenting this letter. Do not call at any other time. Yours truly, for J. Sainsbury.'[51]

Winifred Griffiths was nineteen years old when war broke out, working as a housemaid in Oakley, Hampshire. Her mistress released her so she could answer a local call-out from the co-operative stores; they wanted to train up young women as replacements for the male grocery assistants who had joined the forces. For the first few days Winifred had to stay in a back room bagging up sugar and lump sugar. She was first let out to help at the grocery counter on one of the busiest times of the week, Friday evening. 'I was so bewildered that I am afraid I made a fine mess of things,' she wrote in her unpublished autobiography. 'When trying to serve customers I did not know where things were kept, nor yet had I memorised all the prices. I had not yet acquired the knack of making tidy packets for goods like dried fruit, rice and tapioca … To crown all, most customers expected their goods to be done up in a large paper parcel.' Things soon improved for Winifred, as she made friends with two other new girls, Jennie and Daisy, who had been drafted in from Yorkshire and Somerset. Together they went to evening classes, or the cinema on their half day, or to church on Sundays.

Winifred left the Co-op for a new position in a grocery called Walkers, where she was to be trained up to take the place of a young man about to leave for the front. Much to her consternation, not only did he leave but so did his boss. 'So that after only two or three months of training, as against several years that an old-time apprentice would have had, I found myself in charge of the provision side in a very busy store, where we sold thirty sides of bacon a week.'[52]

Other young women, though, stood little chance of promotion. Grocer Mr Headey, who had had difficulty before the Great War with his one female cashier, Miss Owen, among his twelve male staff, was drafted from Tonbridge to run a large grocery store in Reading which employed twenty-two people. Twenty of the twenty-two were women. It was to prove another unhappy experience. His son recalled how Mr Headey senior disapproved heartily of the female shop assistants. Matters came to a head when one of the women made a mistake, selling a customer powdered borax instead of ground arrowroot. There was 'a hell of a to-do' and she rushed into the girls' restroom crying, the other female assistants hurrying after in order to comfort her, leaving the huge shop empty of staff. Mr Headey promptly sacked the lot. He then had to restaff, hiring *any* kind of man he could get hold of, 'old joshers' including a man with a club foot and another who had left the army on account of his religion.[53]

Of course, it wasn't just in retail that women were stepping into roles traditionally occupied by men. Industrial, clerical, agricultural and transport jobs were suddenly open to them too. *Pathé Gazette* newsreels, which were shown in the newly built, hugely popular picture palaces, had titles like *Navvies in Skirts*, *Zoo's First Woman Keeper* and *While Mother Works*. Over the course of the war, the number of women in employment increased by more than 1.5 million.[54] Women became land girls, tram-drivers, firefighters and prototype policewomen. They heaved coal, built airships and worked behind the front line in France. Thousands also stepped up to do one of the most dangerous and highly lucrative jobs of all: munitions work.

At its height, the Woolwich Arsenal in south-east London was the biggest munitions factory in Britain. Some thirty thousand women walked through the massive wrought-iron gates for each twelve-hour shift. Among them were thousands of ex-shopgirls, attracted by significantly higher pay and a certain independence away from the shopfloor managers. The most difficult jobs they were trained to take on were bomb-making and chemical processing. The women who came into direct contact with sulphur were nicknamed the canaries, as the chemical turned their skin yellow: a far cry from the clean white hands, neat dress and gentility of the counter assistant. What's more, the munitionettes occasionally had a discreet drink together in the pub after work, before returning to their lodgings on the bus, moving about the city unchaperoned.[55] The strict, petty rules of the living-in system must have felt part of a different universe.

Now that they were experiencing working life with good wages, increased training and promotions, regulated hours, controlled working conditions and often workplace childcare, women joined unions as never before. There was a staggering 160 per cent increase in female union membership across all unions during the war. Female shop assistants in stores as well as co-operatives were part of this trend, with both the shop assistants' union (the NAUSAW&C) and the co-operative workers union (the AUCE) seeing huge rises; the AUCE went from having 7,000 female assistants on its books to over 36,000. Some shop-owners still forbad union membership, but in other stores, particularly in the bigger co-operatives and department stores, a large part of the workforce was now unionised. This gave union officer Philip Hoffman more bargaining power than ever, which he was to exercise in the turbulent times ahead.

WEST END SHOP GIRLS' STRIKE.

'Shopgirl As Strike Leader': Hilda Canham and the strike committee during the John Lewis & Co. strike, May 1920.

CHAPTER 6

STRIKE!

After the armistice, with 900,000 British and Empire members of the armed forces dead and thousands more wounded, the weary veterans returning home faced not only the flu pandemic, but also very insecure job prospects. The staple industries such as cotton and coal mining that had earned Britain its nickname of the 'workshop of the world' were in decline, as Britain's industrial and trading dominance was challenged by Germany and the USA. Now that the war was over, this decline was exposed and unemployment shot up.

Female war workers were made to relinquish their jobs for the returning men – munitions workers were sacked and the Restoration of Pre-War Practices Act in 1919 excluded women from most forms of industrial work. Women were expected to return to their former jobs, like domestic service, textile work and shopwork, and married women were expected to devote themselves to their domestic duties again. As the Ministry of Labour put it, 'As soldiers return to their homes their wives are reverting to housewifery.' Shopgirls who had taken the place of shopmen all across the retail trade were also required to step back down as the men returned. Some women missed their war work, its new horizons and camaraderie; others were glad to leave their wartime roles, seeing it as an extraordinary but circumscribed period in their lives.[1]

In spite of all these women having vacated their temporary positions, there were still simply not enough jobs to go around. Working-class wages crashed and many families suffered extreme hardship. Shopworkers were included in this. Stores throughout the country, from Costigan & Co. in Glasgow to John Lewis in London, had hardly raised their wages since the beginning of the war. At the point the union tested its increased strength, picking up the cudgels from where it had left off pre-war, targeting individual shops with demands for minimum wage scales, longer holidays and trade union recognition.

Despite its co-operative beginnings, one of the very worst offenders in terms of low pay was the Army & Navy Co-operative Society, known as 'The Stores', on Victoria Street in London. It was a historic establishment, set in its ways, its huge premises taking up a whole block. Before the war, Edwardian shopper Olivia waxed lyrical about its unchanging reliability. 'The British Parliament is one institution, the Stores are another,' she wrote in her *Prejudiced Guide* to London shopping. It was still a members-only store, where you had to present your membership number on entry, though it is clear that friends would pass their number on to each other. Olivia confessed that one particular membership number served hundreds of friends. 'Who first gave it away, or to whom it really belonged, no one knew, but they all quoted it assiduously for spun silk underwear, and dreamed of bargains.'[2] After eventually getting behind the War Office demands, the Stores had had a good war and profits were up. Yet none of this was being passed on to the employees. Fifty saleswomen in one department were averaging a miserly twenty-two shillings a week, which was less than half of what the union felt would be a fair living wage.[3]

And so, the Great Shop Strike began. With the admirals, generals and commanders of the Stores' board refusing to increase wages significantly, the largest stoppage in retail trade that the country had ever witnessed was under way. At 6.30 a.m. on 4 December 1919, four thousand Army & Navy employees refused to go to work, with picketing shopworkers acting as sentries round the whole block, making sure their fellow staff did not break ranks. The directors made a brave show of continuing as if everything was normal: the lights were on, including the little gas jets at the entrance doorways where customers could light their cigars and pipes. At opening time, a frock-coated and top-hatted under-manager stood explaining to the few confused customers that the shop assistants were 'out'. One large, fur-clad lady did not understand the term, according to unionist Philip Hoffman's account. 'Out, did you say out? It's all very strange, very strange indeed. Out! I never heard of such a thing! Just fancy! Out!' Another customer was insistent that she have her sugar ration, as she had important guests for tea, but the flustered under-manager could not help her either. 'Sorry, Madam, we don't know where the sugar is. If you leave your address, we'll send it.' She was extremely unhappy with that.[4]

Much to Hoffman's delight, the strike became a popular cause, supported by the press and even some shareholders, one lady offering her year's dividends, another her drawing room for the convenience of the staff. On the second day of the strike Hoffman was summoned to meet Alfred Harmsworth, now Lord Northcliffe, the undisputed chief of the British press establishment. In his private office at *The Times*, Northcliffe offered Hoffman a cigar and then proceeded to quiz the trade unionist with short, sharp questions. 'How are your funds? Have they met you yet? Are you going to win?' Northcliffe, perhaps unexpectedly, revealed an in-depth knowledge of shoplife, gleaned from years of readers' letters, and pressed Hoffman on whether conditions at Whiteley's had improved over the years, as well as running through West End shop gossip. He congratulated Hoffman on the modesty of the union's demands, told him that he himself could not run his papers without the help of the print union, and promised his papers' support.

That night, the shop assistants' union met the Army & Navy directors, and after seven hours of negotiations the directors agreed to put the wage demands to the Industrial Court. This new tribunal had been set up that same year in order to arbitrate in industrial disputes. There was great hope among the Army & Navy shop assistants that this tribunal would back them in a momentous ruling for shop assistants around the country. So on the last day of the year, the union invited seven thousand shop assistants to the Albert Hall to hear the Industrial Court ruling read out. Hoffman claimed it was the largest gathering of shop employees ever seen. 'They cheered everybody and everything, for they were in a cheerful mood.' They cried 'Shame!' during the opening speeches, when they heard about the paltry wages of a London saleswoman with three years' service and those of a twenty-year-old shop model. Then they fell silent as the tribunal award was read out, their silence soon turning to joy as the result was announced: a huge 35 per cent increase for those over twenty-one, and fixed minimum wages, a forty-eight-hour week and improved holidays. It had been worth hiring out the Albert Hall, for the effects of this award spread around the country, with wage increases reported across the board.

Despite this triumph of collective action, John Lewis, now aged eighty-four and with a full white beard and whiskers, slightly stooped but still going strong, had no truck with the 'accursed trade unionists', as he called them. [5] Like other proprietors, Lewis initially agreed to pay increases with fixed minimum wages, as well as shorter hours, longer holidays and sick pay. But then he started sacking staff and engaged new employees on condition that they didn't join the union.[6] Lewis was summoned to the Industrial

Court, where he was represented by his barrister son, Oswald Lewis, and advised to comply with his initial agreements. But Lewis senior simply ignored the court ruling. In a last-ditch attempt to change his mind, a deputation of staff was sent to meet their boss. A buyer, a shopwalker, a shopboy and a shopgirl, Hilda Canham, were told by Lewis that he 'feared neither God nor Devil' and wouldn't budge on the matter. So that May Monday morning in 1920, the first day of the Silk Department sale, 400 John Lewis employees went out on strike, including the char ladies. Claiming to be amazed at the action, Lewis railed against the 'vapourings of the accursed trade unionists' that caused such mischief.[7]

Shopgirl Hilda Canham, seven years in John Lewis's employment, became the heroine of the strike. She 'radiated energy and enthusiasm', according to the *Daily Mail*, telling their reporter that she had seen trouble coming for a long time.[8] 'The Island of Lewis', 'The Battle of Oxford Street', 'John Says Nothing,' screamed the supportive newspaper headlines, with Hilda's photograph as the 'girl in brown' splashed beside them. Shop assistants from other stores supported their fellows, with Harrods' and Army & Navy store staff contributing £300 per store to the strike fund and the Wholesale Textile houses £250. Theatres sent complimentary tickets, music hall artists volunteered to give concerts and even Queen Mary made sure her contributions were popped into the Oxford Street collection boxes. The striking staff were astonished and overwhelmed by such support. They needed it, for this one was to be a long haul.

Miss Bobbie Stirling had travelled from the north of Ireland to find work in John Lewis's juvenile department. She was one of the two hundred shopgirls who lived in and who were now out on strike, and at first Oswald Lewis tried to talk each of them round to returning to work. In spite of her precarious situation, Stirling stood up to Oswald Lewis with spirit according to Hoffman's account:

'Do your parents understand the steps you have taken in this matter?' Lewis asked.

'Yes, they are quite aware. I have explained the whole matter to them,' Stirling replied, composed.

'You're very silly – a young girl like you with no friends in London. If this strike lasts out, what are you going to do?'

'We've got plenty of support … I intend to stop out until we all go in together.'[9]

The strike was indeed lasting out; a notice was issued that those who were living in the John Lewis hostels were not welcome to return: they should either go home or find work elsewhere. Their first problem was food, so the strike organisers made sure that the girls could get their meals at the YWCA headquarters canteen. Then the public rallied and offered them alternative living accommodation. After five long weeks, the striking staff realised that their old proprietor would never give in to their demands. So they called off the strike and simply left the firm; a 'wise retirement' said Hoffman, describing it as a 'defeat which was victory'. The strikers were high-spirited to the end, singing 'Pack Up Your Troubles' and 'Auld Lang Syne', and within days they were snapped up by stores on Kensington High Street, with the general manager of Pontings phoning up Hoffman to request as many former John Lewis shopgirls as possible for his establishment. 'I haven't had such girls come into the trade for years,' the Pontings manager said.

The battle to win a decent living wage for shopworkers all around the country continued against the backdrop of the economic slump and soaring unemployment, which reached new heights in 1921 with two million out of work. Once again Spedan Lewis picked a difficult moment to launch an expensive project. Just two months before his father's employees walked out on strike, Lewis had launched the radical profit-sharing scheme that he had been dreaming of for years. In the spring of 1920, his Peter Jones store introduced 'share promises' for its employees, which twice a year could be exchanged for a cash dividend. For the first time ever, members of staff were getting a share in the profits and were part-owners in the business. Lewis tried to encourage them to treat the promises as savings, though many wanted the cash immediately. So he ruled that people had to make a good case for cashing them in. Florrie, who worked in the staff kitchen, had a pretty good one: she was unmarried and expecting a child. Spedan's father would probably have sacked her; instead the younger Lewis sanctioned the cashing in of her £16 holding. Matron in charge of the staff kitchen told him of the 'flurry of excitement' that ensued among the girls. One girl ran up to her, exclaiming:

'Oh, Matron, Florrie's got her share money!'

'What about it?'

'But are these things really money?'

'Of course they are really money, as I keep on telling you silly girls, and now perhaps you'll believe it.'

'But I have got thirty of them! Fancy me worth thirty pounds!'

The young woman then ran off in tears.[10]

Florrie and some of her girlfriends might have succeeded in cashing in their share promises, but the depression of the early 1920s affected upmarket stores badly, including Peter Jones, which made a loss in both 1921 and 1922. Old John Lewis helped out his son with a cash injection, but there was no dividend to pay out to the shop assistants, now 'partners', for another few years. Unperturbed, Spedan Lewis pursued his radical agenda. He had a second 'big idea'. During the war he had realised that, due to the extraordinary working conditions, it had become acceptable – 'the thing' – for professional and better-educated men unable to join up to work in a shop, but only a particular type of shop: 'a shop, of course, of a certain status and Peter Jones came within that line.'[11] Now he wanted to apply the same thinking to educated women. Shopwork for women was no longer associated with trashiness and prostitution. Nevertheless, for the daughters of upper-middle-class families it was considered 'infra dig' to work in a shop – it was just not what a respectable young lady did, particularly not if they were one of the few to have gone on to further education. Yet it was precisely these women Spedan set his sights on.

Letters were sent out to the women's colleges at Cambridge University and Oxford University, as well as Bedford College, London and Royal Holloway College, asking for a list of their top female graduates. Spedan offered these women jobs as 'learners', on the selling floor and as buyers, with the same pay as the male buyers. One such learner was Beatrice Hunter, who after leaving Oxford had worked in the civil service during the war and had become a factory inspector. Like many women, she faced unemployment in the immediate aftermath. One of her letters to a friend in 1922 describes her new opportunity: 'I am going into trade. I've been offered a buyership at Peter Jones, Sloane Square. It's a cheapish drapers and ladies' outfitters … The Chairman is the son of John Lewis of Oxford Street … He has a mad stunt of employing University women.' Beatrice acknowledged that the stunt was risky. 'The commercial world is very suspicious of outsiders – the idea of taking in completely inexperienced people in responsible positions is quite a new one.'

She was nervous on her first day, as her notebook jottings reveal: 'Begin at PJ today. Feel as one does at first when trying to speak a foreign language in its own country.' She was right to be nervous, for many of the old shopfloor hands took 'a dim view of this new experiment and one heard criticisms from all sides', according to shopman Robert Bichan. He used to tease the 'young lady learners', chanting 'Boots, boots, boots, boots' at Beatrice Hunter as she passed by him in the second-hand furniture department carrying six boxes of shoes.

By 1928 there were over seventy learners at Peter Jones, and while some stuck it out for only a few weeks, others were propelled quickly through the ranks to become linens buyers, umbrella buyers and fashion vendeuses. Florence Lorimer was even given £5,000 by Spedan Lewis to fund a far-flung buying tour of Punjab, Kashmir and Afghanistan to purchase antiquities and carpets. In a series of memos Spedan Lewis instructed her to look out for embroidered felt rugs, bedspreads and semi-precious stones, as well as owls and hummingbirds for his personal ornithology collection. She returned with a haul of treasures, whose exotic influence could be traced in a number of fabric ranges.

Beatrice Hunter thrived too. Just a month after she started, she scribbled in her notebook, 'It's terrifying to be plunged into full responsibility without any experience at all. I have four shop girls under me from whom I have to conceal my ignorance ... After years of working on paper it's alarming to be so concrete – real money and real shoes and, worst of, real individual customers to cope with.' Clearly Spedan Lewis was rather taken with her from the start, being 'awfully nice' and 'a real idealist, a wild enthusiast but also a rather sharp business man'. He could also be capricious and mercurial, but she seemed quite to enjoy the rollercoaster of working closely with the chairman, writing, 'The whole thing, of course, is more like a Musical Comedy than real life, priceless from morning to night.' It became even more like a theatrical romance when he whisked her off during the working day to play tennis at Roehampton with his brother Oswald, and later proposed. Beatrice became Mrs Spedan Lewis in October 1923, just a year after she started working at Peter

Jones.[12] Together they had three children and from 1929 to 1951 Beatrice served as vice-chairman of the Partnership.

Dorothy Bouchier, who had felt so hungry as a child during the war, longed for the glamour of working in a famous department store – she would never have put it as derogatorily as Beatrice's comment, 'I'm going into trade.' As a teenage girl she spent all her pocket money on the pictures, dreaming of becoming a movie star, and what better place to start than at Harrods? She left school aged fourteen in 1923 and followed her older brother, who had landed a job in the estate agency department at the store. Soon Dorothy was working in the sumptuous 'small ladies department', selling dresses to women of a petite figure, 'a step nearer to my heart's desire', as she put it in her autobiography. 'How elegant it was, how perfumed, how glamorous, with lovely dresses on display and beautifully made-up, beautifully coiffured sales ladies standing around in pretty sage green dresses.'[13]

Wearing just such a green dress, Dorothy was assigned as 'junior' to one of the sales ladies. However junior she might have been, she was soon thrown into the limelight when her mother entered her portrait photo into a *Daily Mirror* beauty competition. Dorothy had unruly dark locks and big dreamy eyes and clearly awakened men's most atavistic instincts. Alerted by the newspaper, the Harrods photographic department took pictures of Dorothy and hung them from the entrance. 'To be honoured by being displayed at the main entrance of the most famous emporium in the world should have filled me with pride. But it didn't. I would walk past it with eyes averted.'[14] Now fifteen and entering puberty, Dorothy was embarrassed, but the embarrassment did not last long. Soon she started hanging out with a rather fast set of Harrods assistants, including rich young men, sons of store proprietors who were learning the trade at Harrods. After work on a Saturday morning the clique would play rugger and netball at Harrods Sports Club in Barnes, west London, following that with enormous teas and then evening festivities with drinks and dancing the Charleston. 'Sometimes our high heels would catch in the turn-ups of the boys' Oxford Bags and we'd all fall in a giggling heap onto the dance floor.'

Soon everyone was in love with everyone else: Dorothy was in love with 'Slushy' Freshwater, and a Welsh boy was in love with Dorothy. It was the Welsh boy who nicknamed Dorothy 'Chili', and the name stuck. Yet such coursing passions were dangerous in a place like Harrods. 'They demanded a strict moral code from their employees and anyone with a whiff of scandal about them would be sent packing.' When Dorothy/Chili excitedly confided in her fellow junior that she had lost her virginity to Slushy the night before, the truth came out and Chili's mother was summoned to the store 'to be told that my disgusting presence must be removed from the august house of Harrods'.[15] Chili, Slushy and several other colourful characters were given the sack.

Luckily for Chili, the pall of her shame, as she put it, did not waft as far as Kensington High Street, where she was promptly hired by Derry & Toms to model dresses in the model gowns department. By the age of seventeen in 1927, Chili had wangled her way into the movie business, acting first in shorts and then in feature-length silent movies like *Carnival*. Soon she was touted as 'England's "IT" Girl' and she successfully made the transition into talkies. Ahead of her lay the rollercoaster life of a movie star, with its triumphs and failures, its moments of glory and deep personal sorrows.

Another young woman leading a 'butterfly-life' in the late 1920s was Flora Solomon, daughter of a Russian gold tycoon, who received £1,000 a month from her father to live on. An heiress with servants to take care of her household and childcare needs, she attended charity committees by day and danced in nightclubs at night. Following the Wall Street crash in 1929, however, the high-life came to a sudden end when her father's finances hit the rocks and her monthly allowance was stopped. She was widowed soon after and with no income, for the first time in her life she had to make money for herself and her young son. She sold her jewellery, moved to the upper floor of her house, let out the ground floor to her aunt, and found new jobs for her butler and chauffeurs; her maid married her footman, 'solving that problem'.[16] A job was the next thing on the agenda.

At a dinner party in 1931 she found herself sitting next to Simon Marks. Marks' father Michael had fled the Jewish pogroms in what was then Russian Poland, and had started as a pedlar and then stall-holder in Leeds' Kirkgate Market. He had called his stall Marks' Penny Bazaar and since he spoke no English the story goes that the slogan 'Don't Ask the Price, It's a Penny' came from his attaching this permanent sign to his sales tray.[17] After opening other stalls around the north of England, including in Birkenhead, Chesterfield and Warrington, he teamed up with Yorkshireman Tom Spencer and together they opened the first Marks & Spencer Penny Bazaar shop at 63 Stretford Road, Manchester. By the time Michael Marks died in 1907, the company had over fifty outlets, both in city markets and on the high street; the headline read, 'Pioneer of Penny Bazaars − Death of a Generous Manchester Jew'. A photograph of the stall in Newcastle's Grainger Market shows broad counters with young shopgirls in attendance; other images document the pride the company already demonstrated in its heritage, the signs above the open-fronted shops proclaiming, 'Marks & Spencer Ltd, Originators of Penny Bazaars − Admission Free'.[18]

Simon Marks continued his father's expansion programme with dynamism, taking the company on to the stock exchange, so that on the night Flora Solomon sat next to him at dinner he was able to reel off an impressive list of 160 Marks & Spencer stores around the country. 'Now we are going to show what a British company can do,' he said, explaining that his biggest competitor was Woolworths.

Frank W. Woolworth, a farmer's son from Great Bend, Jefferson County, New York State, had been a pioneer in cheap retailing; his five-and-ten-cent stores, with their bright lights and mahogany counter tops split into sections showing off a wide variety of goods, had taken America by storm. He had spotted potential for expansion in Britain, and fixed on Liverpool's Church Street for his first experimental premises in 1909, the same year that Selfridges opened. With gold letters on warm red gloss paint, 'F.W. Woolworth' was topped with the sign 'Nothing In These Stores Over 6d'. Prices were low, price tags were clearly displayed, and pic'n'mix was instantly popular. The Woolworth family had gunned for rapid expansion, so that by the time Marks and Solomon were dining, the four-hundredth Woolworths store had just been opened, in Southport.[19]

This then was the rival chain store that most worried Marks. He explained his plans to move away from the low-cost end of retail, adding that, 'the days of the "Penny Bazaar" are finished'. It sounds as though Marks was showing off and Flora Solomon certainly wasn't in the mood for admiring his achievements. Instead, according to her memoir, she attacked him.

'You know you have a shocking reputation in the country,' she flung at him.

'What do you mean?'

'Your labour conditions are notorious.'

'But how do you know, Flora? When was the last time you ventured into one of my stores?'

Marks had a point. In her memoir Solomon admitted that she rarely went into shops of any kind and that she had 'complete ignorance of the industry', but this didn't stop her.

'I have it from Margaret Bondfield.'

Tenacious Bondfield was by now minister of labour in Ramsay MacDonald's Labour government, the first ever woman Cabinet minister and privy councillor. Solomon had friends in the Labour

Party and knew of Bondfield's undercover and political work to improve shop conditions. And so Solomon threw a final grenade: 'Your company is growing by exploiting its workers.'

Marks apparently quivered with anger. Then he offered her a job. He suggested she might come up with a plan to improve things. Solomon was delighted with Marks' offer and went to seek Bondfield's advice. 'Don't rush it,' Margaret warned. 'Take a good look at the stores first. And if you're wise you'll go across to Europe and investigate conditions there. You may pick up some ideas.'[20]

So Solomon, armed with a letter of introduction from Marks, started her tour of British high streets, until then an alien land to her. She described herself as 'a fat woman with a heavy accent', 'an exotic spectacle'. She was certainly received with suspicion as she questioned shopgirls, interviewed managers and sniffed behind broom cupboards. What she discovered was a country of extreme contrasts. For, in spite of the searing memory of the General Strike of 1926, the ongoing deep recession and ever-increasing unemployment, some parts of the economy were booming. Since the cost of living was falling, those who were actually in work enjoyed increased spending power. Before the First World War, 90 per cent of the population had rented their homes; but now that mortgage regulations had been loosened and planning laws relaxed, private developers had begun building new suburbs, serviced by extensive rail networks, the 'Metro-land' of John Betjeman. With optimism, young families were moving out of old urban housing stock, some of it slums, into new semi-detached homes with gardens. The new homes demanded a new type of owner, and so the twentieth-century suburban housewife was born.

The Great War, with its temporary rise in working-class wages, had already given housewives in industrial cities a taste for buying home furnishings. Liverpool housewives, for example, had not only bought furniture beyond what was absolutely necessary during the war, some had even stretched to buying unpractical items, such as a piano.[19] The *Daily Mail* Home Exhibition (now the Ideal Home Show) was held annually at Olympia in London, its aim to encourage women to buy and use new household technologies and products. The annual catalogues were attractively bound books entitled *The Ideal Labour-Saving Home*, with prints of award-winning idyllic suburban houses on the front cover. Inside they were packed full of advertisements for 'Labour-Saving Devices which solve the problem of domestic drudgery',[22] such as Thor electric washing machines and Daisy vacuum cleaners, and they gave advice on the entire spectrum of household fixtures and appliances, from stainless-steel cutlery to plastic flooring.

Chain stores and co-operative societies like Littlewoods, Marks & Spencer, Woolworths, Home & Colonial and British Home Stores now mushroomed in cities but also on suburban and provincial high streets, bringing such novel home furnishings and household devices within reach of lower-middle-class and some working-class families. And it wasn't just household goods that were more affordable; previously housewives had sewn or knitted the majority of their families' clothes, but now ready-to-wear swept the high street and affordable fashion as we know it today was born. Ready-to-wear had already existed for a century, but it had been associated with poor quality and poor tailoring. The looser-fitting, less complex women's fashions of the interwar years, combined with the advent of revolutionary new fabrics such as rayon, meant that ready-mades underwent a revolution in this period. Vera May Ashby worked as a teenage shopgirl in Witham, Essex, and years later she remembered the shift quite clearly: 'I saw the fashions change … you know, to the silk underwear and ready-made slips. The old corsets went out of fashion, those that laced up at the back.'[23]

Gradually, the shopping experience was becoming democratised. For chain stores and co-operatives were not simply breaking new ground by making goods affordable to a wider customer base. A handful of forward-looking chain-store managers even started reshaping the shopping etiquette which had predominated for over half a century.[24] Large-scale retailing in spacious new stores was a boom industry in the interwar years, growing at a faster rate than many other trades. The market share of what was technically known as the 'variety' chain stores, that is, stores offering a wide variety of goods on open display (M&S, Woolworths, British Home Stores, Littlewoods), rose from less than 3 per cent in 1920 to nearly 20 per cent by 1938.[25] This was a staggering growth rate. The shopgirls employed in these new enterprises not only sold modern consumer goods; they were trained differently too. Customer service was taking on a new meaning. Instead of leaping forward to assist or even lambast hesitant shoppers, assistants now had to keep a discreet distance from their clientele, passively waiting to be approached. Deference had by no means disappeared yet; it was simply less obtrusive than before. As a customer you could now easily find your way to the underwear and hosiery department without being guided by a member of staff; once you got there the goods were more openly displayed, with clearly marked low prices and descriptions. You no longer had to wait for a shopgirl to unearth a single item from behind a counter; independent of her, you could now touch and feel the Wolsey men's vests and long underpants, weighing up the merits of unshrinkable flannel against pure cotton.

The new approach – or rather lack of approach – proved popular, particularly among suburban customers, who found it less stuffy and formal. The trade journal *Store Management* grasped the importance for the shopocracy of these new social complexities, identifying 'quick changing social values and shifting boundaries between classes'. It divided society into three social groups: 'the very rich, the upper middle classes, and a third group comprising the lower middle and artisan classes'. Yet, while admitting that the boundaries between classes were 'not absolutely clear cut', it was adamant that 'you cannot trade with more than one section of the community at a time'.[26]

Those shopkeepers who did not recognise these shifting social patterns were in trouble. The more progressive department stores recognised that chain stores had become stiff competition, so they poured millions into advertising – a colossal 50 per cent of national advertising revenue in retail came from department and drapery stores in the interwar period even though their goods accounted for only 7.5 per cent of all sales in British shops during that time.[27] Some advertisements were clever and funny, like the Harrods ads that printed the refusal letters of famous writers H.G. Wells, Arnold Bennett and George Bernard Shaw, who had all turned down Harrods' invitation to contribute testimonials. Arnold Bennett wrote a long, eloquent refusal, explaining how his novel *Hugo* had been inspired by Harrods, how he loved 'departmental stores', the 'picturesque spectacle' they provided, their window displays, crowds of customers and armies of employees. But 'with lively regret' he felt forced to turn down Harrods' writing offer, for he would 'lose caste' – a strong way of expressing his fear that he would be accused of selling out, of losing his independence as a writer.[28]

Other department stores indulged in publicity stunts, known as 'tie-ins', offering pure entertainment in the form of staged events, which proprietors hoped would generate newspaper copy and thus free advertising. John Logie Baird's very first demonstration of a television set was staged at Selfridges in 1925; the press thought it a mere novelty, though Harry Gordon Selfridge insisted that television was 'not a toy'. In the 1930s Bentalls in Kingston not only provided a daily 'Goblin Cabaret', featuring Marsana the long-necked woman, but also enticed Swedish diver Annie Kittner to jump off a 63-foot-high board into a small pool of water – all inside the store.[29]

Nonetheless, despite the trend for attention-seeking stunts in the capital, and the democratisation process in suburban chain stores, the majority of the upscale department stores in provincial centres sleepily continued with their Edwardian ways. They assumed that they could trade on reputation alone, doing little to accommodate new types of customers. Photographs and sketches of the interiors of Mawer & Collingham of Lincoln and Bainbridge's of Newcastle in the 1930s testify to the continuing formality of the shopping experience there. Goods were still inaccessible, dresses and coats untouchable in glass cases, handkerchiefs and scarves shut up in boxes and mahogany drawers. Tall chairs still awaited unhurried customers; no speedy hustle and bustle here, with Bainbridge's shopgirls waiting patiently behind the counters for their well-to-do clientele.[30]

Shoplife behind the scenes was still extremely challenging. Certain progressive department stores had been providing staff facilities like restrooms, leisure activities and staff outings since the late nineteenth century. But this had not spread in any significant way to other types of shops, and in the rushed expansion of large-scale retail between the wars, shop assistants' welfare issues had often been sidelined. Flora Solomon on her tour of 'the High Streets of towns without number' noted 'apathy, condescension and fear' in all the chain stores she entered, not just Marks & Spencer.[31] A Leeds shopgirl, Miss E.B., remembered the complete lack of staff facilities at the time – no dining rooms, restrooms or cloakrooms – with meals being eaten in the stockroom with a stockroom girl parcelling up at one end. She wrote that an 'atmosphere of fear' pervaded the place, with girls warning each other that 'the terrible monster, "The Supervisor",' was on the prowl by switching lights off in parts of the shop to signal their approach.[32]

Some aspects of a shopgirl's life had got better – since the 1928 Reform Act, those aged twenty-one and over had finally been able to vote; fewer and fewer shop assistants now lived in; and shop assistant wages were improving slightly. But only slightly: women's wages were still significantly lower than men's. One shopgirl confessed blushingly to Solomon that if she couldn't last the week out, she would help herself to the till or pinch a pair of stockings.[33] Unemployment was cancerous, climbing to its peak of around three million people out of work in 1933, and since many shopgirls felt that they were lucky to have a job at all, they continued to put up with despotic old-fashioned managers who could sack them on the spot. Others were ruled by versions of Frederick Winslow Taylor's scientific management and systems theory that Owen Owen had first encountered in North America, and which had now spread to Europe.

At Macy's in New York, cashier girls, who handled around six hundred transactions a day in a room with a cash tube system, had been captured on film beside a large, fast-moving clock. This enabled time and motion to be measured to the one-thousandth of a minute. These films were then projected in slow motion, the motions broken down and analysed minutely. From this study, it was possible to glean what was the 'one best way' of cashiering, and productivity among Macy's cashier girls duly rose by 25 per cent.[34] Such studies were noted in Britain, particularly by the National Institute of Industrial Psychology, whose investigators were hired by the likes of Harrods, R.S. McColl's, Littlewoods and Marks & Spencer to increase efficiency and productivity in their stores. The NIIP represented the cutting-edge of modern management theory in Britain. At Harrods, for example, the NIIP investigators made studies of hiring policies for sales assistants, supervision techniques and fashion workroom management.

Simon Marks was also a fan. In his weekly bulletins to his store managers, time and again he used the language of this 'Guiding Principle in Store Management', explaining that this scientific approach should enable the efficient running of every aspect of the store, from ordering goods to putting them on display, from office routine to stockroom organisation. It also required the 'tactical use of manpower', wrote Marks, citing Napoleon. Marks felt that, in terms of staffing, it was 'no use trying to fit a square peg in a round hole'. A dreamy floorwalker would never make a good manager, while 'a salesgirl who is mentally slow, whose fingers appear always to be fumbling, is useless on the Gramophone Records counter'.[35]

Still, an efficient workforce didn't automatically make a happy workforce. It is easier to record and tabulate sales figures and productivity than it is to measure human emotions. While retailers certainly deemed the NIIP reports a success, what the staff thought went unnoted. What we do know is that Flora Solomon was depressed by what she found on British high streets. As advised by Bondfield, she travelled abroad to Berlin to visit her friends who owned the famous Kaufhaus N. Israel department store. This was the decadent, dangerous capital city that Christopher Isherwood portrays so intensely in his novel *Goodbye to Berlin*. Expertly run by its Jewish proprietors, Kaufhaus N. Israel was one of the largest retail establishments in Europe, employing over two thousand people in its massive block on the Alexanderplatz. The Israels opened their address book for Solomon, enabling her to study stores and clothing factories throughout Berlin. She described Israel as an enlightened employer who impressed upon her the importance of good management. Solomon flew back to London full of ideas; for the Israels, impossibly difficult times lay ahead. In 1932, the Nazi party was already Germany's largest political party, with Berlin's bohemianism and Jewish population in their sights. The following year, Nazi stormtroopers called for a boycott of the store, shouting, 'Don't buy from Jews!', and during Kristallnacht the block was ransacked and set alight. Ultimately the Kaufhaus, this emporium of shopping delights, would be 'Aryanised' and handed over to non-Jewish owners.

Back in London in 1932, Solomon sketched out a memorandum for Simon Marks about what she felt was wrong with his retail chain, and she included concrete proposals on how to rectify matters. Her central argument was that M&S, along with its competitors, was missing a key element in the treatment of its staff: human dignity.

She felt that most stores she had visited 'were providing work for women and girls under conditions that made it impossible for them to face the public as the female sex desired to be observed – presentable in appearance, relaxed in manner, worthy of respect'. Having delivered her memorandum, she heard nothing for three days. Then Simon Marks made it clear that he endorsed her ideas, and that, provided that she never troubled him personally, she was welcome to roll out her suggestions as a permanent member of staff. 'It was really happening to me, a purpose in life!' she rejoiced. 'Friends were amazed. What was she doing with herself, enlisting as a glorified draper's assistant?' Solomon had no such misgivings, throwing herself wholeheartedly into a task she felt was worthwhile, not simply for Marks & Spencer workers, but perhaps for retail employees across the country.

She set up a small crack team, 'a little resistance movement, ever scheming against heartless company bureaucracy'.[36] Despite often encountering resentment from the male managers, her committee worked on persuading each one of them to appoint a welfare officer. They set up restrooms for shopgirls to take a break, particularly important in those stores that were still open-fronted. Marks & Spencer then provided a cheap hot meal each day, plus a cup of tea and a biscuit for a penny. The company built new washing facilities, subsidised canteens and even began offering staff outings and holiday camps. A photograph of Dymchurch holiday camp in 1936 shows ten young women from Windsor's Marks & Spencer store larking about in a field in mid-thigh bathing costumes, tousled hair and low heels, looking just like carefree schoolgirls.

Above all, there was training. Centres were set up in Brixton, Leeds, Manchester and Glasgow to run courses for hundreds of new girls and advanced sales assistants covering topics such as customer service, display, merchandise ordering, till practice, shoplifting and time wastage. Now, instead of Marks' eulogies on the benefits of scientific management, in-house journals explained that 'The Human Approach is vital in running a business harmoniously and successfully'. Likely written by Solomon, the article broke down the 'Human Approach' into six points, the first being 'Look after the physical comfort of your girls,' and the second, 'Create a friendly atmosphere by cooperating and keeping in close contact with everyone.' Miss E.B. from Leeds, who had earlier noted the pervading atmosphere of fear, now felt that staff 'should consider themselves fortunate to be reaping the benefits which were not available to old employees'.[37]

The new training and welfare system seemed to produce extremely positive results, as staff turnover plummeted from nearly 70 per cent in 1932 to 25 per cent just five years later.[38] The staff magazine *Sparks* was now even able to joke about rules and regulations, something that might have caused instant dismissal in earlier times. Hours of work were defined as being 'from the time you arrive to the time your boy friend calls for you'. Wage increases took into account 'youth, sex-appeal and any special ability', while 'making the best cup of tea for the Manager' helped chances of promotion.[39]

In groceries and draperies, department stores and the growing number of chain stores, 'the manager' was still highly likely to be male. But with around half a million women now in shopwork and training improving across the industry, an increasingly large proportion of senior staff were female. Some even used the training they had received to start their own businesses. Ethel May Jupp from Epping Forest, Essex, had started out at Sainsbury's as a twenty-year-old and had been trained up to shop management level. In 1925 she had been hired as a buyer by J. Lyons & Co. in order to establish a delicatessen department, since the famous Lyons Corner Houses had food halls on the ground floor. Lyons sent her to France to gain knowledge of ham processing, salami smoking, truffle hunting and the production of foie gras. She also learnt about American specialities such as Grape-Nuts breakfast cereal. Five years later, now aged thirty-four, Mrs Jupp opened her first business bank account and set up shop herself, initially trading as Mrs Jupp's Pantry in Bayswater, west London and then simply as Jupp, on Kensington High Street. Specialising in delicatessen and fancy groceries, Jupp's was heralded in a magazine article as 'the up-to-date foodstore' and photographs testify to its state-of-the-art decor, with dark chrome counters and optimistic sunburst motifs above the shop window. They also show off Jupp's ultra-modern appliance, a large refrigerator, trumpeted in the magazine article as 'excellent refrigeration ensuring the preservation of all perishable goods'. The formula clearly worked, for the photographs show that shortly before five o'clock, according to the octagonal wall clock, Jupp's was thronging with ladies jostling at the counters.[40]

Mrs Jupp was one of the outriders: trained as a shopgirl, trained as a buyer, and using her merchandising, business and international experience – as well as her thoroughly modern personal taste – to set up her own store. Her customers in the 1930s clearly enjoyed the fruits of her experience; the question was, whether such city-centre shops could survive the bombings and crises of another war.

A Shopgirl in an Oxford Street store, London, conducts business as usual, despite her shop's windows having been blown in by bomb blasts from German air raids, *c.*1940.

CHAPTER 7

KEEP CALM AND CARRY ON SHOPPING

At 16.30 on Monday 26 April 1937, the first German bomber aircraft flew over Guernica, dropping twelve bombs onto the Basque town. For the next two hours, wave after wave of Luftwaffe and Italian fascist air force bombers dropped explosive bombs, hand grenades and incendiaries, accompanied by fighter planes strafing the town with machine-gun fire. War correspondent George Steer, reporting on the Spanish Civil War for *The Times*, was at the scene. His eye-witness report was published two days later, setting the tone for the shock and outrage which reverberated the world over. 'The Tragedy of Guernica' was his headline, 'Town Destroyed in Air Attack'. He wrote, 'The raid on Guernica is unparalleled in military history', describing how 'heavy and incendiary bombs wreck the houses and burn them on top of their victims'. News crews arrived to film the devastation, capturing haunting images of silhouetted house walls, despairing survivors pulling at mountains of rubble and nuns scurrying into still-smoking ruins.

Steer's message was clear: the Nazis were directly involved in this attack, and their capacity and appetite for bombing both military and civilian targets was strong. Britain had already lived through German Zeppelin air raids on its cities during the First World War; Guernica strengthened fears that much worse was to come. But this time round, the government was determined to be prepared. The Committee for Imperial Defence, the forerunner of the wartime Ministry of Information, came up with a grisly estimate that in the event of war with Nazi Germany there would be 1,800,000 casualties on British soil, a third of them fatal, three million refugees and most of London would be destroyed within the first two months. So the Air Raid Wardens' Service and the Women's Voluntary Service were created: voluntary civilian organisations that were to protect and help the population during air raids. With the first Air Raid Precautions posts set up in shops, offices and homes, the ARP wardens' initial tasks were to register the population in their sector and to help establish blackout precautions. The wardens and WVS learnt first aid and basic firefighting. And from the very start, Britain's shopworkers were roped in to contribute to the Air Raid Precautions already under way.

There was fear and urgency in the air. At Woolworths, by now one of the biggest chains with over six hundred branches across Britain, stores and warehouses were examined to identify basements that would be suitable as air-raid shelters. The John Lewis *Gazette* soon claimed that they had the best-prepared shops and staff in the country: they had covered the roofs with fire-resistant material and were instituting regular ARP drills. At Marks & Spencer the chief ARP officer Ralph Salaman produced a manual which spelt out the procedure in case of emergency: staff to use tin helmets, customers to move away from windows, skylights and entrances, newly trained first-aiders to be on standby. Under the gathering clouds of war, normal business rivalries were suspended. Salaman also organised 'the Chain Gang', whereby Marks & Spencer teamed up with its high-street competitors, Woolworths, Boots, British Home Stores and Lyons, agreeing to share staff canteens and restrooms in the event of air-raid damage. And in the years ahead, the Chain Gang pact would indeed be put into action.

Being prepared, however, ran much deeper than laying down fire-resistant roofing. 'Business as usual' had been the motto at the start of the last war but it had led to rampant price inflation, instability and food riots. There was to be no rerun of that chaos this time around. In a series of moves, which retrospectively seem quite breathtaking in their boldness, the government effectively became the nation's shopkeeper. Every level of the supply chain, from overseas shipments to inland distribution to store delivery, came to be directly run or directly influenced by the government. On the flipside, demand was controlled too, through rationing and price fixing. The Board of Trade stated the explicit aims of its rationing policy as being that 'every member of the public would be able to obtain a fair share of the national food supply at a reasonable price'.[1] It sounds a pretty straightforward policy, but what lay ahead politically, economically and emotionally was to challenge every element of that deceptively simple statement. 'Every member', 'fair share', 'national food supply' and 'reasonable price' – standing by these commitments was to prove nigh on impossible. And with shop assistants at the vanguard of implementing rationing and stock-taking, they were effectively being roped into becoming the enforcers of government war policy.

At first, nothing much happened. In the early summer of 1939, two months before war was declared, a documentary crew was filming in the offices of *The Times* in Printing House Square, London.[2] The paper reported on the Eton versus Harrow cricket match at Lord's, the Court Circular brought titbits from the London Season, and the Foreign Telephone Room received news from a Himalayan climbing expedition and from Washington, where a US senator argued in favour of neutrality in the coming war. The advertising was still full-page. After the declaration of war in September 1939, the headlines changed, but the mood of anxious waiting did not. Doris was working as a draper's assistant at Madam Burton's in Newport on the Isle of Wight when war broke out. Years later, she remembered quite clearly how 'it took a long, long time for it to make any difference actually to the trade'. She was then twenty-one years old and explained why it took time for her and her fellow shopgirls to take in the new reality. 'Things were still coming in quite regularly in the drapery shop and as far as I could see there was no difficulty in the goods arriving.' Doris concluded, 'It was the very early days of the war, it hadn't made that impact on shopping.'[3]

Christmas was particularly strange. There were no '1,800,000 casualties' or 'destroyed' cities. Yet nobody quite trusted the quiet. The government ordered the compulsory closing of shops at 6 p.m. except for one late night a week, while the chancellor of the exchequer encouraged people to save as much as possible and not to make frivolous Christmas purchases. With such clear exhortations to hunker down, people bought fewer clothes and began stockpiling dried, preserved and canned foodstuffs. The tinned food departments in Woolworths stores were particularly busy with 'canny' customers buying up stock; the old Scottish word took on a whole new nuance.

But then, Blitzkrieg. On 10 May 1940, Nazi Germany started its massive offensive on the Western Front, its army units attacking France, Belgium, the Netherlands and Luxembourg. Neville Chamberlain resigned and when Winston Churchill addressed the House of Commons for the very first time as prime minister, he called for 'Victory – victory at all costs, victory in spite of all terror, victory however long and hard the road may be; for without victory there is no survival.' With the Allied retreat from France and the evacuation at Dunkirk, Churchill saw Britain as standing alone against Hitler, the only nation defending not just its own country but the whole of Christian civilisation against the 'abyss of a new Dark Age'.[4]

Twelve days later, Luftwaffe boots were treading on British soil. Germany invaded the Channel Islands, with Jersey becoming Feldkommandantur 515. Supplies from Britain ceased entirely; the Channel Islands were now part of the German Reich. The Nazis changed the time from GMT to Central European Time and made everyone drive on the right-hand side of the road. Betty Yvonne Costard was a young shopgirl when the occupation started, working in a baby-wear shop in Jersey's capital, St Helier. She remembered being very frightened and crying when the Germans arrived, having heard terrible things about how the German army had mistreated the civilian population in Poland. Betty was 'saying to my mother all the time, we should have gone away, we should have gone'. In spite of her fear she ventured out to look at the German soldiers on guard in front of the general post office, discovering to her surprise that they were 'only men, we didn't know what to expect'. After a while the fear ebbed as it became clear that there were rules and regulations, and Betty realised she was not going to get raped. Instead she noticed that the soldiers went shopping.[5]

'They emptied the food shops, and came into the little shops. They bought baby things, presumably for their wives back home,' Betty explained. The new shoppers were well mannered and paid for what they wanted, but within weeks most of St Helier's stores were extremely low on stock. This included the Channel Islands' largest department store, de Gruchy. De Gruchy had been trading in St Helier since 1810 and was run by a board of directors and general manager Arthur Harvey. Before the war Arthur Harvey, an aggressive and skilled businessman, had overhauled de Gruchy's still-Victorian working practices – and its building. He had replaced the original shop fittings, ladders and steps and had insisted that in-house buyers be told what the turnover and profits were, so that they could make more informed, strategic decisions. His eye had fallen on the fashion department, where some of the shopgirls were rumoured to be on the take. He immediately issued spot checks as they were leaving, and caught one shopgirl red-handed as she tried to walk out wearing nine pairs of knickers.[6]

Now faced with the Nazi buying spree, which was decimating their stock levels, Arthur Harvey and the board decided that they must stay open regardless. They felt it was their patriotic duty to serve the community and to keep their loyal staff employed, but also to make sure that the premises were not requisitioned by the occupying force. So Harvey joined up with the other St Helier traders to form a committee, of which he was elected chairman, and went to see the Kommandant. Much to the shopkeepers' surprise, the Kommandant understood the problem. He agreed to issue shopping permits to his officers, without which they couldn't buy anything.

The shopping permits successfully slowed down the rate of Nazi purchases. Nonetheless, the Germans had quite a good go at requisitioning de Gruchy, piece by piece. Demands for motor vehicles, the chairman's horse, banqueting glasses, portable cold rooms and carved Wehrmacht crosses all had to be met. The restaurant was taken over to store German uniforms and ammunition. Soon, de Gruchy was running at a loss for the first time in its history. Staff wages had to be cut, and the store could stay open just two days a week.

Back on the mainland, though housewives had no Nazi soldiers as rival shoppers, their household duties had rarely been so difficult. Sponsored by the Ministry of Information, film-maker Ruby Grierson shot a short dramatised documentary called *They Also Serve*, dedicated to the 'Housewives of Britain'. In the film, main character Mrs Anderson, known as 'Mother', has a son at the front, a working daughter and a husband on night shift; Mother spends her day dealing with her myriad duties, including picking vegetables, mending the blackout and going shopping. The final lines read, 'Housewives of Britain, Thank-you for Your Courage and Your Help.'[7] Shown in cinemas around the country as a prelude to

Hollywood escapist movies and British war films, *They Also Serve* clearly positioned housewives as patriotic heroines. Their daily food shop and tasks around the home were also a form of war work, or so went the propaganda.

They had their work cut out. The first rationing of food, namely butter, bacon and sugar, had been introduced at the start of 1940 by the Ministry of Food and was proving fiendishly complex to implement. Even before the war began, five million ration books had been printed; now every family had to register with a local shop, in effect committing themselves to using that particular shop for buying their rationed goods. Which shop to choose was a matter of heated debate; some families preferred their local corner shop, hoping for preferential treatment regarding unrationed items. Others went for big grocery chains where they could obtain most goods under the same roof. Sainsbury's certainly banked on this, putting up posters listing five reasons why it was wisest to register with them. Number one: 'You can obtain all rationed, registered and "free" provisions, groceries and meat under one roof. No rushing about in black-outs and winter weather.'[8]

For shops, the paperwork for each registration was complicated: separate counterfoils had to be detached for each member of the family, names and addresses checked, and then a card-file register updated with detailed records. At Sainsbury's on Watney Street in Stepney, east London, manager William Guest and his shop assistants were overwhelmed with local customers unable to work out how to deal with their ration books. The Sainsbury's staff simply couldn't keep up and ultimately referred the problem to their head office at Blackfriars in the City of London. Sainsbury's was now the nation's largest grocery concern and they needed to stay on top of the Ministry of Food's rationing regulations and frequent changes, so they set up their own rationing department at head office. And it was on a certain Miss Potter's desk in the rationing department that

William Guest's plea for help landed. Guest recalled how the very next day a taxi drew up on Watney Street and out stepped Miss Potter with some of her clerical staff. They loaded the ration books into the taxi, 'returning 24 hours later with a perfectly ordered filing system and several thousand ration books immaculately filled in'.[9]

The man in charge of the Ministry of Food – indeed the man who *was* the Ministry of Food in many housewives' eyes – was Frederick Marquis, Lord Woolton. Here was a man who knew about shopkeeping, having run Lewis's department store in Liverpool before the war (not to be confused with the John Lewis Partnership). And it was arguably down to his marketing and organisational flair that there was neither food rioting nor starvation in the Second World War. For the risk was there. Before the war Britain had imported an astonishing 75 per cent of its foodstuffs by ship, including 90 per cent of its flour and cereals and over 50 per cent of its meat.[10] Now, as mainland Europe was occupied and the Battle of the Atlantic raged with German U-boats torpedoing British supply ships, imports plummeted and food started to become scarce. While the Land Army and every allotment holder started to dig for Britain to increase home production, the remaining foods were rationed one after another. Meat and preserves came next, then tea, margarine and cooking fats in July 1940 and cheese the following year.

Part of Lord Woolton's genius lay in recognising that his job was not simply to implement rationing. It was also to win over the shoppers and housewives who had to live with the consequences. When they walked into Sainsbury's or the corner grocery store, housewives were now confronted with a much smaller selection of goods, rationed or unrationed. Favourite brands disappeared as factories were forced to consolidate their different lines – the 350 pre-war brands of biscuit were reduced to just twenty. And some branded packaging was simply eliminated, so that soft drinks appeared under labels like 'Orange Squash, SW 153'. Although

'Mother' in the documentary film stoically put up with these constant changes and long queues, others were less sanguine.

Woolton went on the offensive with a press, radio and film blitz to inform and woo British housewives. He broadcast on the radio about the need for food control; his ministry sponsored ads with the slogan 'Food is a munition of war. Don't waste it', and coined the phrase 'the Kitchen Front'. Potatoes and carrots were a great source of nutrition, the ministry trumpeted, and offered recipes for dishes such as 'Pigs in Clover – a novel way with baked potatoes and sausage'. Woolton Pie, however, a stodgy mix of parsnips, turnips, carrots and potatoes covered in white sauce and pastry, proved almost inedible. His offensive worked; one Dorchester housewife explained, 'Lord Woolton was always so sympathetic and if he could not give us more butter he added an extra ounce to the margarine. We all trusted and loved him.'[11]

Since the outbreak of war, all men between the ages of eighteen and forty-one had been liable to conscription. As the men were successively called up, staff numbers in retail plummeted, just as they had in the Great War, so those shop assistants selling the butter, margarine and other foodstuffs were more and more likely to be women. Mrs Sheppard applied for a job at Sainsbury's in April 1941; the firm's correspondence was explicit as to why they needed her services. 'Dear Madam, You are aware that we have already lost a large number of our male employees,' the letter from Alan J. Sainsbury began. 'As the call-up of men continues, women with aptitude and enthusiasm will be called upon in increasing numbers to take on greater responsibilities.' Alan Sainsbury invited Mrs Sheppard for interview, and within a few weeks she became relief manager in the Woking branch.[12]

Women also started taking on traditionally male professions within the retail industry; Grace on the Isle of Wight moved from a confectioner's to a pork butcher's. 'I took the place of someone who had joined the Royal Navy.' Grace explained how machinery and tasks usually out of bounds for women were suddenly unproblematic: 'Of course we came into using choppers and boning bacon and various things, cleaning all the machines.'[13]

The problem that many shops had, however, extended further than the loss of their shopmen. Many shopgirls were leaving too. Conscription for women started in December 1941 for single women and childless widows aged twenty to thirty, but from the very beginning of the war women had been leaving shopwork in droves to volunteer for more obviously patriotic work. Doris on the Isle of Wight left Madam Burton's drapery. As she put it so succinctly, 'I had to do something other than being a draper's assistant.' She felt she had to contribute to the war effort, 'especially after Dunkirk when we were really fighting for our lives, never knew when the church bells might go which meant Herman the German had arrived'. Doris went to work at the Saunders-Roe plane factory in East Cowes. 'I went from fitting out ladies for their dresses and hats to fitting out parts of aeroplanes.'[14] She enjoyed her factory work as much as being a shopgirl, but her factory colleague Annie didn't. Annie only left her Woolworths' position for Saunders-Roe 'because it was the best money'.[15]

Throughout the raging hot summer of 1940, in the Battle of Britain, the German Luftwaffe attacked British shipping, airports, radar stations and landing strips − two thousand Luftwaffe fighter planes versus just six hundred from the RAF. Once Hitler realised he was failing to wipe out the British air force, however, he switched tactics and began bombing city centres. First in his sights were Liverpool and Birmingham. Then the Blitz intensified: on 7 September London experienced its first and last mass daylight raid, heralding the start of fifty-seven consecutive nights of bombardment. Thousands of children, mothers, patients and pensioners had been evacuated in the preceding months and now thousands more

Londoners left the city for the comparative safety of the country. But most stayed behind.

Mrs Jupp, who ran Jupp's delicatessen on Kensington High Street, decided to brave it out, feeling she had a duty to help feed her London customers, staying put even after her son was evacuated. Shops began to close at 5 p.m. in order to allow staff time to get home before the bombing began. In the famous documentary *London Can Take It!*, American journalist Quentin Reynolds laconically recounted the tale of eighteen hours in the life of the London Blitz, starting in late afternoon.[16] As Londoners entered their air-raid shelters at nightfall, footage of darts games was intercut with searchlights in the night sky, shots of sleeping grandparents with bombed buildings up in flames. The next day, Londoners picked themselves up, housewives brushing broken glass from their front steps, working men in suits carefully winding their way through rubble heaps on their way to work, even though their normal bus was upended and the Tube bridge was in a state of collapse. Quentin Reynolds drawled, 'London manages to get to work on time, one way or another', pointing out that 'in the centre of the city, the shops are open as usual. In fact, many of them are more open than usual', while showing a smartly dressed shopgirl stepping through a shattered display window straight into her store.

The documentary certainly captured something of the Blitz spirit. Off camera, defiance and bravery were shown in myriad ways too: shop assistants faced with severe bomb damage at a branch of Woolworths, which had stores throughout Germany too, put up a sign which read, 'This is nothing! You ought to see what the RAF have done to our Berlin branch.' There was a certain humour too in the blackout accessories on sale at Selfridges. The department store offered a whole range of merchandise aimed at increasing human and canine visibility in the pitch-black nights. They ranged from white raincoats to luminous flower brooches, and even stretched to little blackout coats for dogs.[17]

But most people could spare not a moment's thought for accessories. On 18 September Miss Katherine Austin, secretary to the staff manager at John Lewis Oxford Street, was on duty for the eleventh night in a row, part of a team 'mothering' two hundred evacuees in the basement. Some were local residents, others John Lewis partners, in other words staff, and many were 'terribly nervy' on account of having lost their homes. On top of this the Langham Hotel close by had been bombed the previous night.[18] Then at midnight the first direct hit struck John Lewis. Miss Austin's first reaction was confusion. 'I put my trousers on back to front – I was very annoyed because it must have wasted a quarter of a minute.' Miss Austin started to try to evacuate her flock when the second bomb landed. She had a moment of sheer panic. 'I could have sworn that the walls in front were going to collapse. It was a curious feeling: it was not so much seen as felt – as though someone had put far too much into a cardboard hat-box and you know it must give way.'

But her training and pluck soon kicked in. Miss Austin ushered the shelter's occupants into the staff dining room as fire swept through the building. Duty manager Captain Burnett tried to close the fire doors to prevent the blaze spreading, but to no avail. Gradually all two hundred people were evacuated and sent from basement shelter to basement shelter, looking for space, all the way down Oxford Street westwards to Selfridges. They were safe. But the next day it was clear that John Lewis Oxford Street, the powerhouse of the whole business, was all but destroyed. Spedan Lewis sent every employee in the Oxford Street branch a postcard the next day, letting them know that their pay would be ready for collection on Friday as normal, and he tried to find temporary positions for them in his other branches. However, the John Lewis partners claimed they received a rather frosty, snobbish reception at Peter Jones, whose existing staff accused the new lot of 'incessant rudeness'.[19]

As the bombing campaign widened to industrial cities and coastal port towns, hundreds of shops were directly or indirectly damaged by bombs and fire. From Marks & Spencer in Coventry to Woolworths in Devonport and Lewis's of Liverpool – Lord Woolton's own store – the destruction was immeasurable. Each morning shop assistants woke up not knowing whether their workplaces would be standing at all. Woolworths even drew up detailed diagrams for 'Establishing a Temporary Store' and sent the plans round to their district managers. All that was needed was three walls that were still structurally intact. 'Remove debris and charred fixtures, wash and whitewash,' and by the time it had a corrugated sheet roof and a splash of blackout paint on the front, you were in business again.[20]

Those who really suffered from the destruction of British cities and the stringent government food controls were the smaller shops. Mastering the new jargon of permits, allocations, basic periods, datum lines, entitlements and points was all very well if you had a Miss Potter in your head office concentrating on making sense of it all. As a small shopkeeper with just two shopgirls for staff, the headaches of extra bureaucracy, goods' shortages and changes in the established network of local suppliers – on top of dealing with sometimes frightened, confused and hungry customers – was often too much. In Leeds, for instance, 25 per cent of the small shops closed down between January 1940 and December 1941;[21] in Glasgow the figure was the same.

Once the Utility clothing and furniture schemes were introduced, with their CC41 logos standing for Civilian Clothing 1941, the bureaucratic burden on shopkeepers and their assistants grew ever heavier. The Utility schemes set standards and prices for material, furniture and consumer goods, rationing the products and aiming at maximum economy and practicality. Every person was issued initially with sixty-six coupons a year for clothing, and there was a set number of coupons per item. A woollen dress required eleven coupons, a nightdress just six. But the exact details of the system were constantly being amended by the Board of Trade. Thus two coupons might get you 'women's non-woollen legless knickers' initially, but after June 1942 this allocation was amended to 'women's non-woollen knickers and panties with side lengths not exceeding 18.5 inches'.[22] And each year of the war the total number of coupons allowed per person was reduced, so that by 1945 you were issued with just twenty-four.

For small shops struggling to make ends meet and to retain their staff, the temptation to make a little money on the side must have been great. There was a lively black market throughout the war, with thieves breaking into shops, factories, warehouses and lorries to steal goods. 'Did it drop off a lorry?' became a well-used expression. There was also an active trade in ration coupons. Some were counterfeit. Others were legal, but since customers were allowed to 'bank' their coupons with their shopkeepers, trusting the retailer to calculate and tear them out correctly, many retailers had control over stacks of coupons, which some abused. Certain shopkeepers turned into coupon dealers, buying clothes coupons from poorer working-class customers and selling them on to middle-class customers, raking in a tidy profit along the way.[23]

Other retailers stockpiled surplus stock, which was against the spirit of rationing. Travel writer Eric Newby in his autobiography wrote about the morning he arrived back in London after his release from a prisoner-of-war camp towards the end of the war. Having nothing civilian to wear, he went to Harrods, which had been clothing him from birth onwards. But he had already mislaid his clothing coupons. He was in search of corduroy trousers. In the men's clothing department he was met by an extremely elderly salesman, who eyed up Newby's 'battledress anti-gas' and sighed. 'We can't have one of our old customers without a change of trousers, can we,' the salesman said. 'Mum's the word, but here in Harrods we've got more gentlemen's trousers than there are coupons in the whole of England.'[24]

Many small shopkeepers were not deeply corrupt; rather they indulged in practices that had been around for centuries (though exacerbated by the war), like giving short weight and adulterating alcohol. In Featherstone, a mining town in the West Riding of Yorkshire, the high-street stores overcharged for basic foods such as eggs, tomatoes and pork dripping. One local store got hold of chocolates and sweets illegally and sold these coupon-free at a high price.[25] These practices were well known, with trade magazines running articles about them and – at the other end of the scale – Sainsbury's boasting that they were cleaner than clean, their poster encouraging families to register their ration books with the claim that 'You are assured of "no profiteering". We guarantee you fair prices and fair dealing.'

Most shops indulging in a little under-the-counter dealing were just trying to get by. Supplies were erratic and could go up as well as down. The Lend-Lease arrangement with the United States and a similar Canadian scheme meant that it wasn't only supplies of military equipment and weapons from across the Atlantic that increased substantially in the summer of 1941; mercifully, food shipments were sent over too. On top of this, the British governmental push to produce as much food 'from our own soil' as possible was highly successful, with the country on track for increasing the production of wheat by 90 per cent, potatoes by 87 per cent and vegetables by 45 per cent over the course of the war.[26] After conscription started for young single women, shopgirl Grace, like many others, joined the Land Army, leaving her butcher's job in order to do so. Her first task was to build a silo; she had no idea what a silo was. She lived in a hostel with other land girls, which was great fun. 'We were just acting like a group of girls in our twenties,' she explained. On the farms they worked alongside German, Italian and Polish prisoners of war. She found the work much harder and filthier than at the confectioner's or butcher's shop. She recalled a long list of new skills that she had to master: 'Hay making, harvesting, threshing, pruning apple trees, picking potatoes, strawberries, sprouts in the frost usually and swedes of course and carrots, stripping and laying a hedge.'[27]

Overall, however, food was in short supply, for as the war wore on, regulations were tightened and rations were repeatedly reduced. People were hungry, though, unlike in the First World War, this never resulted in food riots. In the Channel Islands under Nazi occupation, the hunger was particularly acute. Betty Costard switched from selling baby clothes to working in a chemist's in St Helier. She talked about how in the face of ever-diminishing food supplies her family was 'making do' by gathering moss on the beach to make jelly and collecting a few potatoes from their friend, a farmer, hiding them from the Germans in a baby pram. They had very little meat, and fish only if they could catch it, but as the war continued the Nazis even forbad them from going on to the beaches. Betty made parsnip coffee and sugar-beet syrup as a honey substitute. The Red Cross sent parcels, which helped. But the Germans were hungry too, 'because there was nothing in our shops and they couldn't touch our Red Cross parcels'.

At de Gruchy's, manager Arthur Harvey faced a very different sort of challenge. He fell for a shopgirl named Kay from the store's fashion department and they married in 1941. They had little time to enjoy wedded bliss, however, for the next year Hitler decided to deport all residents not born on the Channel Islands. Arthur had been born in England. De Gruchy's board of directors did everything they could to persuade the authorities not to send Arthur away, but to no avail. Arthur and Kay were sent to Internment Camp Ilag VII in Laufen Castle, Bavaria, for the remaining long years of the war. Months later the board received the following letter from Arthur, written in pencil, which described life in the prisoner-of-war camp. 'All we can do is to sit about on our wooden beds and try to get on each other's nerves as little as possible. My barracks holds 86, ordinary brick floors, unfinished walls.' But he wasn't despairing, just longing for normality to return: 'We hope that all in the shop are set ready for the great word "go". Oh for a real job of work, privacy, freedom and the chance to plan for the future.' He signed off with: 'We are well and my wife joins me in sending best wishes and a soon happy landing. Yours sincerely, A. Harvey.'[28]

Back on the mainland, conscription meant that there were soon one million fewer people employed in the distributive trades – retail and wholesale businesses – than before the war.[29] With bomb-damaged premises, public transport destroyed and few staff, shops had to be inventive. A handful of firms even decided to try operating with just a skeleton team. The key to this lay in the novel concept of self-service. Self-service had been pioneered in the United States, with the first Piggly Wiggly store opening in Memphis, Tennessee in 1916, and was truly revolutionary. Goods were laid out on open shelves, with customers helping themselves by loading merchandise into the newest shopping accessory: a shopping basket. There were no shop assistants to receive lists and retrieve goods from behind counters; instead, the 'clerks' (as they were called in the States) were concentrated at the checkout. The Piggly Wiggly franchise spread rapidly across the USA during the interwar years. British retailers had initially rejected the alien concept, but faced with extreme staff shortages, self-service now looked a little more attractive. So in 1942 the London Co-operatives in Romford experimented with a hybrid system, with certain sections of the shop being completely self-service, while shopgirls were still on hand at the rations counter to help customers with their ration books.[30]

Such experiments were, nevertheless, small scale. The key to being able to open the shop shutters each morning still lay in recruiting and retaining flesh-and-blood employees. In order to keep the staff they had happy, many employers softened the rigid discipline they had imposed for decades. Rules regarding make-up and jewellery were relaxed, and shop assistants were allowed a little more freedom of expression in their dress. It was a far cry from Victorian strictures and fines being docked from weekly pay. William Whiteley would have turned in his grave.

Retailers now turned to those left behind – teenagers, people approaching retirement and above all married women – to fill the vacancies. This signalled the biggest change in shop employment since the arrival of shopgirls in the 1860s and 70s. It was a shift from shopgirls to shopwomen – and an accompanying shift from full-time work to more part-time work. For now the staff who stood behind the counters of drapers' shops and grocery stores, of Woolworths and Kendal Milne, were likely to be women with children, women who had domestic and caring duties as well as fire-warden duties and other voluntary-service duties. Here was the craziness of wartime multitasking, where women were workers, mothers, wives and fire wardens all at once. It was a pattern repeated in other industries too: in 1931, 16 per cent of female workers over fourteen were married; by 1943 this had shot up to 43 per cent.[31]

The great challenge for these women was how to fulfil all these duties at once, and shopping was a particular problem. Many female workers tried to shop after work or in their lunch hour, which led to enormously long queues and discontent among customers and employers alike. Shopkeepers called on employers to give their staff designated hours in which to purchase all they needed for their families; eventually even the government recognised that this was a good idea. The Ministry of Labour communicated this to the Ministry of Food: 'It is found that women workers with domestic responsibilities must be given some time off each week to do their shopping.'[32]

Of course, the problem of when to shop applied just as much to the shop assistants themselves. Amazingly, firms like Sainsbury's granted their assistants a 'shopping time' allowance of one hour per fortnight – arguably much too little, but a step in the right direction. And big employers' willingness to be flexible was about to be stretched even further. Just as it looked like the tide of war was starting to turn, with the Allied success of the Normandy landings in June 1944 beating the Germans back in northern France, Hitler unleashed another deadly form of attack. The V-1 flying bombs, vengeance weapons that also came to be known as doodlebugs, were small pilotless aircraft launched from bases in occupied France and Holland. Their targets were London and south-east England. This time, the bombing took place during the day, when everyone was out of their shelters and going about their business in offices, shops, factories, schools and streets. When the rumbling growl of a V-1 engine overhead suddenly fell silent, people underneath knew it was about to dive to earth. They ran for their lives. Schools were closed to protect children and for the duration of that summer, Sainsbury's allowed its shopwomen to bring their children to work. When lives and profits were on the line, employers found the will and the way to allow women to manage their two worlds of home and work. Unfortunately, if predictably, that flexibility would be much less apparent once the war was over.

At 9.41 a.m. on Friday 28 July, a V-1 rocket succeeded in getting through to Lewisham, south London, undetected by the warning sirens. Its engine cut out and it dove silently down, directly hitting the market stalls on Lewisham High Street. It was a catastrophe. The market had been bustling and the stalls were lined up right outside Marks & Spencer, Sainsbury's and Woolworths, which caught the full force of the blast. Dead and injured people lay everywhere, with whole families wiped out together. Shops were destroyed on both sides of the high street and there were casualties even underground in Woolworths' basement café.[33] Marks & Spencer had been full of shoppers: dozens of its staff and customers were killed or injured. Among the five staff killed were sixteen-year-old shopgirl Doris Taylor; fifteen-year-old Alice Thompson, who had been helping the window dresser to complete a new display; Mrs Ethel Clarke in the general office, who was heavily pregnant; and Mrs Doris Clamp, emergency management reserve. Store manager Sydney Spurling was killed in his office. It fell to staff manageress Miss Hall to comfort the bereaved families. She had to identify the bodies as best she could and visited the injured in hospital. 'Personally I don't mind if I never have to go to a hospital for the rest of my life,' she said. 'My hair turned grey overnight – something I did not believe could happen – but I can assure you it did.'[34] This proved to be one of the worst V-1 attacks on London, with a death toll of more than 50, and 216 injured.

Within a few short weeks the RAF had figured out how to stop the V-1s in mid-air, so by late August the British air force was intercepting the majority of the flying bombs. Paris was liberated and the long march to Berlin was under way; prospects for peace looked strong. It seemed as though victory could be on the horizon and, to use Churchill's words, an end to the long hard road and time of terror was in sight. Lord Woolton left the Ministry of Food and was appointed Minister of Reconstruction, tasked to plan and build a safe, functioning post-war world. At the end of the previous war, the women who had taken up men's jobs in shops and factories and on the land had been demoted, sent back to their pre-war jobs or back to the home. Many women had gladly relinquished their wartime work, but others had felt cheated. This time around, with the menfolk soon to return, women who had been promoted to relief managers and staff managers, married women in butcher's shops and general corner stores, former shopgirls in the Land Army and munitions factories were again faced with an uncertain future.

The government issued a poster called *A West End London Street Scene* in the last year of the war, showing a bustling, colourful spectacle around Oxford Circus, with civilian shoppers thronging the pavements in front of gleaming window displays and spilling across streets busy with red buses and sleek motorcars.[35] It was a hopeful illustration of what post-war life would be like, but this utopian vision had little prospect of turning into reality for many years to come. All over the country shoppers still clutching their Utility coupons and ration books were making do in bomb-damaged city centres. Steel would not be released for rebuilding for another decade; the great John Lewis Oxford Street store was trading from a collection of partially reconstructed separate buildings on a bombsite, some of them open to the elements.[36]

But all anxious uncertainty was temporarily swept away as peace was finally declared. On 8 May 1945, King George VI broadcast to the nation from Buckingham Palace. He thanked God for deliverance and said, 'As your King I thank with a full heart those who bore arms so valiantly on land and sea, or in the air; and all civilians who, shouldering their many burdens, have carried them unflinchingly without complaint.' Kay and Arthur Harvey were released from their Bavarian castle prisoner-of-war camp and made the long journey back through the ruins of central Europe to mainland Britain. They were repatriated to England in June, but couldn't get back to Jersey immediately because of the ongoing travel restrictions. They made good use of the enforced delay, and spent five weeks in England visiting suppliers and ordering stock. Finally, on 29 July 1945, de Gruchy's board of directors welcomed back their general manager to St Helier. They were all determined that it would soon be business as usual and were 'set ready for the great word "go"', as Arthur had longed for in his letter home. The store celebrated by taking out a large yet gloriously understated ad in the *Evening Post*:

Our Mr. Harvey, repatriated to England from
Germany, has taken the opportunity thus afforded of
visiting Manufacturers and Wholesalers, and reports that
a full share of the following goods will be forthcoming:

FASHION GOODS

WOMEN'S & CHILDREN'S WEAR

MEN'S WEAR

HOUSEHOLD GOODS & FURNISHINGS

Some suppliers already have parcels ready packed for dispatch

Shop assistant Valerie Allen, nineteen years old, holds flowers in the
Biba shop in west London, 1969.

CHAPTER 8

CHELSEA GIRLS AND COUNTER-CULTURES

In 1955, just over a year after the end of rationing, 21-year-old art-school graduate Mary Quant set up a new shop in the King's Road, Chelsea. She was frustrated by the failure of high streets, including their flagship stores, to offer anything that she or her friends wanted to wear. As she later wrote, 'the young were tired of wearing the same as their mothers'.[1] With the New Look on the wane, British fashion in the mid 50s had become a dour business. It was aimed at middle-aged middle-class women, was firmly in the grip of the European couture houses, and sold through department stores that were becoming dowdy backwaters. Many stores that had survived a decade of post-war austerity were not moving with the times. 'We were all lamb dressed as mutton in those days,' said pop journalist Maureen Cleave.[2]

Quant 'wanted the young to have fashion of their own ... absolutely twentieth-century fashion'. Coming from a family of teachers, she had little experience of shopkeeping herself. Nevertheless, together with her business partner, Alexander Plunket Greene, she took out a low-rent lease on Kings Road – once the haunt of

Victorian writers, artists and poets, it was now an average high street, albeit one with a hint of the café culture to come. She named the shop Bazaar but discovered that, when it came to filling its rails, she just couldn't find the things she wanted. So she set about sourcing and making clothes and accessories herself, drawing on skills she had learnt as an apprentice couture milliner.[3]

Bazaar's range blew the lid off London fashion. Quant's clothes were inspired by American 'beat' style and its search for free expression in everything from fashion to fiction and film. She used classic children's fabrics, like gingham and flannel, and scaled up children's wear, reworking knee-high socks, short skirts, cardigans and leotards. Gymslips would mutate into mini dresses and shorts would be sexed up into hot pants. Sharp seams replaced fussy frills. At a time when most young girls wore pastel colours, Quant used a bold palette, combining plum with ginger, pale blue and maroon, tobacco brown and purple. She also challenged another convention – the traditional separation between day and evening wear. The result, dubbed 'the Chelsea look', was all about informality, fun and freedom of movement. For many, it was as radical as the rational dress movement that had liberated late-Victorian women from their corsets.[4]

The young Diana Dawson, who would later marry jazz legend George Melly, was one of Quant's first shopgirls, working there on Saturdays from the age of eighteen. She remembers how 'radically different Mary's clothes were from anything else available at the time'. When not working on Bazaar, she was modelling for women's magazines like *Women's Own*, *Vogue* and *Queen*, where 'it was all tweed suits, pinched at the waist, finished off with hats and gloves'. During photo sessions, the young models were 'constantly told' to make themselves 'look older' because 'fashion wasn't something for people of our age'. Diana's wages as a Bazaar assistant 'didn't stretch very far', but she splashed out on 'a bright pink and curvy dress with a scoop neck and bare shoulders' and remembers feeling 'so proud of it'.[5] Diana was wowed and she wasn't alone. At weekends, lines of fledgling fashionistas formed early outside the shop, but those who didn't want to queue for Quant could always head a couple of coffee shops further down, to Kiki Byrne's store, known for her trademark shift dresses. The stores were rivals – Mary had once employed Kiki – but the competition was about to get much tougher.

Within a decade of Bazaar's opening, London boasted nearly seventy boutiques. The new pop magazine *Rave* summed up the 'British boutique boom' for the uninitiated: 'Boutiques are the current "in" places to buy clothes and accessories. The people who run them, with flair and fashion sense, know exactly what YOU like to wear and how it should be worn.' Readers needed to know where to look: 'Boutiques are often hidden away in side streets and their fame spreads by word of mouth. There is usually an air of mystery about them with beat music playing in the background. Boutiques are fun places … and they're often used as rendezvous for friends.'[6] In 1966 a pocket guidebook was compiled for those wanting to find these exclusive hangouts. For the sum of 4s 6d, Millicent Bultitude's *Get Dressed* offered thumbnail profiles of thirty-eight niche stores and listed another twenty-nine, inviting readers to add their own discoveries in the blank pages at the end.[7] One of the most prominent of those profiled was Quorum. Founded in 1964 by Alice Pollock, and also on King's Road, Quorum gave a platform to one of the era's most famous design duos, Celia Birtwell and Ossie Clark, whose bold, nature-inspired prints and free-flowing lines anticipated hippy chic. Birtwell grew up near Manchester and had studied at Salford Art School. She also shopped – or at least window-shopped – at Kendals department store and remembers asking her mother, a seamstress, to make copies of some of the 'little suits and dresses' on sale there. Her father didn't approve of her emerging fashion sense: 'I thought I looked really glamorous but he thought I looked like a real Jezebel. He pretended not to know me in the street.'[8]

Across town, a rival scene was thriving in Soho's Carnaby Street. According to one American journalist, the street was 'no longer just an address' but 'a way of life'. It was Britain's answer to Greenwich Village or St-Germain-des-Prés, 'a colourful sartorial revolt against the Grey Establishment typified by Savile Row'.[9] Where much King's Road style had been created by and for young women, Carnaby Street seemed to be ruled by young men. One name stood out: John Stephen. Dubbed 'the million pound Mod', he would eventually buy up nearly half the street, though he came from much humbler beginnings. Stephen had started out as an apprentice welder in Glasgow's shipyards but came to London as an eighteen-year-old, landing a job in the military tailoring department of Moss Bros in Covent Garden. He soon moved, finding work as an assistant in Britain's first boutique for men, Vince, which was opened by physique photographer Bill Green in 1954 among the Soho workshops that sewed for Savile Row. Vince's clothes were cut to accentuate the figure and catered for a gay market, well over a decade before homosexuality was decriminalised. However, John Stephen recognised that the style could have wider appeal and he set up his own boutiques, first on Beak Street and then on Carnaby Street. His reworking of Italian styling with pop design was an immediate hit, especially with scooter-riding mods.[10] Ever the entrepreneur, Stephen had some of his many shops cater for modettes too, building on the look pioneered by Quant.

Despite all the creativity and ambition in Soho and Chelsea, there was one boutique that would come to rule them all: Biba. Biba was the brainchild of Barbara Hulanicki. Born in Warsaw in 1936, she had moved to England with her mother and younger sisters in 1948. They were fleeing personal tragedy: Barbara's father, a Polish diplomat, had been murdered that year by Zionist extremists in Palestine. The family settled in a small flat in Brighton, just around the corner from Barbara's rich Aunt Sophie who lived in some style in the Metropole Hotel. After Brighton Art College, Barbara found work as a fashion illustrator in Covent Garden and saw her drawings printed in *Vogue* and *Tatler*. In 1961, she married Stephen Fitz-Simon – Fitz to his friends – an advertising account manager and, with him, developed a new mail-order business. Biba's Postal Boutique sold clothes designed by Barbara and stitched together by art students through an arrangement made with one of her former tutors. After a slow start, she adapted a winning look – a gingham dress inspired by Quant but popularised by Brigitte Bardot. An ad for the item in the *Daily Mirror* produced seventeen thousand orders.[11]

In 1964, at the age of twenty-six, Hulanicki set up her first Biba store, not on the King's Road or Carnaby Street, but in a former chemist's on Abingdon Road, in the shadow of three of Kensington's best-known department stores – Barkers, Pontings, and Derry & Toms. It quickly became a London legend, one of the most powerful symbols of the swinging Sixties. Its interior was striking, ornately decorated with Victorian furniture, ostrich feathers, potted palms, mottled mirrors and antiques. Defying post-war modernism, which favoured white walls, clean lines and primary colours, Biba went 'vintage'. Looking back to Art Nouveau, it combined fin-de-siècle decadence with daring new design.

There was nothing vintage about Biba's shopgirls, however. From the start, Hulanicki had strong views on how her shopgirls would be different, would offer a completely new shopping experience and would transform the way shoppers acted in a store. In her auto-biography she explained, 'I was quite adamant that the girls should not impose themselves on the customers. We were not going to become another "Can I help you, madam?" shop. I wanted the customers to feel at home, not hounded by sales assistants.' So she hired Sarah, Irene and Elly from the Harrods export department. In a radical break with shopgirl tradition, they would come out from behind their counters. They would present themselves not as servants or advisors, but as 'friends'. Sarah was 'the red light for the beat offspring of aristocratic families', while Irene and Elly 'knew the young working girls'. As the *Evening Standard* put it, Biba became 'a place of pilgrimage for office girls seeking refuge from … dull dreary department stores'.[12]

Like Quant before her, Hulanicki dispensed with traditional plain sales assistant dresses. Instead, Sarah, Irene, Elly and the 'powerful band of girls', as she described them, wore Biba clothes at work and started modelling Biba clothes for catalogues and magazines. Another London look was born. As a young illustrator, Hulanicki had been inspired by Hollywood films and 'mesmerised' by Audrey Hepburn, 'the first young person's hero to wear couture clothes'. Like Hepburn, the 'classic' Biba girl was a world away from the full figure of 1950s femininity. She was 'square-shouldered and quite flat-chested', her head 'perched on a long, swanlike neck', her face 'a perfect oval' and her eyelids 'heavy with long, spiky lashes'.[13] The look would be famously personified by south London teenager Lesley Hornby, otherwise known as Twiggy.

Biba, and the other 'London looks' embraced by the baby-boom teenagers, may have been inspired by comic-book fantasies of childhood, but this was a generation rewriting the rulebook – at work, at home and in the bedroom. Although a Biba girl may have 'looked sweet', she 'was as hard as nails'. She 'did what she felt like at that moment and had no mum to influence her judgement'. There was no question of the Biba shopgirls living in or abiding by byzantine rules about boyfriends. They rented and shared their own flats and bedsits and, as Hulanicki put it, 'had no mother waiting for them to see if they came home with a crumpled dress'. They seized their independence and, as they did so, played their own part in Britain's sexual revolution. Hulanicki summed it up: 'I don't think our girls were promiscuous; they picked and chose. If they fancied someone they went right out and got what they were after instead of weaving webs and hypocritical traps, as we had to in the Fifties.'[14]

Biba girls became not just shop assistants and models but personalities in their own right, whose very lives embodied the store's challenging brand. When American TV company CBS made a documentary about a young country girl who came to the big city and was transformed into a swinging Sixties dolly, they used Elly as their girl. Sarah Burnett was among four from Biba whisked off 'by a Frenchman to go and dance in a club in the South of France … We were called Les Minis Anglais or something like that. It was very innocent. It was extraordinary.' Her workmate, Madeline Smith, moved from a summer job at the store to find fleeting fame as a horror-film star, with credits on *The Vampire Lovers* and *Theatre of Blood*. And the much-photographed 'Biba Twins', eighteen-year-old assistants Rosie and Susy Young, became two of the most famous faces of the day. They'd dropped out of Bournemouth Art School and travelled around Spain before heading to London. Rosie remembers that 'shop girls were so glamorous then … a real part of the swinging scene … and there we were at the centre of it all'. Over in Fulham, new designs by Zandra Rhodes and Sylvia Ayton drew in the crowds at their Fulham Road Clothes Shop, but so did their staff: 'the shop was like an open house to strange people, who liked sitting on the big banana seat and talking to the shop girl'.[15]

Boutiques certainly placed shopgirls centre stage, accessible to customers who were usually around their age and close enough to them in background to create a personal connection. The stores' appeal was built on this emotional bond between them and their customers, but these faux relationships functioned like real teen friendships, based as much on idolising envy as on empathy and trust. Boutique impresarios were all too aware that this intimacy and insider status, however illusory, kept the shop buzzing and the tills ringing.

From the late 1880s, well-heeled women had flocked to Whiteley's, Harrods, Jenners, Kendals and the rest for their social scene as much as for the shopping. They could meet friends, style gaze, watch the world go by and, in the more adventurous establishments, enjoy the occasional – and, at the time, highly daring – mid-morning glass of wine and a biscuit. From the late 1950s, their great-granddaughters and their friends made a beeline for boutiques. If you could get through the door, you could make the free coffee last a while, hang out and, if you looked the part, maybe pick up an invitation to a party later. Their unique fusion of fashion, art, design and music came to define new British bohemianism. They were Britain's fragmented answer to Andy Warhol's Factory.

Diana Dawson, working at Quant's Bazaar, lapped it up. So did her genuine friends. She recalled that they 'would come in to gossip and giggle, though we tended to shut up when Mary walked in'. The neighbouring boutiques and coffee bars, sometimes combined in one venue, were the 'haunts of the Chelsea Set during the day'. In the evenings, the action switched to local pubs, particularly 'the Markham, round the corner from Bazaar, or the Pheasantry', where 'you went to find out where the nearest party was', following the sound of Paul Anka records, 'armed with a bottle of cheap red wine and some cigarettes'.[16]

Boutiques came with their own distinct soundtrack. And they didn't just play records, they also played host to the singers and bands that made them. According to *Rave*, Sandie Shaw was a regular at Hem and Fringe, while Lulu favoured the Victoria and Albert. The Pennyhapenny Boutique was owned by members of the band The Pretty Things. And Apple's founder, the model Jenny Boyd, found that being the sister-in-law of a Beatle did her business no harm: her sister Patti was married to George. At Top Gear, John Lennon was known to 'sit on the window sill and put 78s on the old record player', while Mick Jagger kept accounts for 'all his girlfriends' there, but 'stopped paying the bills' after each break-up. Quorum's catwalks were in a league of their own. Choreographed by Ossie Clark, they broke with every couture convention, with models moving down the runway to Hendrix, The Doors and the Velvet Underground. These 'happenings' attracted A-listers and rising talent – musicians, journalists, photographers, artists, aristos and assembled hangers-on. The store played another intriguing but less well-known part in British music history. Pink Floyd's Syd Barrett dated Lindsay Corner, one of their shopgirls, and one Dave Gilmour was their van driver.[17]

Outside the central London bubble of King's Road, Carnaby Street and Kensington, boutiques blossomed in other cities across Britain. In Manchester, new stores linked to new bands and new celebrities flourished. In 1965, Tony Bookbinder opened Pygmalia in Back Pool Fold, a small alley a few blocks from Kendals on Deansgate. He was the drummer with Billy J. Kramer's band The Dakotas and his younger sister, Elaine, was breaking into the British blues scene under her stage name Elkie Brooks. Nearby, shop assistant Christine Shipley worked at Contrary in Barton Arcade, selling 'maxi coats with trousers to match, wet look tops, hot pants, split knee velvet trousers, maxi dresses and lurex tops' to 'great customers', including younger members of the cast of new soap *Coronation Street*. On the city's real Bridge Street, Britain's best-known footballer, George Best, opened his Edwardia store in 1969, selling trademark menswear. In Nottingham, young designers Janet Campbell and Paul Smith set up The Birdcage in an old tailor's shop. For Campbell, like so many other young entrepreneurs, it was all an experiment: 'None of us had any formal training in retailing, or worked in a shop before, so nobody knew the "right" way to do it ... I employed a girl called Valerie because she'd got the right sort of hair.' The big difference was that the set-up was, for Campbell at least, 'completely classless', attracting 'girls who worked in banks, students, offices – and rich girls, too'.[18]

In Barnsley, 23-year-old Rita Britton decided she wanted a piece of the action. She wasn't an art student and had no famous friends, but in 1967 she quit her job in a local paper mill, where she'd worked since she was fifteen, borrowed £500 from her dad, rented a dank basement in town and created what would become a legendary store – Pollyanna. With few connections, she jumped in at the deep end. She remembers starting off 'with just two rails of stock from Mary Quant'. Her dad, a lorry driver, had helped her out there, too: 'I can remember my dad coming home at six in the morning after a double shift and driving me down to London. He'd park outside Mary Quant, sleep in the car, drive me back to Barnsley and then go back to work.' She adds, 'Incidentally, I remember the people at Mary Quant serving me tea and cucumber sandwiches with no crusts. I thought: "They must be incredibly hard up."'[19] Britton pressed on: 'I rang up Ossie Clark from a call box at the end of my Gran's road and he agreed that I could buy from him.'[20]

Not surprisingly, the young-blood boutiques rattled the old department stores. Those that had survived the war now faced a challenge from within retail's own ranks to renew their cultural edge for a new generation. Some stores, however, relished the challenge. In the early 1950s, Woollands department store in Knightsbridge was struggling. In its pre-war heyday, it had successfully catered for a servant class whose mistresses shopped a few streets away at Harrods and Harvey Nichols, but now it found itself stuck in an Edwardian time-warp. Its fortunes were turned around in 1961, however, when a young manager named Martin Moss succeeded in bottling some boutique magic by opening the first 21 Shop in pride of place on the ground floor. Moss had gone back to the drawing board, bringing in Terence Conran and interior design students from the Royal College of Art to strip out the stuffy sales space and give it a more open feel. In a bold move, he also promoted Vanessa Denza, a 22-year-old Woollands shopgirl, to the position of fashion buyer for 21. Denza whisked new styles straight from art-student studios to her shopfloor. Among them was a daring needle-cord women's trouser suit designed by Marion Foale and Sally Tuffin. Denza recalls, 'In

1961 you didn't wear trousers. That's when I started buying in a lot of trousers from France. I used to go over to the factories and hand pick what I needed.' In another break with store tradition pioneered by boutiques, she rapidly accelerated turnover by only running a few styles for a short time rather than buying in bulk for an entire season. If customers blinked, they would miss the chance to buy. Fast fashion was born.[21]

Woollands' owners, the Debenhams Group, seized the opportunity and sold Moss's successful concept of an in-store boutique to others. By 1965, there were four new 21 Shops: three in their Marshall and Snelgrove stores in London, Birmingham and Manchester and one in Williams and Hopkins in Bournemouth. Other stores were quick to follow the model of 21. In 1966, Selfridges launched Miss Selfridge as its own boutique brand. The following year, the brand was occupying its own premises in Croydon, Brighton, Regent Street and Brompton. Boutiques were branching out and moving slowly but surely towards the mainstream or, as some would claim, towards their own demise.

Meanwhile, on the high streets the chain stores were also learning fast. The story of one – Chelsea Girl – is particularly telling. For all the hype, the real Chelsea set and the real Chelsea look were still exclusive and expensive. According to Twiggy, a suburbanite catapulted to stardom in this new world, Bazaar and the rest of the better-known boutiques were only 'for rich girls'. Quant had once claimed that boutiques had helped to push 'snobbery out of fashion' and that in her shop 'you will find duchesses jostling with typists to buy the same dresses'. They may have aspired to the same look, but a Quant pinafore featured in *Vogue* in 1960 cost sixteen and a half guineas, almost three weeks' wages for an average office girl.[22] Step forward Chelsea Girl – a 'new' chain that was in fact a bold rebranding of a much more sedate one. Lewis Separates had been a well-known interwar family clothing business and had itself grown out of the family's original stores, which had sold groceries and then knitting wool. In 1965, alert to the money to be made from Quant's Chelsea look, owner Bernard Lewis bit the bullet and rebranded, launching across the country in local high streets. Art-student style immediately became more accessible and more affordable. It was a pivotal moment. Traditionally, the quality of a shop's goods had been guaranteed by the trusted family name above its doors. Now, young customers would only buy clothes where they sniffed style.

The boutique movement and its big store imitators were tapping into a whole new generation of consumers. The post-war baby boom had brought about a massive demographic shift, producing record numbers of teenagers. At the start of the 1950s, there were three million fifteen- to nineteen-year-olds; by the end, there were close to four million. This post-rationing generation now left school at fifteen. They took up jobs in shops, offices, hairdresser's and hotels, on production lines and in manufacturing. Their living costs were low because most lived at home. Nevertheless, many young workers were desperate to escape family houses they found stifling and parents they found overbearing and out of touch. Marriage still offered one escape route and young workers could afford to get hitched earlier than ever. As a result, the average age at which women married fell from twenty-five in the 1920s to twenty-two by the late Sixties. The sexual revolution wasn't all about ripping up the rulebook. Rather, it could shore up old social norms, like marriage.

Of those who didn't head down the aisle, some broke new ground by heading to university. Student numbers doubled in the 1960s, from 100,000 to 200,000, with many admitted to the new 'plate-glass' universities – Sussex, Lancaster, Warwick, Kent, York, Strathclyde, Essex and others – that now joined their red-brick predecessors. The Biba shopgirls and their peers also challenged convention by leaving family homes for bedsits and flat-shares with friends as part of a growing number of Likely Lads and Liver Birds.

All these groups – young single workers, young marrieds and young students – contributed to a burgeoning counter-culture in Britain that marked one of the most decisive breaks with traditional social values ever seen.

Their younger brothers and sisters were not to be left out. As houschold sizes shrank, older siblings left home and new housing stock began to rise in war-torn cities and new towns, many younger teenagers gained their own bedrooms – the first generation to do so en masse. Wherever possible, teenagers started to transform their rooms into self-reflecting shrines to football players, pop stars, bands and models. New kinds of teen magazines fuelled these subcultures, particularly among girls. *Jackie*, *FAB*, *Petticoat* and *Marty* swapped pre-war 'girl's own' adventure stories for fashion features, photo stories and problem pages. *Honey*, launched in 1960, was aimed at readers who were 'young, gay and get ahead!'. By 1967, it had nearly a quarter of a million female readers and in an intriguing move from printed page to fixed premises, Honey boutiques briefly appeared as pop-up outlets in regional department stores.[23]

The teen magazine market was part of a bigger post-war economic transformation. By the late 1960s, 16- to 24-year-olds, were spending over £150 million each year on cosmetics, footwear, knitwear, coats, jackets and suits. And the customers were not just middle class – working-class consumer spending had begun to rise. According to an earlier *Financial Times* report from the mid 1950s, 'the middle-class family of today spends £94 a year on clothes, while the average working-class family manages on £54'.[24] The bigger point here, however, was that 'the latter outnumber the middle class by more than 2 to 1'. Smart retailers, even small independents, would always look to find ways to tap into this mass market.

This spending spree was funded by full employment. In stark contrast to the biting unemployment of the interwar years, work had never been easier to find. In 1959 Tory prime minister Harold

Macmillan came out with the famous line, 'Indeed let us be frank about it — most of our people have never had it so good.' This was a new age of affluence, with rising wages, exports and investment. Unemployment had reached a historic low of just 216,000 in 1955 and then averaged around 2 per cent until the early 1970s. By 1966, retail was employing 1.3 million women or nearly one fifth of the entire female workforce. Many of this generation of shopgirls typically started as fourteen- and fifteen-year-old Saturday girls, most of them still at school. Stores found they needed part-time Saturday assistants once the traditional full-time working week was cut from six days to five, a gradual process that began in the 1930s but was much more widely adopted post-war. Needless to say, Saturday girls were paid a lot less than their weekday counterparts, but for many it was an exciting rite of passage.

Something else was beginning to change, too. Married women, many of them mums in their thirties and forties, began to return to work. Because of such historic low unemployment, many retailers were battling with staff shortages. And as during the Second World War, they turned to married women to fill the gap. Towards the end of that conflict, just as after the First World War, most women who had stepped up into men's roles in shopwork had been required to step down again. But now, in the 1950s, shopkeepers made their job offer even more tempting to the working mother juggling domestic duties: the shopwork available was on a part-time basis and they had no intention of taking it away from women a few years down the line. Part-time work had been pioneered during the war, but this was now on a different scale altogether.

It was a historic and lasting shift. In 1957, only a quarter of shop-workers were part-time. A decade later, nearly a third were, and most of them were women.[25] On the upside, it meant that mothers could fit in paid work around their children. The real downside, however, was that their pay, conditions and pensions were generally poor.

This was a sadly familiar cycle. Back in the 1850s and 60s, the original expansion of the retail industry had been based on the girling of shopwork. To a large extent, shopkeepers who wanted to grow their businesses began employing young women because they could pay them less. A century on, and Britain's success as a maturing retail economy was again built on the cheap labour of its increasingly part-time, and mostly female, workforce. Young female art-and-design students like Quant, Hulanicki, Birtwell and Campbell were breaking exciting new ground through boutiques and everything they stood for. But other young women, including their own shopgirls, sellers and models, were sleepwalking into a lasting low-wage trap.

In the nineteenth century, many girls had opted for shopwork over domestic service because it was better paid. In the early twentieth century this continued to be the case. As their working hours were reduced and new kinds of professional qualifications, such as book-keeping, were introduced, female shopworkers' wages had improved in comparison to other trades. But by the late 1960s, it seemed that these advances were being slowly but surely eroded. An Earnings Survey conducted in 1968 by the Department of Employment showed that for both men and women, the job of sales assistant was 'one of the lowest paid in Britain'. Other researchers, writing in the *Industrial Relations Journal*, would go on to calculate that sales assistants' earnings had actually fallen in relation to other low-paid workers, most of whom were part of Britain's post-war servant class: 'only gardeners, farmworkers and general catering workers, waiters and barmen earned less than salesmen, and only kitchenhands, hairdressers and barmaids earned less than saleswomen. If gratuities were included, the position of sales assistants could be even worse.'[26]

This was the world of the small private business – the countless shops, salons, pubs, restaurants and hotels that made up the sprawling service sector and which seemed so hard to reform. Unions worked behind the scenes to raise standards but the labour movement as a whole was much more concerned with the bigger beasts of British industry – notably car plants, coal mines and manufacturing. The shop assistants' union, known from 1947 as the Union of Shop, Distributive and Allied Workers, or USDAW, had seen its post-war numbers rise. But the number of female members remained fairly low and the number of part-time members even lower.

Hope for pay equality with men came from a different sector. In 1955, female civil servants had submitted mass petitions and marched in demonstrations trying to force a promise of equal pay. By 1961 they had secured this, as had most female teachers. Outside the private sector, this progress was taking longer – but would ultimately result in a countrywide shift. In 1968, a group of female manual workers fought a famous battle of their own, leading, ultimately, to landmark national legislation on equal pay. In June of that year the sewing machinists at Ford's car plant in Dagenham, the European centre of the US motor giant's global operation, walked out. The women worked on the specialised upholstery for car seats. They were incensed by Ford's regrading of its workforce, which had put them on a lower, unskilled grade while men doing very similar work had been put on a higher, semi-skilled grade. Lower grades meant lower pay. When they walked out, no upholstery meant no finished product and no sales.

Ford's entire UK production was brought to a halt for three weeks when women at their Halewood plant on Merseyside joined the Dagenham strike. Things might have ended very differently if anyone other than Barbara Castle had been the secretary of state for employment in Harold Wilson's government. Castle was still only one of a handful of women to have served in the Cabinet. She held personal meetings with the Dagenham machinists and although she wouldn't support their demand to be regraded as skilled workers, she did back their case for a pay rise. More importantly, she used the strike to win support for a momentous piece of legislation that was extremely close to her own heart: the 1970 Equal Pay Act. At long last, wages would – in theory at least – be determined by the nature of the tasks performed, not the body of the person performing them. Employers were given five years to make whatever changes were necessary to ensure that they offered equal pay for equal work. If bohemianism had been made in Chelsea, then equal pay – which was just as counter-cultural – was made in Dagenham.

1970 was proving to be a watershed year for British women in other ways. In February, an event at Ruskin College in Oxford would take the fight for equal rights well beyond women's wage packets. Back in the nineteenth century, artist and social critic John Ruskin had celebrated the dignity of labour and sought to open up more opportunities for working-class men. Now the college named in his honour hosted a very different kind of meeting: Britain's first National Women's Liberation Conference.

The event had come about rather by accident. A few weeks beforehand, a mature student named Sally Alexander had booked college rooms for a conference on women's history. Mother to a young daughter, and a former stage manager, she'd gone to university after her divorce in 1968. Like many others, however, she was increasingly frustrated by the way that history was written and taught. Traditional history books were still dominated by accounts of the power struggles of royal courts, politicians and parliaments. And while some social historians were starting to study the lives of ordinary people, or 'history from below', they were principally interested in writing the story of working men, rather than that of their wives, mothers, sisters and daughters – or, indeed, women who had proven themselves on their own terms. Sally had been particularly exasperated by the sidelining of women's experience at a recent Ruskin history conference, not least because that event was run by the otherwise radical History Workshop group, at the vanguard of the new focus on social history. When young history lecturer Sheila Rowbotham had suggested the group's next meeting might cover women's history, the mostly male crowd had 'roared with laughter'. Sally and Sheila were taken aback but, with the help of several others, got on with organising their own meeting.

It quickly became apparent to them that little had been written about the recent history of women's working and social lives. Undeterred, they decided their meeting would address the position of women in the present day instead. With a small group of co-organisers, they invited some speakers, put out some leaflets and waited. Rowbotham recalls that they were expecting 'perhaps a hundred people'. In fact, five hundred showed up, some with their babies and young children. 'Everybody arrived with their sleeping bags on Friday night, which was turmoil.' Somehow, they wrangled a rapid overspill from Ruskin into the Oxford Union's hallowed debating chamber, described by Rowbotham as 'an extraordinarily stiff environment that was meant to produce male orators who would become prime ministers'. She remembered 'being really scared of speaking in that room'.[27]

Over three days, the National Women's Liberation Conference debated a whole host of subjects, from the family, sex and mother-hood to women's work and pay. For them, these issues were inextricably linked. The reason why most women found themselves restricted to doing certain kinds of jobs – most of which, like shopwork, were quite poorly paid – was that at some point in their lives many would have to juggle earning cash with caring for kids. While some women relished that arrangement, others felt increasingly trapped.

From the outset, the organisers of the Ruskin event were acutely aware of the need to reach out to ordinary working women. To that end, they invited Audrey Wise, trade unionist at USDAW, to give a platform speech. Wise was then in her mid thirties. She had grown up in Newcastle and like so many of her generation, she 'married young', at the age of eighteen, and 'just fitted in jobs mostly part time' around her small children, working as a 'shorthand typist, insurance agent, market researcher', which she regarded as 'going-round-knocking-on-doors type jobs – definitely not a career'. She had joined USDAW when she 'got a job canvassing catalogues'. From then on things changed. She quickly rose to become branch secretary and then, long before the Ruskin conference, an active supporter of the Ford strikers. She would go on to become a Labour MP and a prominent voice in this new wave of women's rights debates. Speaking at an equal rights rally in a rainy Trafalgar Square before all this, in 1969, she'd been struck by the quiet determination of the mostly female crowd: 'These women on this wet day … tipping their umbrellas back so they could see you … drinking in every word.' Many had travelled across the country to be there and Wise gleefully imagined the kinds of responses from husbands shocked to hear that their wives were 'going to London': 'how can we afford it? What about the dinner, who will look after the children?' A man, thought Wise, would 'simply say, "I'm going on a demonstration." Full stop.'[28]

Like Margaret Bondfield before her, Wise was a socialist first and a feminist second. She'd been invited to Ruskin to talk about women and trade unions and although she stuck to the brief, she argued that the only way of improving the lives of working women was to improve the lives of all working people. She remembers that many in the audience found her line 'quite hard going' and that the encounter certainly 'wasn't cosy'. But she 'enjoyed the weekend' and 'went away very friendly to it all', above all, 'thrilled at the size of it'.[29] She later took part in debates on the Working Women's

Charter – a set of proposals that proved too challenging for the TUC, among others.[30]

Back at Ruskin, the landmark conference had ended with a session that opened a whole new question: 'Where are we going?' All those attending voted unanimously to support four demands: equal pay; equal education and opportunity; twenty-four-hour nurseries; free contraception and abortion on demand. Inspired by the US civil rights movement, they also agreed to channel their energies into a new Women's Liberation Movement. The 'women's libbers' were roundly ridiculed by much of the press, many politicians and the wider public for wanting this kind of equality and freedom. They would attract outright hostility, however, when they pulled off one of their most audacious stunts. On 20 November 1970, around fifty demonstrators disrupted the Miss World contest at the Royal Albert Hall. This was the television highlight of the year, watched by over twenty million viewers. Protestors, including Sally Alexander, heckled the startled-looking finalists as they disembarked from their coach, shouting, 'Shame on you!', 'We're not beautiful or ugly, we're angry!' and 'Welcome to the world's largest cattle market!' They brandished banners declaring, 'Beauty contests degrade women' and berating the 'Poor cows' taking part. Inside the venue, they silenced equally startled hosts Michael Aspel and Bob Hope with football rattles and flour bombs.

At the time, many commentators saw the Miss World protest as clear evidence that feminists were sexually repressed men-haters. In fact, they embraced women's sexuality. Many devoured the books of Betty Friedan, Germaine Greer and Erica Jong and, even if they didn't agree with every line, encouraged women to explore their own bodies and find their own sexual pleasures. What they objected to, very vehemently, was not only the continuing economic inequality that kept them dependent on men and marriage, but also their treatment as passive 'sex objects' who existed to please others. As one of their posters pithily put it: 'YES to mini-skirts, NO to mini-wages.' Many of those who disrupted the Miss World contest would happily wear bikinis on the beach and were devotees of Bazaar, Biba and art-school chic – and saw no contradiction in that. For them, there was a world of difference between women running their own businesses and creating styles that made their customers feel more visible and powerful, and a beauty contest in which women paraded in swimwear at the behest of men in bow ties.

The media decried the Miss World protest and accused the Women's Liberation Movement of going way too far. More radical political groups, however, had been preparing to take things much further. They set their targets high, aiming at nothing less than capitalist consumer society itself. 'Never had it so good', with its easy money and beautiful shops, its new fashions and endless household appliances, had a darker side. And certain underground groups were set on exposing it. In the early hours of the day of the Miss World contest, one of these groups had planted not a flour bomb but a small explosive device in a BBC broadcast van parked outside the Albert Hall. It went off, damaging the vehicle but causing no injuries. The incident was not widely reported, mostly because the authorities wanted to starve those suspected of being responsible of publicity. The group in question was the Angry Brigade.

The Angry Brigade was a small band of young men and women who had dropped out of university, determined to challenge post-war authority. Like many of their generation, they had been radicalised by the mass student protests in Paris in 1968 (their name was inspired by French activists Les Enragés) and by struggles against the Vietnam War, the nuclear arms race and the political leaders who presided over these. Their views were forged by a heady mix of Marxism, anarchism and a fair amount of cannabis, but above all by one of the era's most ardent critics of consumerism, French thinker Guy Debord. Debord's book *The Society of the Spectacle* had first appeared in 1967 and informed the thinking of some of those who had led the Paris protests. His argument was simple: people's relationships with each other in modern society had become badly distorted by consumer culture. They were mesmerised by the pursuit of money and the things they could buy to the point where social life was no longer about 'living' but only about 'having'. For Debord, all this was a dangerous illusion, 'a spectacle' generated by mass culture – through its shops, magazines, adverts and films – promising idealised lifestyles that could never be truly attained and which were, in any case, empty.[31]

Plenty of young people were starting to reject consumerism and the 'meaningless' world of work that fed it. Instead, thousands celebrated an alternative hedonism, embodied by the free festival movement that sometimes came with free food, drink, drugs and love. The Angry Brigade understood all that but wanted to push things further. They took Debord's philosophy fiercely to heart. Their early interventions were non-violent – they cranked out posters, pamphlets, communiqués and political tracts on Roneo duplicators and distributed these around the north and west London squats where they lived. They worked with runaways, the homeless, black migrants and others left behind by the post-war consumer boom. But they were also influenced by the increasingly violent tactics adopted by other radical groups, such as Baader-Meinhof in Berlin and The First of May Group, who were taking direct action against General Franco's ongoing and brutal dictator-ship in Spain. Accounts of precisely what the Angry Brigade did and why are deeply conflicting but they did begin to plant small bombs of their own, at the Miss World contest, and also in the offices and homes of civil servants and politicians, judges and other 'high pigs'; among these were employment secretary Robert Carr, Attorney General Sir Peter Rawlinson, and John Davies, the secretary of state for trade and industry, all of whom were involved in a controversial Industrial Relations Bill seeking to rein in the unions. Then, on May Day 1971, they set their sights on a completely new type of target: the Biba boutique and its shopgirls.

On that day, Biba's founder Barbara Hulanicki had 'managed to drag' husband Fitz to Antiquarius, the antique market on Kings Road. He was unhappy to be away from the shop on a busy Saturday afternoon. Leaving her at a stall, he went to make a quick call to ask shopgirl Irene if everything was all right:

'Yes,' she said. 'It's fine, but there has been a bomb scare.'

'What do you mean?' asked Fitz.

'Well, this geezer said we had ten minutes to go before it went off, and then he rang again and said we had five minutes.'

'Do as I say, Irene,' said Fitz. 'Blow smoke into the fire alarm to make it go off and clear the shop.'

With that, Barbara recalls, a white-faced Fitz came running back to her, 'stuffed some money into my hand for a taxi and said, "Now don't worry, there's a bomb in the shop," and shot off'. By the time she reached the shop herself, she remembers that 'crowds of customers were out on the pavement and so were all the staff. I couldn't see Fitz. Someone said the bomb had gone off. I died a thousand deaths before I reached the front door.' Inside, she discovered first of all that no one had died, despite the fact that there had been well over a thousand shoppers in the store just minutes before. Fitz and the manageress were inspecting the damage. Half of the basement had been demolished and a security guard slightly injured. Thousands of pounds' worth of stock had been ruined. And almost just as much had been stolen – 'stuffed up jumpers and into bags' by fleeing customers.[32]

Hulanicki was in shock. And deeply confused as to why anyone might bomb her store. Then in Communiqué #8, published in *The Times*, the Angry Brigade explained their 'rationale'.

All the sales girls in the flash boutiques are made to dress the same and have the same make-up, representing the 1940s. In fashion as in everything else capitalism can only go backwards – they've nowhere to go – they're dead. Life is so boring there is nothing to do except spend all our wages on the latest skirt or shirt.

Brothers and Sisters – what are your real desires? Sit in the drugstore, look distant, empty, bored, drinking some tasteless coffee? Or perhaps BLOW IT UP or BURN IT DOWN. The only thing you can do with modern slave-houses – called boutiques – is WRECK THEM.[33]

In this rhetoric, shopgirls like Irene and Elly were not liberated young women working towards counter-cultures of their own, but zombie agents of capitalist consumerism working in modern slave-houses. For the Angry Brigade, the 'flash boutiques' and their shopgirls were symbols of everything that was wrong with modern life. They peddled impossible dreams that only served to distract and divide people. Salesgirls were 'dead' because they and their goods belonged to a world that was heading for an abyss. Half a century before, G.K. Chesterton had come to a similarly vitriolic conclusion, though from a very different political starting point. For him, it was department stores, rather than boutiques, that symbolised the mesmerising emptiness of early twentieth-century consumerism. He had also turned his fire on shopgirls, presiding over their 'awful interminable emporia', and even fantasised about decapitating them. For all her lowly economic status, the shopgirl exercised enormous and enduring symbolic power. She seemed to embody consumerism and all the conflicting passions bound up with it – desire, envy, guilt and pleasure. She stood at the gateway between goods and those who might buy them – a temptress, whether in a demure black silk dress or a daring mini-skirt.

The Angry Brigade went on to attack more high-profile targets, including the home of William Batty, a director of the Ford car plant. But by December 1972, eight alleged members were on trial, all of them protesting their innocence. Four of them, John Barker, James Greenfield, Anna Mendleson and Hilary Creek, would receive ten-year prison sentences for conspiring to cause explosions.[34] The Angry Brigade's campaign was at an end, but, for better or worse, the consumer culture they had wanted to derail forged ahead.

Back at Biba, Barbara and Fitz had reopened within days. Like their takings, their plans for the boutique continued to grow, supported by a major deal with property magnate British Land and the Dorothy Perkins chain. In 1973, 'Big Biba' took over all seven floors of Derry & Toms' Art Deco building on Kensington High Street, including its famous roof garden. It was a far cry from the concept of the small, quirky, specialist boutique. Big Biba branched out big time, selling cosmetics, household goods, children's clothes, sports gear, furniture, paint, wallpaper and stationery, and offering a food hall and restaurant into the bargain.[35] It proved to be a step too far: Biba fell victim to recession and a bitter management dispute, closing its doors in 1975.

Other boutique entrepreneurs fared better in the mainstream market, taking their skills to the high-street chains. Sylvia Ayton went on to become head of design at Wallis. Lee Bender expanded Bus Stop, opening twelve stores around the country by the early 1970s before selling to French Connection in 1979.[36] But one store on the King's Road stuck two fingers up to the mainstream. In 1971, Vivienne Westwood and Malcolm McLaren opened Let It Rock, selling Fifties rocker gear, now considered vintage in its own right. Three years later, they moved on from biker leathers to bondage leathers, with added zips, chains and whips. They renamed the shop Sex and hired some new assistants, among them Sid Vicious and Glen Matlock. When nineteen-year-old John Lydon walked in one day wearing a slashed T-shirt with the slogan 'I hate Pink Floyd', the line-up for McLaren's band, the Sex Pistols, was complete. Chrissie Hynde, who was one of Sex's shopgirls along with glowering punk icon Jordan, tried to teach Lydon guitar but soon gave up. McLaren never disguised the fact that he'd created a band that pushed counter-culture to new extremes, in part to promote sales in the boutique.

A cultural world away, many of the grand department stores began to go under. London's shopping map was being redrawn. As well as Derry & Toms, neighbour Pontings sold up in Kensington. Gamages of Holborn and Gorringes of Victoria did the same and even Whiteley's, a store that had created so much stir in its day, could only limp on for a few more years. But if some old names were losers in these new times, others emerged as winners. In an era of dramatic takeovers and buyouts, the Debenhams group took over Swan & Edgar on Piccadilly and Marshall and Snelgrove on Oxford Street. House of Fraser became another national powerhouse, absorbing over fifty stores in locations across the country during the decade.[37]

New players, large and small, were joining the retail scrum. A change in immigration law in the late 1960s had encouraged the wives and families of many male migrants to settle in Britain while they still could. Asian women arriving from India, Pakistan, Bangladesh, Uganda and Kenya found work in many areas, but especially on assembly lines, in the garment and textile trades and – perhaps most visibly – in small family-run convenience stores. The Asian corner shop became part of countless shopping landscapes in towns and cities across Britain and, along the way, helped to launch a culinary revolution. These family stores also triggered a lasting change in retail's ethnic make-up. Until this point, shopwork had been largely 'white' work. Earlier generations of migrants from the Caribbean had rarely been taken on behind the counter. The story of this informal but powerful 'colour bar' remains fragmented, unrecorded in store archives and revealed only through personal stories like that of Esther Bruce. Esther was shockingly sacked as a seamstress at Barkers department store in Kensington in the early

1930s because a new manager decided he didn't want 'coloured people' working for him. Her Guyanan father and long-standing Fulham resident, Joseph Bruce, was so outraged he complained to his local MP, but to no avail.[38] In the decades that followed, other black women seeking shopwork were often told that there were 'no positions available';[39] others side-stepped discrimination by setting up stores of their own. Dorothy Owanabae, for example, was one of the first to sell cosmetics for black skin in the 1960s from her Kilburn-based business.[40] Half a century on, retail now has the most ethnically diverse workforce in the country.

In another landmark change with its roots in the 1960s, the large chains were beginning a migration of their own that would, in time, change our high streets for ever. Just as the department stores had shaken up late nineteenth-century shopkeeping, property developers were about to do the same. Arnold Hagenbach ran a major bakery business in Wakefield. His business partner, Sam Chippindale, was a Leeds estate agent. Together, these two Yorkshiremen formed the Arndale Group and set out to bring US-style covered shopping malls to British towns. They started in the north, persuading planning officials with straight talk and the promise of profitable business rates. The first Arndale Centre was built in Jarrow in 1961 and the largest was in Manchester, completed in the late Seventies. Altogether a further eighteen Arndale complexes would be built across the country, from Poole and Eastbourne on the south coast to Aberdeen in the north of Scotland, a blaze of modernist optimism.[41] Loved or loathed, they attracted big-name stores and quickly became part of the British shopping psyche.

The Arndale Group tended to favour town centres. Other developers, however, began to look further afield, eyeing up the profits to be made from a growing suburban population who now owned cars, fridges and freezers. In 1976, the Brent Cross shopping centre opened in a north London suburb. Britain's first out-of-town stand-alone shopping mall was built on top of a disused dog track, wasteland and much-loved allotment plots. Its location was sanctioned by the Greater London Council in an effort to ease West End traffic jams. Everything about it was immense. Covering 800,000 square feet over 52 acres, it employed over four thousand people. As in the Arndales, historic brands anchored this new venture: John Lewis, Fenwick, Waitrose, Marks & Spencer, W.H. Smith and Boots.[42]

The small-time shopkeepers in the surrounding areas – in Hendon, Barnet and Finchley – were very nervous of their new supersized neighbour and angry at the threat it posed to their livelihoods. Hendon traders were so outraged they were moved to resign en masse from the Barnet Chamber of Commerce and the latter's chairman faced a vote of no confidence.[43] Finchley traders organised a 'shop locally' campaign, but, very tellingly, they couldn't count on the support of their own local MP: one Margaret Thatcher.

Elected as leader of the Conservative opposition in 1975, Margaret Thatcher embraced Brent Cross and its enterprising spirit. She was a politician who understood shops. She had, famously, been brought up in one, living above the Roberts' family grocer's in Grantham and helping out behind the counter as a schoolgirl in the 1930s.

> Behind the counter there were three rows of splendid mahogany spice drawers with sparkling brass handles, and on top of these stood large, black, lacquered tea canisters. One of the tasks I sometimes shared was the weighing out of tea, sugar and biscuits from the sacks and boxes in which they arrived into 1lb and 2lb bags. In a cool back room we called 'the old bake house' hung sides of bacon which had to be boned and cut up for slicing. Wonderful aromas of spices, coffees and smoked hams would waft through the house.[44]

For all her apparently warm memories, Thatcher rarely returned to her 'boring' home town once she'd left for Oxford in 1943.[45] But her brand of Conservatism would always pull in two different directions – on the one hand, looking back to the traditional community values that had shaped her upbringing and, on the other, forwards to an unfettered free market that she believed held the key to future prosperity.

In February 1978 she made an official visit to Brent Cross where these two worlds momentarily collided. A brief note in the Thatcher Foundation archive records the event:

> MT was accompanied by Monty Modlyn, who lived in the area. The *Finchley Times*, 23 February 1978, reported an enthusiastic reception. MT played 'Michael, Row the Boat Ashore' on an electric organ at Minns Music Store, met Mrs Margaret Lyon who went to school with her in Grantham, and wrote 'Margaret Thatcher for No. 10' on a postcard. Another shopper handed her an Abba record for signature. Seeing the title – 'Take a Chance on Me' – MT observed, 'I think that's appropriate for a politician'. She revealed that the dress she was wearing came from Marks and Spencer when Marcus Sieff welcomed her to the local branch.[46]

As this tantalising note doesn't record it, we can only imagine the fleeting conversation between Mrs Thatcher and Mrs Lyon, her former classmate. Grantham was still a quiet market town, untouched by boutique counter-culture or concrete shopping precincts. What would its residents, and her grocer father in particular, have made of Brent Cross and the new Britain which had made it possible? Significantly, the archivist at the Thatcher Foundation has categorised the Brent Cross visit as 'trivial'. Perhaps it is, compared to the more momentous events documented in the collection. But Mrs Thatcher herself might beg to differ. More than most politicians of her day, she understood the place of shopping in many people's – especially women's – lives and played on it throughout her own political life. Married to a millionaire, she still knew how to work a crowd in an everyday M&S dress.

Shoplife shaped her politics. Concepts like value, choice, competition, prudence and, above all, service, were second nature to her. As she put it, 'Life "over the shop" is much more than a phrase. It is something which those who have lived it know to be quite distinctive. For one thing, you are always on duty. People would knock on the door at almost any hour of the night or weekend if they ran out of bacon, sugar, butter or eggs.' She learnt a sharp lesson from this: 'Everyone knew we lived by serving the customer; it was pointless to complain – and so nobody did.'[47] This Margaret would have had little sympathy for the earlier efforts of another – Margaret Bondfield, similarly steeped in shoplife, but a very different kind of political pioneer – to encourage shopworkers to stand up for their rights.

One right that Margaret Thatcher most certainly believed in was the 'right to buy'. She may have been the first to put it in those terms but she wasn't the first to see the appeal of the broad idea. Earlier generations of activists – on the left, on the right and in the co-op movement – had shared this basic belief. Badged in different ways, it had underpinned rival political platforms for over a century, from co-operatism and struggles for a 'living wage' to campaigns for free trade. Opinions differed sharply, of course, on the best and most practical ways to ensure that people across the social scale had 'enough' in their purses and pockets to buy not only the goods and services on which they depended but also those they desired.

The women working in Britain's post-war shops – from art-school boutiques to the all-encompassing Brent Cross – understood that they too 'lived by serving the customer'. But they also lived by leading the customer, helping to shape their needs and desires, their self-image and expectations. Ultimately, these shopgirls and their successors have played a vital part in creating a world in which the speed, scale and sensations of 'shopping' as we have known it have been utterly transformed.

EPILOGUE

Brent Cross marked the beginning of a new era of out-of-town buying, but it also opened in the midst of a dramatic decline in the number of Britain's shops. The move of many shoppers to out-of-town developments played a part in this, but it wasn't entirely to blame. While the total number of stores had peaked at nearly a million in the 1920s, it had been falling ever since. For a period after the Second World War, it looked as though the decline had slowed, but by the time that Margaret Thatcher played 'Row the Boat Ashore' in a Brent Cross music outlet, there were fewer than 400,000 stores in Britain.[1] Some researchers now predict that the total number will continue to shrink to 220,000 by 2018 as 'bricks' give way to 'clicks' with the inexorable rise of online retail. Shopping as we have known it is changing fast.

Retail gurus are alternately gung-ho and gloomy. Mary 'Queen of Shops' Portas has called for a radical overhaul of the high street. Her sparring partner, Bill Grimsey, former head of leading DIY and other chain stores, insists that her efforts are too little too late, given that around fifty independent businesses are closing each week and nearly one sixth of all retail space lies vacant. Meanwhile, the British already buy more online than any other country. Topshop

233

boss Philip Green was recently asked to offer some top tips to fellow traders and he put it bluntly: 'If you were starting out from scratch today, would you have shops at all?'[2] The William Whiteleys of today are more likely to begin with a website.

Surprisingly, in spite of this slow decline in the number of bricks-and-mortar shops, there have been plenty of job opportunities to be had in retail. Retail encompasses not just shopwork in physical stores, but employment in sales, store operations, security, management, buying and merchandising, and also distribution, e-commerce, finance and human resources. Taken together, retail remains Britain's largest private sector employer and makes up around 10 per cent of all jobs across the country.[3] Until now, while actual shops have been closing, shopwork has not been disappearing. With British people spending increasing amounts on consumer goods, the number of people employed in the sector reached an all-time high of 2.7 million in 2012, of which 1.7 million were women employed in sales and customer service.[4] These are our shopgirls and shopwomen of today.

As throughout the last 150 years, retail continues to employ a young workforce: one million of our shopworkers are under twenty-five years of age and over 40 per cent of all sixteen- to nineteen- year-olds in work are employed in this sector. It is also now a firmly female workforce. Over two thirds of our shopworkers are women – a figure unthinkable to those early nineteenth-century shopkeepers such as the Glaswegian provisions dealer who dismissed his 'Romantic Freak' shop assistant on discovering that 'he' was, in fact, 'of the feminine gender', and those hundreds of Victorian proprietors who fretted over opening up their craft to shopgirls.

Many aspects of retail have changed since those early days: basic working conditions, living-in, shopgirls' moral status as women in the public eye. Despite this, many shops still largely depend on low-paid workers willing to work flexible hours: school leavers and working mums. Today, as in the past, only a minority of the country's shopworkers belong to a trade union and in some respects working conditions have come full circle. In 1994, a century's worth of hard-won reforms were repealed at a stroke by the Deregulation Act, one of Prime Minister John Major's most far-reaching parting shots. The legislation annulled all previous Shop Acts, freeing up trading hours to meet our apparently insatiable consumer demand. Ever since then, large stores have been able to open for twenty-four hours Monday through Saturday and for six hours on a Sunday. Small stores face no restrictions at all and can, if they wish, open 24/7 for 365 days of the year, including Easter Sunday and Christmas Day. This has helped turn the majority of shop assistants into part-time workers. If Margaret Bondfield were alive today, she'd still be champing at the bit, trying to coax shop assistants to join a union, and fiercely championing shopworkers' rights to better pay and conditions.

However, it now looks like we are at a tipping point in terms of shopworker numbers too. For the first time in decades, the number of shop assistants seems likely to fall. Indeed, the job profile for 'Sales Assistant' on the government's National Careers Service website predicts a drop in the number of people employed in sales and customer service over the next five years – a drop linked to the combined effect of efficiencies, recession and the ongoing online revolution.[5] Mary Portas, who started out as a John Lewis Saturday girl before becoming one of the youngest members of the board of Harvey Nichols, believes that the stores that will survive these seismic shifts will be those that treat their staff with respect and offer customers not just expertise and value for money but an all-round experience.

For though sweeping change is afoot, we are still shopping and being served in physical shops. High streets may be losing ground but they still account for over 40 per cent of all consumer spending. Over the past two centuries shopping has become nothing less than our national past time and many will find it a hard habit to break.

Collectively, we still spend more time shopping than we do on any other single activity outside work – as much as eighteen hours a week according to one recent survey and a combined total of eight years of our lives, according to another.

Part of what drives us to do this, of course, is that we shop out of necessity for the food, clothes and other essentials that we cannot get any other way. After all, most of our nineteenth-century ancestors didn't become consumers for fun: if they were among the working poor, they became consumers to live. But along the way, together with the better-off, they found new pleasures and developed new kinds of sociability in and around shopping. And it's arguably these things that continue to draw so many of us to the shops today: we have strong emotional attachments to both the stores and, very often, the people who help us within them.

Shops suffuse our earliest memories.[6] As babies and children, it's quite likely that we spent a fair amount of time in and around shops for the simple reason that shopping is one of the few tasks that can be achieved with young children in tow. Beyond that, particular visits to specific shops are often markers of personal milestones: being taken to buy our first pair of shoes, school uniform, wristwatch or teenage party outfit; spending our first wage packet; choosing gifts for birthdays, engagements, weddings and retirements. Equally, being unable to afford to be part of these modern rituals of buying and giving can hurt and be a source of shame.

The fact that shopping allows us to give to others – and to give much more than formal gifts and presents – is hugely important. Everyday shopping is nothing less than an act of love.[7] Buying things for others – food, clothes, toys or treats – is an everyday way of showing we care, that we've thought about what others need or want. In effect, we 'say it through shopping'. To view consumer culture this way – as an intensely social part of life, built on relationships – is to challenge the more wearily familiar line that it is shallow, self-centred and individualizing. Perhaps the pursuit of small personal pleasures, alongside the promise of the 'experience', may yet keep our shopping rituals alive.

At one level, we still crave convenience and low prices over all other considerations. To that end, we will never come face to face with many of the 'shop assistants' who serve us from cavernous warehouses and distribution centres as we 'click and collect' in ever greater numbers. Where Amazon has led, big supermarkets, department stores, chains and many others have closely followed.

But convenience has never been everything. The Angry Brigade were certainly right that shopping was about spectacle. What they would never understand, however, is why so many shoppers – quite knowingly – lapped it up. On Regent Street in London today, for example, luxury stores are reinventing the shopping experience yet again and, as so often in the past, fashion is leading the charge. Modern shop assistants must work with, and alongside, interactive technologies, as well as being expert at good old-fashioned selling techniques. The Burberry store features a huge interactive screen, five hundred hidden speakers, a hydraulic stage and microchipped clothes. If they are so inclined, customers trying an outfit can check themselves out sashaying down an interactive catwalk. A few doors away, Karl Lagerfeld's store has iPads on its rails that help customers to assemble a complete look. Having made your selection and found the changing room, you can upload a 'selfie' featuring your new gear to the store's – and your own – social media streams. And the actual buying is more likely to happen later – on the customer's smartphone or tablet.

When Steve Jobs launched the world's first smartphone – Apple's iPhone – in 2007, he challenged customers to buy what they 'didn't know they wanted.'[8] Jobs knew that even some Apple devotees didn't quite get the point of this new device, but he also knew that this wouldn't matter in the least once they experienced what it had

237

to offer and what they could view – and acquire – in a few touches of the screen. He was right. In under a decade, smartphones have revolutionized retail. In the next five years, online purchases are predicted to account for a fifth of all UK sales and most of these will have been made on a mobile. You can, of course, buy a smartphone itself without setting foot in a real store, but Apple wants it both ways. Their new stores, like the one on Regent Street, have done away with conventional trappings – no counters, no checkouts. Almost the minute you cross the threshold, you will be greeted by one of a team of blue T-shirted assistants – all eager converts to the cause – and guided through what is certainly a new kind of 'experience', which may involve propping up the instore 'genius bar' for a time. Apple say that their assistants defy rigid definition. They are definitely not 'sales staff'. Instead they are 'people who love technology and people who love people' as well as 'musicians, photographers, mountain climbers, students and artists whose interests can't be defined by a job description'.

Apple's assertion brings the shopgirls' story full circle. Over the past 150 years, shopgirls have defied firm categorization, performing as servants, specialists, muses, models and much more besides in their everyday encounters with customers. These were young women with spirit and vim: from the pioneering wave of shopgirls entering drapery stores in Southport and Stourbridge in the 1860s to the Selfridges' "businesswomen", and arsonist suffragette Gladys Evans, from impoverished chain-store assistants stealing stockings in the 1930s to Chili Bouchier's journey from Harrods small ladies' department to star of the silver screen; and from the raw courage of Miss Austin during the Blitz to the Biba girls' glamorous embodiment of a hip brand, and Dorothy Owanabae selling cosmetics for black skin.

These women were all at the forefront of social change. Shopgirls have always been on the cutting edge – either in modernizing stores, with drapery and fashion leading the way, or sometimes more reluctantly dragged into the modern world in the grocery trade through technological and commercial advances, such as canning, refrigeration and self-service. Today, shopgirls continue to be key players in the constant reinvention of commerce, either as active agents or as embodiments of the new, reflecting the constant shifts in our consumer society. Take a trip to any kind of store – down the road, out of town or online – and you'll still see all this played out before you. Britain's shops, and the people who work in them, are doing nothing less than helping shape our sense of who we are, who we'd like to be and what we want from life.

ACKNOWLEDGEMENTS

Many wonderful people made this book possible. Lauren Bennie is a tenacious and talented researcher and we owe her a very great deal. We would like to thank those who believed in the idea from its inception, especially Sarah Rigby, Georgina Capel, Anita Land, Julian Alexander, Liz Warner, Lisette Black and Walter Iuzzolino. The book accompanies a BBC Two series made by betty and we are also indebted to all those who shaped each of the three episodes and lifted this story to the screen.

Lise Shapiro Sanders' book on shopgirls inspired us from the start. Anna Davin very generously shared her thoughts and research notes on nineteenth-century life and gave us many early leads. Many other academics shared valuable ideas, including Geoffrey Crossick, Leonore Davidoff, Peter Gurney, Sean Nixon, Lynne Pettinger, Laura Ugolini, Amanda Wilkinson and Mike Winstanley.

A host of archivists and curators helped us to unearth the experiences of shopworkers from within their amazing collections. In particular we'd like to thank Laura Outterside (Sainsbury's), Hannah Jenkinson (Marks & Spencer), Judy Faraday (John Lewis Partnership), Sebastian Wormell (Harrods), Janet Foster (Selfridges),

Jane Holt (London College of Fashion), Celia Joicey (Fashion & Textile Museum) and Polly Russell (British Library, Social Sciences) for their time, expertise and enthusiasm.

Our book research was funded by the Economic and Social Research Council (with particular thanks to Bruce Jackson) and the University of Essex. Our editor at Hutchinson, Sarah Rigby, kept us to a tight schedule and offered incisive comment and tireless support throughout. The British Library was a working haven, providing obscure texts, musical scores, digitized newspapers, a calm space and great cake.

Personal thanks from Annabel Hobley
I would like to thank the circle of support that has helped me with my children and home during the creation of this book and TV series, particularly wonderful grandparents John Hobley and Frances and Stephen O'Malley, and also Julia Frommhold. Also part of the circle are Emma Benson, Christopher Hobley and Rahila Hobley, Nicholas Hobley and Roberta Natalucci, Edward O'Malley, Frederike Helwig, Gordon Scott, Marie Hiller and Gloria Curpan. I have been inspired in her intellectual rigour by my mother, Uta von Tschurtschenthaler-Hobley – tragically no longer with us – and by my father, John Hobley, in his fascination for the minutiae of business, local history and working lives. Very special love and thanks to my husband, Thomas O'Malley, for his constant love and support, for his belief in me and for teaching me how to shop.

Personal thanks from Pamela Cox
Huge thanks and much love, as ever, to everyone who has kept me smiling and kept the domestic show on the road over the past year, especially my partner and trusted critic, Bill Hayton, and our children, Tess and Patrick Hayton; my sisters, Gill Knight and

Alison Johnson; my parents, Allan and Maureen Cox; my parents-in-law, Alec and Pat Hayton, and my colleagues and friends at the University of Essex.

NOTES

Chapter 1: The Girling of Shopwork

1. 'Romantic Freak of a Glasgow Girl of Sixteen', *Glasgow Daily Herald*, 20 July 1861.

2. Hudson, Derek, ed., *Man of Two Worlds: The Life and Diaries of Arthur J. Munby, 1828–1910*, London: John Murray, 1972, vol. 8, 2 June 1861, pp.192–204.

3. *Victorian Townscape: The Work of Samuel Smith*, compiled by Michael Millward and Brian Coe, London: Ward Lock, 1974.

4. Geoffrey Crossick, social historian of nineteenth- and twentieth-century Britain and Europe: research conversation with Pamela Cox.

5. John Copeman & Sons, *Copeman's of Norwich 1879–1946*, Norwich: Jarrold & Sons, 1946, p.23.

6. Lee Holcombe, *Victorian Ladies at Work: Middle-Class Working Women in England and Wales, 1850–1914*, Newton Abbot: David and Charles, 1973, p.104.

7. John Tallis, *London Street Views 1838–40 and 1847*, London: London Topographical Society, 1969.

8. Francis Wey, *Les Anglais Chez Eux (A Frenchman Sees the*

English in the Fifties), London: Sidgwick & Jackson, 1935.

9. Lady Jeune, 'The Ethics of Shopping', *Fortnightly Review*, vol. 63, January 1895, p.123.

10. Ibid., p.124.

11. William Ablett, *Reminiscences of an Old Draper*, London: S. Low, Marston, Searle and Rivington, 1876, p.9.

12. Lise Shapiro Sanders, *Consuming Fantasies: Labor, Leisure, and the London Shopgirl, 1880–1920*, Columbus: Ohio State University Press, 2006, p.24.

13. Obituary of Jessie Boucherett, *The Times*, 21 October 1905.

14. 'Association for Promoting the Employment of Women', *English Woman's Journal*, vol. 4, September 1859, p.57.

15. Ibid.

16. Ibid., p.56.

17. 'On the Obstacles to the Employment of Women', *English Woman's Journal*, vol. 4, February 1860.

18. Simon Gunn and Rachel Bell, *Middle Classes: Their Rise and Sprawl*, London: Phoenix, 2003, p.18.

19. Quoted in Holcombe, *Victorian Ladies at Work*, p.4.

20. Thomas Austin Bullock, *Bradshaw's Descriptive Guide to Manchester & Surrounding Districts*, Manchester: Bradshaw & Blacklock, 1857, p.57.

21. For extended discussion, see Erica Rappaport, '"The Hall of Temptation": Gender, Politics and the Construction of the Department Store in Late Victorian London', *Journal of British Studies*, vol. 35, no. 1, January 1996, pp.62–4.

22. 'Success in Business: How the Late Mr Whiteley Made his Fortune', *The Daily Chronicle*, 25 January 1907.

23. Linda Stratmann, *Whiteley's Folly: The Life and Death of a Salesman*, Stroud: Sutton, 2004, p.25.

24. *London Magazine*, vol. 9, September/October 1902, pp.189–92.

25. 'A Commercial Eutopia', *Essex Weekly News*, 3 November 1876.

26. Rappaport, 'The Hall of Temptation', *Journal of British Studies*, vol. 35, pp.58–83.

27. Robert Storch (ed.), *Popular Culture and Custom in Nineteenth-Century England*, London: Croom Helm, 1982, p.74.

28. *Bayswater Chronicle*, 11 November 1876 (known as the *Paddington, Kensington, and Bayswater Chronicle* until 1875).

29. 'More Whiteleyana! Cheap Meat!', *Bayswater Chronicle*, 10 March 1877.

30. 'Local Gossip', *Bayswater Chronicle*, 26 March 1881.

31. Harrods, *A Story of British Achievement: 1849–1949*, London: Harrods, 1949; and Bill Lancaster, *The Department Store: A Social History*, London: Leicester University Press, 1995, p.22.

32. Lancaster, *The Department Store*, p.195.

33. Holcombe, *Victorian Ladies at Work*, p.104.

34. Hudson, *Man of Two Worlds*, vol. 12, 22 February 1862, p.142.

35. Ibid, vol. 8, 2 June 1861, pp.192–204.

36. Hudson, *Man of Two Worlds*, vol. 8, 2 June 1861, pp.192–204.

37. Thomas Darlington (ed.), *Memoir of Emerson Muschamp Bainbridge of Newcastle-on-Tyne*, Edinburgh: R & R Clark, 1893, pp.15–16.

38. Lancaster, *The Department Store*, p.181.

39. 1882 [C 3183] Report of the Chief Inspector of Factories and Workshops to Her Majesty's Principal Secretary of State for the Home Department, for the year ending 31st October 1881, p.35.

40. Peter Sell and Gina Murrell, *Flora of Great Britain and Ireland*, Cambridge: Cambridge University Press, 2006, vol. 4, p.78.

41. Lancaster, *The Department Store*, p.31.

42. Christopher Hosgood, '"Mercantile Monasteries": Shops, Shop Assistants, and Shop Life in Late-Victorian and Edwardian Britain', *Journal of British Studies*, vol. 38, no. 3, July 1999, pp.324–5.

43. *The Drapers Record* (26 Nov. 1875, 1 Feb. 1878, 8 Feb. 1878), quoted in Hosgood, 'Mercantile Monasteries', p.345.

44. 'Life Behind the Counter', *Young Woman*, January 1893, p.128.

45. Hudson, *Man of Two Worlds*, vol. 8, 2 June 1861, pp.192–204.

46. 'Women Who Work Behind a Counter', *Cassell's Magazine*, vol. 9, 1874, p.349–51.

47. Hudson, *Man of Two Worlds*, vol. 12, 22 February 1862, p.142.

48. *City Press*, 20 August 1870.

49. Holcombe, *Victorian Ladies at Work*, pp.18, 106: between 1861 and 1911 the number of female shopworkers increased by 319 per cent, the number of male shopworkers by 118 per cent.

50. Jeune, 'The Ethics of Shopping', *Fortnightly Review*, vol. 63, p.126.

51. Holcombe, *Victorian Ladies at Work*, p.107.

52. Miss Fowle, March 1921, miscellaneous unmarked box of short histories at Harrods Store Archive, quoted in Erika Rappaport, *Shopping for Pleasure: Women in the Making of London's West End*, Chichester: Princeton University Press, 2000, p.201.

53. 'Miss Fowle', *Harrodian Gazette*, vol. 3, no. 6, 4 June 1915, pp.14–15.

Chapter 2: Servants of the Counter

1. Margaret Bondfield, *A Life's Work*, London: Hutchinson & Co., 1948, p.24.

2. John Benson, *The Working Class in Britain 1850–1939*, London: Longman, 1989, p.24; Elizabeth Roberts, *Women's Work 1840–1940*, Basingstoke: Macmillan, 1988, p.34; 1891 census report for England and Wales.

3. William Ablett, *Reminiscences of an Old Draper*, London: S. Low, Marston, Searle and Rivington, 1876.

4. Bill Lancaster, *The Department Store: A Social History*, Leicester: Leicester University Press, 1995, p.126.

5. Miss Fowle, March 1921, miscellaneous unmarked box of short histories at Harrods Store Archive, quoted in Erika Rappaport, *Shopping for Pleasure: Women in the Making of London's West End*, Chichester: Princeton University Press, 2000, p.201.

6. Anna Davin, 'City Girls: Young Women, New Employment, and the City: London, 1880–1910', in Mary Jo Maynes, Birgitte Soland and Christina Benninghaus (eds.), *Secret Gardens, Satanic Mills: Placing Girls in European History, 1750–1960*, Bloomington: Indiana University Press, 2005.

7. Lee Holcombe, *Victorian Ladies at Work: Middle-Class Working Women in England and Wales, 1850–1914*, Newton Abbot: David and Charles, 1973, p.114.

8. Lancaster, *The Department Store*, pp.130–1; Jan Whitaker, *The Department Store: History, Design, Display,* London: Thames & Hudson, 2011, p.31.

9. Richard S. Lambert, *The Universal Provider: A Study of William Whiteley and the Rise of the London Department Store*, London: Harrap, 1938, pp.152–3; see also Richard Patterson, 'The Cost of Living in 1888', The Victorian Web, www.victorianweb. org/economics/wages4.html (accessed 25 March 2014).

10. 'Why is Whiteley's so often burned down?', *The Pall Mall Gazette*, 16 August 1887.

11. Holcombe, *Victorian Ladies at Work*, p.113.

12. Philip Christopher Hoffman, *They Also Serve: The Story of the Shop Worker*, London: Porcupine Press, 1949, p.24.

13. Bondfield, *A Life's Work*, p.25.

14. 'Disgraceful Affair at Cardiff', *The Drapers Record*, 10 January 1887, p.421.

15. Lambert, *The Universal Provider*, p.75.

16. Holcombe, *Victorian Ladies at Work*, p.114.

17. Henry Mayhew, *The Shops and Companies of London and the Trades and Manufactories of Great Britain*, London: 1865, p.5.

18. Bondfield, *A Life's Work*, p.62; also cited in Holcombe, *Victorian Ladies at Work*, p.109.

19. 'Women Who Work – Behind a Counter', *Cassell's Magazine*, vol. 9, November 1873, p.349.

20. Mark Patton, *Science, Politics, and Business in the Work of Sir John Lubbock: A Man of Universal Mind*, Aldershot: Ashgate, 2007; R.J. Pumphrey, 'The Forgotten Man: Sir John Lubbock, F.R.S.', *Notes and Records of the Royal Society of London*, vol. 13, no. 1, June 1958, pp.49–58; Ursula Lubbock Grant Duff, *The Life-work of Lord Avebury (Sir John Lubbock), 1834–1913*, London: Watts and Co., 1924.

21. Letter to the editor, 'The Shop Hours Regulation Bill', *The Spectator*, 26 July 1873, p.13 (a response to this letter identifies Boucherett as the author).

22. Letter to the editor, *The Spectator*, 26 July 1873, p.13. See also 'The Nine Hours Bill and the Shop Hours Regulation Bill', *Englishwoman's Review*, 1873, pp.209–12.

23. Holcombe, *Victorian Ladies at Work*, p.125.

24. Dr Arthur Edis, 'Slavery in the West-End', Letter to the Editor, *The Times*, 7 November 1878, p.9; Mrs Strange Butson, 'The Standing Evil – A plea for shopgirls', *The Girl's Own Paper*, vol. 1, 1880, p.612.

25. 'Lecture at National Health Society on London Shopwomen

– Letter to Dr Edis', *House and Home*, 29 March 1879, p.10.

26. Joseph Chitty and John Mounteney Lely, *The Statutes of Practical Utility, 1235–1895*, London: Sweet and Maxwell, 1902, p.809.

27. Thomas Sutherst, *Death and Disease Behind the Counter*, London: Kegan Paul, Trench and Co., 1884, pp.20–22.

28. Ibid., pp.135–6.

29. Select Committee on the Shop Hours Regulation Bill, Parliamentary Papers, vol. IXX, 1886, p.102.

30. Richard Foster, *F. Cape & Co. of St Ebbe's Street, Oxford*, Oxford: Oxford City and County Museum, 1973 [not paginated].

31. Mrs Loftie, *Social Twitters*, London: Macmillan and Co., 1879, p.144.

32. *Social Notes*, 6 April 1878, p.93.

33. Jane Rendell, '"Industrious Females" and "Professional Beauties", Or, Fine Articles for Sale in the Burlington Arcade', in Iain Borden et al. (eds.), *Strangely Familiar: Narratives of Architecture in the City*, London: Routledge, 1996, pp.32–6.

34. Ibid.

35. Amanda Wilkinson, 'Women and Occupations in the Census of England and Wales: 1851–1901', unpub. Ph.D. thesis, University of Essex, 2012.

36. Ibid.

37. *Reynolds's Newspaper*, issue 79, 15 February 1852. With thanks to Amanda Wilkinson.

38. Sir William Acton, *Prostitution: Its Moral, Social and Sanitary Aspects*, London: J. Churchill, 1857, p.64.

39. William Tait, *Magdalenism: An Inquiry into the Extent, Causes and Consequences of Prostitution in Edinburgh*, Edinburgh: 1840, p.146.

40. 'The Great Social Question Revived', *The Morning Post*, 11 January 1859, p.5.

41. Judith Walkowitz, *Prostitution and Victorian Society*, Cambridge: Cambridge University Press, 1980.

42. *Manchester Times*, 20 August 1887, p.16. With thanks to Amanda Wilkinson.

43. 'The Black Flag Hoisted in Regent Street', *The Pall Mall Gazette*, 8 July 1887.

44. 'Intemperance and Immorality', Letter to the Editor, *Reynolds's Newspaper*, 26 September 1886, p.2. With thanks to Amanda Wilkinson.

Chapter 3: Scandalous Shopgirls

1. 'The Whiteley Tragedy', *The Daily Chronicle*, 28 January 1907.

2. Linda Stratmann, *Whiteley's Folly: The Life and Death of a Salesman*, London: The History Press, 2004, pp.109–117.

3. Royal Commission on the Ancient and Historic Monuments of Scotland, http://canmore.rcahms.gov.uk/en/site/115649/digital_images/edinburgh+47+48+49+50+51+52+princes+street+jenners/?show=all (accessed 21 February 2014).

4. Anthony Trollope, *London Tradesmen*, London: E. Mathews & Marrot, 1928, reprinted from *The Pall Mall Gazette*, 1880.

5. Zuzanna Shonfield, *The Precariously Privileged: a professional family in Victorian London*, Oxford: Oxford University Press, 1987, p.44.

6. Osbert Lancaster, *All From Memory*, Cambridge, Mass.: John Murray, 1953, pp.62–9.

7. Henry Mayhew, *London Labour and the London Poor, Volume 1: The London Street Folk*, London: 1861–2 (a portion duplicate of 1851 edition), index for first 5 vols., pp.478–9.

8. John Thomson and Adolphe Smith, *Street Life in London*, London: S. Low, Marston, Searle and Rivington, 1877, auctioned 7 November 2001, see lib–161.lse.ac.uk/archives/digital/street_life_in_london.pdf. See *Telegraph*, 6 November 2013, p.21, or www.telegraph.co.uk/culture/art/artsales/10428053/The-world-of-Charles-Dickens-lives-on-in-Street-Life-in-London.html (accessed 3 March 2014).

9. 'Resting-Places for Women Wayfarers', *Women's Gazette* and *Weekly News*, 3 July 1878, p.100.

10. Harriet Jordan, 'Public Parks, 1885–1914', *Garden History*, vol. 22, no. 3, 1994, p.89.

11. Bill Lancaster, *The Department Store: A Social History*, London: Leicester University Press, 1995, pp.25–8.

12. 'Paddington Licensing Meeting', *Bayswater Chronicle*, 23 March 1872; see extended discussion in Erica Rappaport, '"The Halls of Temptation": Gender, Politics and the Construction of the Department Store in Late Victorian London', *Journal of British Studies*, vol. 35, no. 1, January 1996, pp.67–75.

13. 'Lunch with the Linendrapers', *The Graphic*, 3 August 1872, p.98.

14. Eliza Linton, 'The Girl of the Period', *Saturday Review*, 14 March 1868, pp.339–40.

15. Eliza Linton, 'The Philosophy of Shopping', *Saturday Review*, 16 October 1875, pp.488–9.

16. William Ablett, *Reminiscences of an Old Draper*, London: S. Low, Marston, Searle and Rivington, 1876, p.36.

17. Charles Cavers, *Hades! The Ladies! Being Extracts from the Diary of a Draper, Charles Cavers, Esq.*, London: Gurney & Jackson, 1933.

18. Lancaster, *The Department Store*, p.185.

19. *London Standard*, 21 January 1885.

20. Answers section, *The Girl's Own Paper*, December 1886, p.192.

21. Judith Coffin, *The Politics of Women's Work: The Paris Garment Trades, 1750–1915*, Chichester: Princeton University Press, 1996, p.89.

22. 'Women Who Work Behind a Counter', *Cassell's Magazine*, vol. 9, 1874, p.351.

23. J.E. Davidson, *What Our Daughters Can Do for Themselves*, London: Smith, Elder & Co., 1894, pp.49–51.

24. Sanders, *Consuming Fantasies*, p.28.

25. 'Women Who Work Behind a Counter', *Cassell's Magazine*, vol. 9, 1874, p.350.

26. 'Crib-hunting', *Cassell's Saturday Journal*, 2 April 1910.

27. Anthea Jarvis, *Liverpool Fashion, Its Makers and Wearers: The Dressmaking Trade in Liverpool, 1830–1940*, Liverpool: Merseyside County Museums, 1981, p.34.

28. Lucy Duff Gordon, *Discretions and Indiscretions*, London: Jarrolds, 1932, p.67.

29. For extended discussion, see Joel Kaplan and Sheila Stowell, *Theatre and Fashion: Oscar Wilde to the Suffragettes*, Cambridge: Cambridge University Press, 1994, p.116.

30. *Bystander*, 27 July 1904, pp.437–8.

31. Duff Gordon, *Discretions and Indiscretions*, p.77.

32. 'Rev. J. Campbell's Libel on the West-End Trade', *The Drapers Record*, 9 January 1909, pp.96–7.

33. Lancaster, *The Department Store*, p.181.

34. Sanders, *Consuming Fantasies*, p.159.

35. 'Careers for Women', *Forget-Me-Not*, 12 December 1903, p.661.

36. *Forget-Me-Not*, 23 August 1902, p.368.

37. 'Life in the Shop: A Word on Living in. No Married Man Need Apply, by Our Special Commissioner', *The Daily*

Chronicle, 24 February 1898.

38. Dora Day column, *The Shop Assistant: A Monthly Journal of Shop Life, Social Advancement and Reform*, vol. 2., no. 13, July 1897, p.7.

39. Agnes Repplier, 'English Railway Fiction', in *Points of View*, Boston: Houghton and Mifflin, 1891, pp.209–10.

40. Arthur Applin, *Shop Girls: A Novel with Purpose*, London: Mills & Boon, 1914.

41. Francis Bacon, 'Of Studies', in Michael Kiernan (ed.), *The Essayes or Counsels, Civill and Morall*, Oxford: Clarendon, 1985, p.153.

42. Lady Laura Ridding. 'What Should Women Read?', *Woman at Home*, 37, 1896, p.29. Cited in Kate Flint, *The Woman Reader*, Oxford: Clarendon, 1993, p.52.

43. Geo Humphrey, 'The Reading of the Working Classes in the Nineteenth Century', *Nineteenth Century*, vol. 33, April 1893 pp.692–3.

44. For extended discussion, see Sanders, *Consuming Fantasies*, Chapter 4.

45. Dr Mary Wood-Allen, *What a Young Woman Ought to Know*, Philadelphia: Vir Publishing Co., 1905.

46. M. J. Loftie, *Social Twitters*, London: Macmillan and Co., 1879, p.44.

47. Sanders, *Consuming Fantasies*, footnote 28, p.241.

48. William Archer, *The Theatrical 'World' of 1896*, London: Walter Scott, 1897.

49. Mario Borsa, *The English Stage of To-Day*, London: John Lane, 1908, p.5.

50. Sanders, *Consuming Fantasies*, p.182.

51. *Old Bailey Proceedings Online* (www.oldbaileyonline.org, version 7.0, accessed 21 February 2014), Whiteley inquest, 18 March 1907 (t19070318-31), testimony of Mrs Elizabeth

Lloyd, Horace Rayner's wife's aunt.

52. Ibid., testimony of George McConnell, messenger to an umbrella-maker.

53. Ibid., testimony of Dr Herbert Ernest Batten, casualty surgeon at St Mary's Hospital.

Chapter 4: Grace Dare Undercover

1. Margaret Bondfield, *A Life's Work*, London: Hutchinson & Co., 1948, p.28.

2. Hilda Martindale, *From One Generation to Another, 1839–1944: A Book of Memoirs*, London: George Allen & Unwin, 1944, pp.34–5.

3. Bondfield, *A Life's Work*, p.32.

4. 'Life in the Shop: Crib Hunting. Extracts from an Assistant's Diary, by Our Special Commissioner', *The Daily Chronicle*, 10 February 1898.

5. Bondfield, *A Life's Work*, p.63.

6. Grace Dare, 'Our Women's Page', *The Shop Assistant*, August 1896, p.7.

7. 'Life in the Shop: A Word on Living in. No Married Man Need Apply, by Our Special Commissioner', *The Daily Chronicle*, 24 February 1898.

8. Ibid.

9. 'Usdaw's History', Usdaw, www.usdaw.org.uk/aboutus/usdawshistory.aspx (accessed 20 March 2014).

10. *Fabian Tract No. 80*, London: The Fabian Society, 1897, pp.11–12.

11. Bondfield, *A Life's Work*, p.29.

12. Ibid., p.51.

13. 'Miss Bondfield on Tour', *The Shop Assistant*, July 1898, p.3.

14. 'Life in the Shop: The Woes of a Forgotten Class, by Our Special Commissioner', *The Daily Chronicle*, 4 February 1898, p.8.

15. Ibid.

16. 'Miss Bondfield on Tour', *The Shop Assistant*, p.3.

17. Marilyn French, *From Eve to Dawn: Infernos and Paradises, the Triumph of Capitalism in the Nineteenth Century*, New York: Feminist Press, 2008, p.283.

18. Mary Agnes Hamilton, *Margaret Bondfield*, London: Leonard Parsons, 1924, pp.95–6.

19. Nicole Robertson, *The Co-operative Movement and Communities in Britain, 1914–1960: Minding Their Own Business*, Farnham: Ashgate 2010; Peter Gurney, *Co-operative Culture and the Politics of Consumption in England, 1870–1930*, Manchester: Manchester University Press, 1996; Michael Winstanley, *The Shopkeeper's World, 1830–1914*, Manchester: Manchester University Press, 1983, p.36.

20. George Jacob Holyoake, *Self-Help by the People: History of the Rochdale Equitable Pioneers, Part 1, 1844–1857*, London: Swan Sonnenschein & Co., 1907, p.41.

21. Winstanley, *The Shopkeeper's World*, pp.87–8; C.P. Hosgood, 'The "Pigmies of Commerce" and the Working-Class Community: Small Shopkeepers in England, 1870–1914', *Journal of Social History*, vol. 22, issue 3, 1989, pp.439–60.

22. Alison Adburgham, 'Introduction', *Army and Navy, Yesterday's Shopping: The Army & Navy Stores Catalogue 1907*, Newton Abbot: David & Charles Ltd, 1969.

23. Jean Gaffin and David Thoms, *Caring and Sharing: The Centenary History of the Co-operative Women's Guild*, Manchester: Holyoake Books, 1993, p.48.

24. Grace Dare, 'Our Women's Page', *The Shop Assistant*, August 1898, p.32.

25. Harris's report was discussed in Grace Dare, 'Some Resolutions for the New Year', *The Shop Assistant*, January 1898, p.129. See also Robertson, *The Co-operative Movement*.

26. Muriel Jeffs, 'Margaret Llewelyn Davies and the Women's Co-operative Guild', in Bill Lancaster and Paddy Maguire (eds.), *Towards the Co-operative Commonwealth: Essays in the History of Co-operation*, Loughborough: Co-operative College, 1996; Gillian Scott, *Feminism and the Politics of Working Women: The Women's Co-operative Guild, 1880s to the Second World War*, London: UCL Press, 1998.

27. 'Good Food Cheap', *Daily News*, 1903, and 'The Opening', *Co-operative News*, October 1902, p.4, both in COLL MISC 0268: Women's Co-operative Guild: Sunderland Scrapbook 2, London School of Economics, Women's Library Archive.

28. Philip Christopher Hoffman, *They Also Serve: The Story of the Shop Worker*, London: Porcupine Press, 1949, pp.48–9.

29. Ibid., p.54.

30. Dare, 'Some Resolutions for the New Year'.

31. Cicely Hamilton, *Diana of Dobson's. A Romantic Comedy in Four Acts*, London: Century, 1909, Act 1, Scene 1.

32. Bondfield, *A Life's Work*, p.72. For commentary and contemporary reviews, see Diane F. Gillespie and Doryjane Birrer, *Diana of Dobson's*, Ontario: Broadview Press, 2003.

33. Richard Foster, *F. Cape & Co. of St Ebbe's Street, Oxford*, Oxford: Oxford City and County Museum, 1973; Angela Airey and John Airey, *The Bainbridges of Newcastle: A Family History 1679–1976* [imprint unknown], 1979, pp.67, 115; David Wyn Davies, *Owen Owen: Victorian Draper*, Aberystwyth: Gwasg Cambria, 1983, p.80; Robertson, *The Co-operative Movement*.

34. Winstanley, *The Shopkeeper's World*, pp.96–100.

35. *Harrodian Gazette*, 1909–13. For a longer discussion see

Lise Shapiro Sanders, *Consuming Fantasies: Labor, Leisure, and the London Shopgirl, 1880–1920*, Columbus: Ohio State University Press, 2006, ch. 2.

36. Gordon Honeycombe, *Selfridges: Seventy-Five Years, The Story of the Store 1909–1984*, London: Park Lane Press, 1984, p.186.

37. Winstanley, *The Shopkeeper's World*, pp.72–3.

38. Philip Snowden, *The Living Wage*, London: Hodder and Stoughton, 1912, p.35.

39. Mrs Carl Meyer and Clementina Black, *Makers of Our Clothes: A Case for Trade Boards, Being the Result of a Year's Investigation into the Work of Women in London in the Tailoring, Dressmaking and Underclothing Trades*, London: Duckworth and Co., 1909, pp.15–17.

40. Ibid., pp.17–18.

41. Ibid., p.190.

42. Ibid., p.184.

43. Hansard, House of Commons, vol. 155, col. 1888, 24 April 1906. See also James Thompson, 'Political Economy, Labour and the Minimum Wage', in Ewen Green and Duncan Tanner (eds.), *The Strange Survival of Liberal England*, Cambridge: Cambridge University Press, 2007, pp.62–8.

44. Scott, *Feminism and the Politics of Working Women*, pp.100–101.

45. Hoffman, *They Also Serve*, p.78.

46. Ibid., pp.82–3.

47. Ibid., p.58.

48. James Kenyon and Sagar Mitchell, *Mitchell and Kenyon 484: Crewe Hospital Procession and Pageant*, Blackburn: Mitchell & Kenyon, 1907, held at the British Film Institute, London.

49. *Votes for Women*, 1 October 1908, p.5.

50. Diane Atkinson, *Votes for Women: Women and the Suffrage Movement*, Cambridge: Cambridge University Press, 1988, p.27.

51. Elizabeth Crawford, *The Women's Suffrage Movement in Britain*

and Ireland: A Regional Survey, London: Routledge, 2000, pp.90, 132.

52. Christabel Pankhurst, *Unshackled: The Story of How We Won the Vote*, London: Hutchinson, 1959, pp.43–4.

53. Crawford, *The Women's Suffrage Movement*, p.387; Martindale, *From One Generation to Another*, pp.34, 35, 172.

54. Molly Housego and Neil R. Storey, *The Women's Suffrage Movement*, Oxford: Shire Library, 2012, p.34.

55. Women's Social and Political Union, Handbill, March 1912.

56. 'Citizens, Awake!', *Votes for Women*, 8 March 1912; Patricia Greenwood Harrison, *Connecting Links: The British and American Woman Suffrage Movements, 1900–1914*, Westport, Conn.: Greenwood, 2000, p.165.

57. Notes on Alice Ker's and Alice Davies' court appearances, Harrods Store Archive, April 1912.

58. *Irish Times*, 19 July 1912.

59. Letter published in *Votes for Women*, 6 September 1912.

60. Housego and Storey, *The Women's Suffrage Movement*, p.46.

Chapter 5: Thoroughly Modern Management

1. David Wyn Davies, *Owen Owen: Victorian Draper*, Aberystwyth: Gwasg Cambria, 1983, p.18.

2. Ibid., p.22.

3. 'American Business Methods', *The Drapers Record*, 21 July 1906, p.153.

4. Susan Porter Benson, *Counter Cultures: Saleswomen, Managers, and Customers in American Department Stores 1890–1940*, Urbana: University of Illinois Press, 1986, p.231.

5. Ibid., pp.128–9.

6. Davies, *Owen Owen*, p.119.

7. 'American versus English Shopping', *The Drapers Record*, 28 April 1906, p.185.

8. For extended discussion, see Mica Nava, *Visceral Cosmopolitanism: Gender, Culture and the Normalisation of Difference*, New York: Berg, 2007, pp.41–54.

9. 'American Business Methods', *The Drapers Record*, 21 July 1906, p.153.

10. Michael Winstanley, *The Shopkeeper's World, 1830–1914*, Manchester: Manchester University Press, 1983, p.120.

11. Bill Lancaster, *The Department Store: A Social History*, London: Leicester University Press, 1995, p.195.

12. Winstanley, *The Shopkeeper's World*, pp.127–32.

13. Christopher Hosgood, '"Mercantile Monasteries": Shops, Shop Assistants, and Shop Life in Late-Victorian and Edwardian Britain', *Journal of British Studies*, vol. 38, no. 3, July 1999, p.336.

14. Joseph Lewis della-Porta, *Manchester House, Guest's Hosier and Draper*, Shropshire Archives.

15. Winstanley, *The Shopkeeper's World*, p.12.

16. G.K. Chesterton, 'The Big Shop', *Daily News*, 27 January 1912.

17. H.G. Selfridge, Selfridge Editorial (Selfridge's syndicated daily press column), 31 January 1912.

18. *Daily Express*, 1 February 1912.

19. *Daily News*, 2 February 1912.

20. Olivia [surname unknown], *Olivia's Shopping and How She Does It: A Prejudiced Guide to the London Shops*, London: Gay and Bird, 1906, p.80.

21. Gordon Honeycombe, *Selfridges: Seventy-Five Years: The Story of the Store 1909–1984*, London: Park Lane Press, 1984, pp.37–42.

22. Honeycombe, *Selfridges*, p.233.

23. Lindy Woodhead, *Shopping, Seduction & Mr Selfridge*, London: Profile Books, 2007, p.96.

24. Harry Gordon Selfridge, 'Spirit of the House', and other items from the Selfridges Archives Collection.

25. From HAT (History of the Advertising Trust Archive, Norwich), cited in Lise Shapiro Sanders, *Consuming Fantasies: Labor, Leisure, and the London Shopgirl 1880–1920*, Columbus: Ohio State University Press, 2006.

26. Sanders, *Consuming Fantasies*, p.79.

27. Honeycombe, *Selfridges*, p.189, and Selfridges Archives Collection.

28. Olive Christian Malvery, *A Year and a Day*, London: Hutchinson, 1912, p.151.

29. Susan Frances Lomax, 'The Department Store and the Creation of the Spectacle 1880–1940', Colchester: University of Essex, Ph.D. thesis, 2005, p.124.

30. 'Crowds and Shop Windows', *The Times*, 2 November 1910, p.8.

31. Lomax, 'The Department Store', p.50.

32. *Bainbridge*, 524/J/1, Doc 524 E2 Manuscript, Walter Brittain c.1948, John Lewis Partnership Archives Collection, quoted in Lomax, *The Department Store* [no page number].

33. 'The European Crisis', *The Drapers Record*, 8 August 1914, p.269.

34. 'Meeting to Maintain Home Trade', *The Drapers Record*, 28 August 1914, p.366.

35. 'Trade Recruits', *The Drapers Record*, 5 September 1914.

36. Michael Moss and Alison Turton, *A Legend of Retailing – House of Fraser*, London: Weidenfeld & Nicolson, 1989, p.108.

37. Philip Christopher Hoffman, *They Also Serve: The Story of the Shop Worker*, London: Porcupine Press, 1949, p.180.

38. Peter Cox, *Spedan's Partnership: The Story of John Lewis and Waitrose*, London: Labatie Books, 2010, p.17.

39. Hoffman, *They Also Serve*, quoting John Lewis employee Mr

L.R. Pritchard, p.182.

40. John Spedan Lewis, *Partnership for All*, London: Kerr-Cross Publishing Co., 1948, pp.5–10.

41. Grancey, Jonathan, *A Very British Revolution: 150 Years of John Lewis*, London: Laurence King Publishing, 2014, p.49.

42. John Spedan Lewis, 'Dear to My Heart', BBC Radio broadcast, 15 April 1957.

43. Jon Henley, 'Is John Lewis the Best Company in Britain to work for?', *Guardian*, 16 March 2010.

44. Spedan Lewis, *Partnership for All*, p.xv.

45. Cox, *Spedan's Partnership*, p.47.

46. *The Gazette*, 1967, John Lewis Partnership Archives Collection.

47. Lewis, *Partnership for All*, pp.32–5.

48. Chili Bouchier, *Shooting Star*, London: Atlantis, 1995, p.28.

49. Karen Hunt, 'Negotiating the Boundaries of the Domestic: British Socialist Women and Politics of Consumption', *Women's History Review*, 2000, vol. 9, no. 2, p.404.

50. Deborah Thom, 'Women and Work in Wartime Britain', in Richard Wall and Jay Winter (eds.), *The Upheaval of War*, Cambridge: Cambridge University Press, 1988, pp.302–6; Appendix 11.1, p.318.

51. SA/WAR/1/1: WW1 female staff recruitment letter template [1914-1918], The Sainsbury Archive, Museum of London Docklands.

52. John Burnett, *Useful Toil: Autobiographies of Working People from the 1820s to the 1920s*, London: Allen Lane, 1974, pp.115–24.

53. Winstanley, *The Shopkeeper's World*, p.133.

54. Margaret Bondfield, *A Life's Work*, London: Hutchinson & Co., 1948, ch.10.

55. Lilian Wyles, *A Woman at Scotland Yard*, London: Faber & Faber, 1952.

Chapter 6: Strike!

1. Deborah Thom, *Nice Girls and Rude Girls: Women Workers in World War One*, Cambridge: Cambridge University Press, 1998, pp.188–93.

2. Olivia [surname unknown], *Olivia's Shopping and How She Does It. A Prejudiced Guide to the London Shops*, London: Gay and Bird, 1906, p.40.

3. Philip Christopher Hoffman, *They Also Serve: The Story of the Shop Worker*, London: Porcupine Press, 1949, p.171.

4. Ibid., pp.175–6.

5. 'Shop Girls' Strike', *Daily Mail*, 27 April 1920, p.5.

6. Peter Cox, *Spedan's Partnership: The Story of John Lewis and Waitrose*, London: Labatie Books, 2010, pp.67–8.

7. Hoffman, *They Also Serve*, pp.187; 'Shop Girls' Strike', *Daily Mail*, 27 April 1920, p.5.

8. Hoffman, *They Also Serve*, p.187.

9. Ibid., pp.192–3.

10. John Spedan Lewis, *Partnership for All*, London: Kerr Cross Publishing Co., 1948, p.45.

11. Ibid., p.30.

12. Cox, *Spedan's Partnership*, pp.70–75.

13. Chili Bouchier, *Shooting Star*, London: Atlantis, 1995, p.35.

14. Ibid., p.38.

15. Ibid, p.45.

16. Flora Solomon and Barnet Litvinoff, *Baku to Baker Street: The Memoirs of Flora Soloman*, London: Collins, 1984, p.152.

17. Helen Chislett, *Marks in Time: 125 Years of Marks & Spencer*, London: Weidenfeld & Nicolson, 2009, pp.9–12.

18. Photographs of Grainger Market, 1906; Lowestoft, 1910; Staff, Broad Street, Reading, 1912, Marks & Spencer Company Archive.

19. Paul Seaton, *A Sixpenny Romance: Celebrating a Century of*

Value at Woolworths, London: 3D and 6D Pictures Ltd, 2009.

20. Solomon and Litvinoff, *Baku to Baker Street*, p.151.

21. 'Report for 1917', in *Liverpool University Settlement Reports (1908–1918)*, Archive of the University of Liverpool.

22. *Daily Mail*, 'General Electric Stand 69', in *Ideal Labour-Saving Home*, 1920, p.vi.

23. Vera May Ashby, born 1911, audio interview, *Witham Oral Histories*, recorded by Janet Gyford, Essex University, 5 May 1981, Tape 46.

24. Susan Frances Lomax, 'The Department Store & Modern Spectacle 1880–1940', Ph.D. thesis, University of Essex, 2005, p.56.

25. James B. Jefferys, *Retail Trading in Britain*, Cambridge: Cambridge University Press, 1954, pp.50–70.

26. *Store Management*, April 1937, p.209.

27. P. Scott & J. Walker, 'Advertising, Promotion, and the Competitive Advantage of Interwar British Department Stores', *Economic History Review*, vol. 63, no. 4, 2010, p.2.

28. Arnold Bennett letter, 13 March 1929, Harrods Archive, Press Cuttings vol. 156.

29. Bill Lancaster, *The Department Store: A Social History*, London: Leicester University Press, 1995, p.96.

30. Lomax, 'The Department Store', pp.58–65.

31. Solomon and Litvinoff, *Baku to Baker Street*, p.156.

32. E.B. from Leeds, 'Progress 1926–1936', *Sparks Magazine*, Christmas 1936.

33. Solomon and Litvinoff, *Baku to Baker Street*, p.157.

34. Michael Weatherburn, Imperial College Doctoral researcher, specialising in work efficiency and incentive methods in industrial Britain: research conversation with Lauren Bennie; Laurel Graham, 'Lillian Gilbreth and the Mental Revolution at Macy's, 1925–28', *Journal of Management History*, vol. 6, issue 7, 2000, p.285.

35. 'A Guiding Principle in Store Management', *Marks & Spencer Weekly Bulletin*, 4 February 1928.

36. Solomon and Litvinoff, *Baku to Baker Street*, p.162.

37. E.B. from Leeds, 'Progress 1926–1936', *Sparks Magazine*, Christmas 1936.

38. Marks & Spencer, *Staff Management News*, vol. 1, June 1938.

39. Marks & Spencer, 'Brighter Staff Regulations', *Sparks Magazine*, Summer 1937.

40. Private collection of Jemma Jupp, granddaughter of Ethel May Jupp.

Chapter 7: Keep Calm and Carry On Shopping

1. Board of Trade reports, 1937, p.10, cited in Ina Zweiniger-Bargielowska, *Austerity in Britain: Rationing, Controls, and Consumption, 1939–1955*, Oxford: Oxford University Press, 2000, pp.13–14.

2. Paul Rotha, dir. *The Fourth Estate*, London: Realist Film Unit, 1940.

3. Doris, audio interview by Daniel Swan, University of Portsmouth, 2012.

4. Winston Churchill speech to House of Commons, 18 June 1940.

5. Betty Yvonne Costard, audio interview, Imperial War Museum 1989, cat. no. 10879.

6. Beth Lloyd, *De Gruchy's: The History of Jersey's Department Store of Distinction*, London: Hale, 1982, p.119.

7. Ruby Grierson, dir., *They Also Serve*, London: Realist Film unit, 1940.

8. SA/WAR/2/IMA/1/7: Rationing notice, 1940, The Sainsbury Archive, Museum of London Docklands.

9. Sainsbury's Archives Virtual Museum, 2001, http://sainsburys.

lgfl.org.uk/ration_reg.htm (accessed 2 April 2014).

10. HMSO, *How Britain Was Fed in Wartime*, London, 1946.

11. Norman Longmate, *How We Lived Then: A History of Everyday Life during the Second World War*, London: Pimlico, 2002, pp.153–5.

12. SA/WAR/2/1/5: Letter from Alan J. Sainsbury to Mrs E. Sheppard, 25th April 1941, The Sainsbury Archive, Museum of London Docklands.

13. Grace, audio interview by Daniel Swan, University of Portsmouth, 2012.

14. Doris, audio interview by Daniel Swan, University of Portsmouth, 2012.

15. Annie, audio interview by Daniel Swan, University of Portsmouth, 2012.

16. Humphrey Jennings and Harry Watt, dirs, *London Can Take It!*, London, G.P.O, Fim Unit, 1940.

17. Ministry of Information Second World War Official Collection.

18. *The Gazette*, John Lewis Partnership Archives Collection, cited in Peter Cox, *Spedan's Partnership: The Story of John Lewis and Waitrose*, London: Labatie Books, 2010, ch. 11.

19. *The Gazette*, quoted in Cox, *Spedan's Partnership*, p.127.

20. 'Establishing a Temporary Store', www.woolworthsmuseum.co.uk/1940s-defiance.htm, Woolworths Virtual Museum, created by Paul Seaton.

21. Mark Roodhouse, *Black Market Britain 1939–55*, Oxford: Oxford University Press, 2013, p.80.

22. Michael Moss and Alison Turton, *A Legend of Retailing – House of Fraser*, London: Weidenfeld & Nicolson, 1989, p.164.

23. Roodhouse, *Black Market Britain*, p.94.

24. Eric Newby, *A Traveller's Life*, London: Harper Press, 2010, p.43.

25. Featherstone study cited in Roodhouse, *Black Market Britain*, p.99.

26. HMSO, *How Britain Was Fed in Wartime*, p.5. Statistics apply to 1944.

27. Grace, audio interview by Daniel Swan, University of Portsmouth, 2012.

28. Lloyd, *De Gruchy's*, p.126.

29. HMSO, *How Britain was Fed in Wartime*.

30. *Self-Service: The Journal for the Progressive Retailer*, vol. 1, no. 2, December 1951, pp.8–10.

31. Penny Summerfield, *Women Workers in the Second World War: Production and Patriarchy in Conflict*, London: Routledge, 1989, p.31.

32. MOL to MOF, 6 June 1942, cited in Summerfield, ibid., p.113.

33. 'Word War II Air Raid', *Lewisham War Memorials,* Local History and Archives Centre, Lewisham, http://lewisham warmemorials.wikidot.com, accessed 30 March 2014.

34. Helen Chislett, *Marks in Time: 125 Years of Marks & Spencer*, London: Weidenfeld & Nicolson, 2009, p.179.

35. Grace Golden, *A West End Street Scene*, 1945, catalogue ref. INF 3/1738, National Archives.

36. Cox, *Spedan's Partnership*, p.138.

Chapter 8: Chelsea Girls and Counter-Cultures

1. Mary Quant, *Quant by Quant,* London: Pan Books, 1967, pp.46–8; Richard Lester, *Boutique London: A History: King's Road to Carnaby Street*, London: ACC Editions, 2010, pp.10–11.

2. Cited in Alwyn Turner, *The Biba Experience*, Woodbridge: Antique Collectors Club, *c.*2004, p.9.

3. Quant, *Quant by Quant*, pp.46–8.

4. Marnie Fogg, *Boutique: A '60s Cultural Phenomenon*, London: Mitchell Beazley, 2003, p.26.

5. Peter Stanford, Interview with Diana Melly, *Independent on Sunday*, 30 October 2005.

6. 'The British Boutique Boom! Part 1', *Rave*, September 1965.

7. Millicent Bultitude, *Get Dressed: A Useful Guide to London's Boutiques*, The Garnstone Press, 1966.

8. Kate Finnigan, Interview with Celia Birtwell, *Telegraph*, 21 August 2011.

9. Nancy R. Ross, 'Britain's Fashion Revolution', *Spokesman Review*, 27 May 1966.

10. Veronica Horwell, Obituary of John Stephen, *Guardian*, 9 February 2004; Clare Lomas, '"Men Don't Wear Velvet You Know!" Fashionable Gay Masculinity and the Shopping Experience', *Oral History*, vol. 35, issue 1, 2007, pp.85–6.

11. Turner, *The Biba Experience*, p.12.

12. Barbara Hulanicki, *From A to Biba: The Autobiography of Barbara Hulanicki*, London: V&A Publishing, 1983, p.79; Turner, *The Biba Experience*, p.16.

13. Turner, *The Biba Experience*, p.11.

14. Hulanicki, *From A to Biba*, p.78.

15. Turner, *The Biba Experience*, pp.23–4; Interview with Rosie Young, *Marshwood Vale Magazine*, 31 January 2013, www.marshwoodvale.com/people/articles/people/rosie-young (accessed 21 March 2014); Fogg, *Boutique*, p.179.

16. Peter Stanford, Interview with Diana Melly, *Independent on Sunday*, 30 October 2005.

17. Fogg, *Boutique*, p.47; British Style Genius, www.bbc.co.uk/britishstylegenius/archive.shtml (accessed 21 March 2014); The Look, http://rockpopfashion.com/blog/?p=43 (accessed 21 March 2014).

18. Manchester Beat, www.manchesterbeat.com/shops/clothes/

index.php (accessed 21 March 2014); Fogg, *Boutique*, p.126.

19. Tony Greenway, 'Pollyanna's Rita Britton talks to *Yorkshire Life* about Barnsley roots', *Yorkshire Life*, 12 December 2010, http://www.yorkshirelife.co.uk/people/celebrity-interviews/pollyanna_s_rita_britton_talks_to_yorkshire_life about_barnsley_roots_1_1631706 (accessed 21 March 2014).

20. Pollyanna, www.pollyanna.com/page/about-us (accessed 21 March 2014).

21. Interview with Vanessa Denza, Victoria and Albert Museum, http://www.vam.ac.uk/content/articles/i/vanessa-denza-mbe/ (accessed 21 March 2014).

22. Fogg, *Boutique*, p.22; Quant, *Quant by Quant*, p.80.

23. Brian Braithwaite, *Women's Magazines*, London: Peter Owen, 1995, p.88.

24. Ibid.

25. Olive Robinson and John Wallace, 'Part-time Employment and Low Pay in Retail Distribution in Britain', *Industrial Relations Journal*, vol. 5, issue 1, 1974, p.39.

26. Ibid.

27. Kira Cochrane, 'Forty Years of Women's Liberation', *Guardian*, 26 February 2010, http://www.theguardian.com/lifeandstyle/2010/feb/26/forty-years-womens-liberation (accessed 21 March 2014). See also Michelene Wandor's collection of interviews with those present: *Once a Feminist: Stories of a Generation*, London: Virago, 1990.

28. Michelene Wandor, 'Interview with Audrey Wise', in her *Once a Feminist: Stories of a Generation*, London: Virago, 1990, pp.200–205.

29. Ibid., p.210. See also Julie Langdon and Hilary Wainwright, Obituary of Audrey Wise, *Guardian*, 5 September 2000.

30. 'Women's Charter Falls By the Wayside', *Guardian*, 3 September 1975, p.7.

270

31. Gordon Carr, *The Angry Brigade: The Cause and the Case*, London: Victor Gollancz, 1975.

32. Hulanicki, *From A to Biba*, p.120; Turner, *The Biba Experience*, pp.47–9.

33. Carr, *The Angry Brigade*, p.104.

34. Martin Bright, 'Look Back in Anger', *Observer*, 3 February 2002, www.theguardian.com/theobserver/2002/feb/03/features.magazine27 (accessed 21 March 2014).

35. BBC: On This Day, 10 September 1973, http://news.bbc.co.uk/onthisday/hi/dates/stories/september/10/newsid_3914000/3914415.stm (accessed 21 March 2014).

36. 'British Boutique Labels of the 1960s and 1970s: Bus Stop', Candy Says, www.candysays.co.uk/blogs/vintage-blog/6972642-british-boutique-labels-of-the-1960s-and-1970s-bus-stop (accessed 21 March 2014); see also Lee Bender, *Bus Stop and the Influence of the 70s on Fashion Today*, London: A&C Black Visual Arts, 2010.

37. 'House of Fraser: Brief Summary of Company History', version 2, December 2011, University of Glasgow Archive Services.

38. Obituary of Josephine Esther Bruce', *Independent*, 29 August 1994.

39. Personal communication with Stephen Bourne, nephew of Esther Bruce and historian of black British life, April 2014; see also John Rex and Sally Tomlinson, *Colonial Immigrants in a British City: A Class Analysis*, London, Routledge and Kegan Paul, 1979.

40. Susan Okokon, *Black Londoners: A History*, Stroud: The History Press, 2009.

41. Christopher Middleton, 'The Changing face of Britain's Arndale Centres', *Guardian*, 4 April 2001.

42. Daniel Miller, Peter Jackson, Nigel Thrift, Beverley Holbrook and Michael Rowlands, *Shopping, Place and Identity*, London: Routledge, 1998, p.33.

43. Ibid., p.35.

44. Margaret Thatcher, *The Path to Power*, London: HarperCollins, 1995, p.5.

45. Penny Junor, *Margaret Thatcher: Wife, Mother, Politician*, London: Sidgwick and Jackson, 1984, p.44.

46. Margaret Thatcher Foundation, 'Remarks visiting Brent Cross Shopping Centre', 17 February 1978.

47. Thatcher, *The Path to Power*, p.4.

Epilogue

1. For extended discussion, see J.A.N. Bamfield, *Retail Futures 2018: Shop Numbers, Online and The High Street*, Nottingham: Centre for Retail Research, 2013.

2. Mary Portas, 'The Portas Review: An independent review into the future of our high streets', December 2011, www.maryportas.com (accessed February 2014); Bill Grimsey, *Sold Out*, Croydon: Filament Publishing, 2012; Rosamund Urwin, 'How to get your PG tips', *Evening Standard* (London), 27 February 2014.

3. British Retail Consortium, *Retail in Society: Britain's Favourite Job*, November 2011, p.19.

4. UK Commission for Employment and Skills, *Working Futures 2012–1022*, Evidence Report 83, March 2014. See Table 4.2: Females. Occupational Categories.

5. https://nationalcareersservice.direct.gov.uk/advice/planning/jobprofiles/Pages/salesassistant.aspx (accessed 8 May 2014).

6. Jenny Shaw, *Shopping: Social and Cultural Perspectives*, London: Polity Press, 2010.

7. Daniel Miller, *A Theory of Shopping*, London: Polity Press, 1998.

8. Tim Walker, 'We bought what we didn't want', *Independent*, 19 June 2009, p.32.

SELECT BIBLIOGRAPHY

Primary Sources

Ablett, William, *Reminiscences of an Old Draper*, London: S. Low, Marston, Searle & Rivington, 1876

Acton, Sir William, *Prostitution: Its Moral, Social and Sanitary Aspects*, London: J. Churchill, 1857

Applin, Arthur, *Shop Girls: A Novel with Purpose*, London: Mills & Boon, 1914

Ashby, Vera May, born 1911, audio interview, Witham Oral Histories, recorded by Janet Gyford, University of Essex, 5 May 1981, Tape 46

Bender, Lee, *Bus Stop and the Influence of the 70s on Fashion Today*, London: A&C Black Visual Arts, 2010

Bondfield, Margaret, *Socialism for Shop Assistants*, London: Clarion Press, 1909

Bondfield, Margaret, *A Life's Work*, London: Hutchinson & Co., 1948

Borsa, Mario, *The English Stage of To-day*, London: John Lane, 1908

Boucherett, Jesse, 'On the Obstacles to the Employment of Women', *English Woman's Journal*, vol. 4, February 1860, pp. 54–60

Boucherett, Jesse, 'Association for Promoting the Employment of Women', *English Woman's Journal*, vol. 4, September 1859

Boucherett, Jesse, 'Letter to the Editor', *The Spectator*, 26 July 1873

Boucherett, Jesse, 'The Nine Hours Bill and the Shop Hours Regulation Bill', *The Englishwoman's Review*, 1873, pp. 209–12

Bouchier, Chili, *Shooting Star*, London: Atlantis, 1995

Bullock, Thomas Austin, *Bradshaw's Illustrated Guide to Manchester*, Manchester: Bradshaw & Blacklock, 1857

Briggs, Asa, *Friends of the People: The Centenary History of Lewis's*, [no publication place]: Batsford, 1956

Butson, Mrs Strange, 'The Standing Evil – A Plea for Shopgirls', *The Girl's Own Paper*, Vol 1, 1880, p. 612

Cavers, Charles, *Hades! The Ladies!,* London: Gurney & Jackson, 1933

Chitty, Joseph and Lely, J.M., *The Statutes of Practical Utility, 1235– 1895*, London: Sweet and Maxwell, 1902

Copeman, John, and sons, *Copeman's of Norwich*, Norwich: Jarrold, 1946

Corina, Maurice, *Fine Silks and Oak Counters: Debenhams, 1778- 1978*, London: Hutchinson, 1978

Costard, Betty Yvonne, audio interview, Imperial War Museum, 1989, cat. no. 10879

Dam, H.J.W., *The Shop Girl. A Musical Comedy*, London: 1894

Darlington, Thomas (ed.), *Memoir of Emerson Muschamp Bainbridge of Newcastle-on-Tyne*, Edinburgh: R&R Clark, 1893

Davidson, J.E., *What Our Daughters Can Do For Themselves, A Handbook of Women's Employments*, London: Smith, Elder & Co., 1894

Dickens, Charles, *Dickens' Dictionary of London*, London: 1879

Duff Gordon, Lucy, *Discretions and Indiscretions*, London: Jarrolds, 1932

Foster, Richard, *F. Cape & Co. of St Ebbe's Street, Oxford*, Oxford: Oxford City and County Museum, 1973

Goldsman, E.N., *Show Window Backgrounds*, London: Blandford Press, 1930

Grace, Doris and Annie, audio interviews by Daniel Swan, University of Portsmouth, 2012

Grierson, Ruby, dir., *They Also Serve*, British Film Institute, London: Realist Film Unit, 1940

Grogan, Mercy, *How Women May Earn a Living*, London: Cassell, Petter, 1880

Hall, Owen, *The Girl from Kay's. A New and Original Musical Play* (lyrics by Adrian Ross and Claude Aveling), London: Chappell & Co., 1903

Hallsworth, Joseph and Davies, Rhys, *Life of Shop Assistants*, Manchester, 1910

Hamilton, Cicely, *Diana of Dobson's. A Romantic Comedy in Four Acts*, London: Century, 1909

Hamilton, Mary Agnes, *Margaret Bondfield*, London: Leonard Parsons, 1924

Harrods, *A Story of British Achievement, 1849–1949*, London: Harrods, 1949

HMSO, *How Britain Was Fed in Wartime*, London, 1946

Hoffman, Phillip Christopher, *They Also Serve: The Story of the Shop Worker*, London: Porcupine Press, 1949

Holyoake, George Jacob, *Self-Help by the People: History of the Rochdale Equitable Pioneers, Part 1, 1844–1857*, London, Swan Sonnenschein & Co, 1907

Howard, Delisia, *In Biba*, London: Hazard Books, 2004

Hudson, Derek (ed.), *Munby: Man of Two Worlds: The Life and Diaries of Arthur J. Munby, 1828–1910*, London: John Murray, 1972

Hulanicki, Barbara, *From A to Biba: The Autobiography of Barbara Hulanicki*, London: V&A Publishing, 1983

Jefferys, James B., *Retail Trading in Britain, 1850–1950*, Cambridge: Cambridge University Press, 1954

Jennings, Humphrey and Watt, Harry, dirs., *London Can Take It!*, London: G.P.O. Film Unit, 1940

Jeune, Lady, 'The Ethics of Shopping', *Fortnightly Review*, vol. 63, 1895, p.123

Lancaster, Osbert, *All From Memory*, Cambridge: Mass.: John Murray, 1953

Lewis, John Spedan, *Partnership for All*, London: Kerr-Cross Publishing Co., 1948

Linton, Eliza, 'The Girl of the Period', *The Saturday Review*, 14 March 1868, pp.339–40

Linton, Eliza, 'The Philosophy of Shopping', *The Saturday Review*, 16 October 1875, pp.488–9

Llewelyn Davies, Margaret (ed.), *Life As We Have Known It*, London: Hogarth Press, 1931

Loftie, M. J., *Social Twitters*, London: Macmillan and Co., 1879

Malvery, Olive Christian, *A Year and a Day*, London: Hutchinson, 1912

Martindale, Hilda, *From One Generation to Another, 1839–1944: A Book of Memoirs*, London: George Allen & Unwin, 1944

Mayhew, Henry, *London Labour and the London Poor. Volume 1: The London Street Folk*, London: [no named publisher], 1851

Mayhew, Henry, *The Shops and Companies of London and the Trades and Manufactories of Great Britain*, London: [no named publisher], 1865

Melly, Diana, *Take a Girl Like Me*, London: Chatto & Windus, 2005

Meyer, Mrs Carl and Black, Clementina, *Makers of Our Clothes: A Case for Trade Boards, Being the Result of a Year's Investigation into the Work of Women in London in the Tailoring, Dressmaking and Underclothing Trades*, London: Duckworth and Co., 1909

Millward, Michael and Coe, Brian, compiled by, *Victorian Townscape: The Work of Samuel Smith*, London: Ward Lock, 1974

Newby, Eric, *Something Wholesale: My life and Times in the Rag Trade*, London: Pan, 1985.

Newby, Eric, *A Traveller's Life*, London: Harper Press, 2010

Obituary of Jesse Boucherett, *The Times*, 21 October 1905

Olivia [surname unknown], *Olivia's Shopping and How She Does It: A Prejudiced Guide to the London Shops*, London: Gay and Bird, 1906

Pankhurst, Christabel, *Unshackled: The Story of How We Won the Vote*, London: Hutchinson, 1959

Pearce, Charles E., *The Soul of a Shopgirl*, London: Aldine serial novels, 1915

Philipps, Leonora, *Dictionary of Employments Open to Women*, London: Women's Institute, 1898

Rotha, Paul, dir., *The Fourth Estate*, London: Realist Film Unit, 1940

Quant, Mary, *Quant by Quant*, London: Pan Books Ltd, 1967

Smith, Thomas Davidson, unpublished autobiography, Lancaster, 1902–3

Snowden, Philip, *The Living Wage*, London: Hodder and Stoughton, 1912

Solomon, Flora and Litvinoff, Barnet, *Baku to Baker Street: The Memoirs of Flora Solomon*, London: Collins, 1984

Sutherst, Thomas, *Death and Disease Behind the Counter*, London: Kegan Paul, Trench & Co., 1884

Tait, William, *Magdalenism: An Inquiry into the Extent, Causes and Consequences of Prostitution in Edinburgh*, Edinburgh: 1840

Tallis, John, *London Street Views*, London: London Topographical Society, 1969

Thatcher, Margaret, *The Path to Power*, London: HarperCollins, 1995

Thomson, John and Smith, Adolphe, *Street Life in London*, London: S. Low, Marston, Searle and Rivington, 1877

Trollope, Anthony, *London Tradesmen*, London: E. Mathews & Marrot, 1928, (reprinted from *The Pall Mall Gazette*)

Wey, Francis, *Les Anglais Chez Eux (A Frenchman Sees the English in the Fifties)*, London: Sidgwick & Jackson, 1935

Wood-Allen, Dr Mary, *What a Young Woman Ought to Know*, Philadelphia: Vir Publishing Co.,1905

Principal newspapers and journals

The Daily Chronicle

Daily Express

Daily Mail

The Daily News

The Drapers Record

English Woman's Journal

Forget-Me-Not

The Pall Mall Gazette

The Shop Assistant

The Spectator

Store Management

The Times

T. P.'s and Cassell's Weekly

Votes for Women

Women's Industrial News

Principal store archives and store journals

Co-operative News

The Gazette (John Lewis)

Harrodian Gazette

Harrods Store Archive, Harrods, London

House of Fraser Archive, University of Glasgow Archive Services

John Lewis Partnership Archives Collection, Heritage Centre, Cookham

Marks and Spencer Company Archive, University of Leeds

The Sainsbury Archive, Museum of London Docklands

Selfridges Archives Collection, Selfridges, London
Sparks Magazine
Whiteley's Store Archives, City of Westminster Archive Centre
Woolworth Virtual Museum, www.woolworthsmuseum.co.uk

Secondary Sources

Adburgham, Alison, *Army and Navy, Yesterday's Shopping: The Army & Navy Stores Catalogue 1907*, Newton Abbot, David & Charles Ltd, 1969

Airey, Angela and Airey, John, *The Bainbridges of Newcastle: A Family History 1679–1976*, [imprint unknown], 1979

Atkinson, Diane, *Votes for Women: Women and the Suffrage Movement*, Cambridge: Cambridge University Press, 1988

Benson, John, *The Working Class in Britain 1850–1939*, London: Longman, 1989

Bowlby, Rachel, *Carried Away: The Invention of Modern Shopping*, London: Faber and Faber, 2000

Braithwaite, Brian, *Women's Magazines*, London: Peter Owen, 1995

Burnett, John (ed.), *Useful Toil: Autobiographies of Working People from the 1820s to the 1920s*, London: Allen Lane, 1974.

Carr, Gordon, *The Angry Brigade: The Cause and the Case*, London: Victor Gollancz, 1975

Chislett, Helen, *Marks in Time: 125 Years of Marks & Spencer*, London: Weidenfeld & Nicolson, 2009

Cox, Pamela, *Bad Girls in Britain: Gender, Justice and Welfare 1900–1950*, Basingstoke: Palgrave, 2012

Cox, Peter, *Spedan's Partnership: The Story of John Lewis and Waitrose*, London: Labatie Books, 2010

Crawford, Elizabeth, *The Women's Suffrage Movement in Britain and Ireland: A Regional Survey*, London: Routledge, 2000

Crossick, Geoffrey and Haupt, Heinz-Gerhard (eds.), *Shopkeepers and Artisans in Nineteenth-Century Europe*, London: Methuen, 1984

Crossick, Geoffrey and Haupt, Heinz-Gerhard (eds.), *The Petite Bourgeoisie in Europe 1780–1914: Enterprise, Family and Independence*, London: Routledge, 1995

Crossick, Geoffrey and Jaumin, Serge (eds.), *Cathedrals of Consumption: The European Department Store, 1850–1939*, Aldershot: Ashgate, 1998

Dale, Tim, *Harrods: A Palace in Knightsbridge*, London: Harrods Publishing, 1995

Davies, David Wyn, *Owen Owen: Victorian Draper*, Aberystwyth: Gwasg Cambria, 1983

Davin, Anna, 'City Girls: Young Women, New Employment and the City: London, 1880–1910', in Mary Jo Maynes, Birgitte Soland and Christina Benninghaus (eds.), *Secret Gardens, Satanic Mills: Placing Girls in European History, 1750–1960*, Bloomington: Indiana University Press, 2005

Duff, Ursula Lubbock Grant (ed.), *The life-work of Lord Avebury (Sir John Lubbock), 1834–1913*, London: Watts and Co., 1924

Fogg, Marnie, *Boutique: A '60s Cultural Phenomenon*, London: Mitchell Beazley, 2003

Gaffin, Jean and Thoms, David, *Caring and Sharing: The Centenary History of the Co-operative Women's Guild*, Manchester: Holyoake Books, 1993

Giles, Judy, *The Parlour and the Suburb: Domestic Identities, Class, Femininity and Modernity*, Oxford: Berg, 2004

Graham, Laurel, 'Lillian Gilbreth and the Mental Revolution at Macy's, 1925–1928', *Journal of Management History*, vol. 6, issue 7, 2000, pp.285–305

Gunn, Simon and Bell, Rachel, *Middle Classes: Their Rise and Sprawl*, London: Phoenix, 2003

Gurney, Peter, *Co-operative Culture and the Politics of Consumption in England, 1870–1930*, Manchester: Manchester University Press, 1996

Guyford, Janet, 'Shop People and Their Customers, Witham, Essex, 1900–1939', University of Essex, MA thesis, 1981

Harrison, Patricia Greenwood, *Connecting Links: The British and American Woman Suffrage Movements, 1900–1914*, Westport, Conn.: Greenwood, 2000

Hilton, Matthew, *Consumerism in Twentieth-Century Britain: The Search for a Historical Movement*, Cambridge: Cambridge University Press, 2003

Holcombe, Lee, *Victorian Ladies at Work: Middle-Class Working Women in England and Wales, 1850–1914*, Newton Abbot: David and Charles, 1973

Honeycombe, Gordon, *Selfridges: Seventy-Five Years, The Story of the Store 1909–1984*, London: Park Lane Press, 1984

Hosgood, C. P., 'The "Pigmies of Commerce" and the Working-Class Community: Small Shopkeepers in England, 1870–1914', *Journal of Social History*, vol. 22, issue 3, 1989, pp.439–60

Hosgood, Christopher, '"Mercantile Monasteries": Shops, Shop Assistants, and Shop Life in Late-Victorian and Edwardian Britain', *Journal of British Studies*, vol. 38, no. 3, 1999, pp.322–52

Housego, Molly and Storey, Neil R., *The Women's Suffrage Movement*, Oxford: Shire Library, 2012

Hunt, Karen, 'Negotiating the Boundaries of the Domestic: British Socialist Women and the Politics of Consumption', *Women's History Review*, vol. 9, no. 2, 2000, pp. 389–410

Jarvis, Anthea, *Liverpool Fashion: Its Makers and Wearers: The Dressmaking Trade in Liverpool, 1830–1940*, Liverpool: Merseyside County Museums, 1981

Jeffs, Muriel, 'Margaret Llewelyn Davies and the Women's Co-operative Guild', in Bill Lancaster and Paddy Maguire (eds.), *Towards the Co-operative Commonwealth: Essays in the History of Co-operation*, Loughborough Co-operative College, 1996

Junor, Penny, *Margaret Thatcher: Wife, Mother, Politician*, London: Sidgwick and Jackson, 1984

Kaplan, Joel and Stowell, Sheila, *Theatre and Fashion: Oscar Wilde to the Suffragettes*, Cambridge: Cambridge University Press, 1994

Lambert, Richard S., *The Universal Provider, A Study of William Whiteley and the Rise of the London Department Store*, London: Harrap, 1938

Lancaster, Bill, *The Department Store: A Social History*, London: Leicester University Press, 1995

Lester, Richard, *Boutique London: A History: King's Road to Carnaby Street*, London: ACC Editions, 2010

Lloyd, Beth, *De Gruchy's: The History of Jersey's Department Store of Distinction*, London: Hale, 1982

Longmate, Norman, *How We Lived Then: A History of Everyday Life During the Second World War*, London: Pimlico, 2002

Lomas Clare, '"Men Don't Wear Velvet You Know!" Fashionable Gay Masculinity and the Shopping Experience', *Oral History*, vol. 35, issue 1, 2007, pp. 80–92

Lomax, Susan Frances, 'The Department Store and The Creation of the Spectacle 1880–1940', Colchester: University of Essex, PhD thesis, 2005

McRobbie, Angela, *British Fashion Design: Rag Trade or Image Industry?*, London: Routledge, 1998

McRobbie, Angela, *Feminism and Youth Culture*, Basingstoke: Macmillan, 2000

Miller, Daniel, *A Theory of Shopping*, London: Polity Press, 1998

Miller, Daniel, Jackson, Peter, Thrift, Nigel, Holbrook, Beverley and Rowlands, Michael, *Shopping, Place and Identity*, London: Routledge, 1998

Morrison, Kathryn, *English Shops and Shopping: An Architectural History*, New Haven, Conn., and London: Yale University Press, 2003

Moss, Michael and Turton, Alison, *A Legend of Retailing – House of Fraser*, London: Weidenfeld and Nicolson, 1989

Nava, Mica, *Changing Cultures: Feminism, Youth and Consumerism*, London: Sage, 1992

Nava, Mica, *Visceral Cosmopolitanism: Gender, Culture and the Normalisation of Difference*, New York: Berg, 2007

Okokon, Susan, *Black Londoners: A History*, Stroud: The History Press, 2009

Patton, Mark, *Science, Politics, and Business in the Work of Sir John Lubbock: A Man of Universal Mind*, Aldershot: Ashgate, 2007

Pettinger, Lynne, 'Branded Stores, Branded Workers: Selling and Service in Fashion Retail', Colchester: University of Essex, Ph.D thesis, 2003

Phillips, Derek, *The Wonder of Woolies: Memories from Both Sides of the Counter of Britain's Best-Loved Store*, Gosport: Footplate Publishing, 2009

Porter Benson, Susan, *Counter Cultures: Saleswomen, Managers, and Customers in American Department Stores, 1890–1940*, Urbana: University of Illinois Press, 1986

Pumphrey, R.J., 'The Forgotten Man: Sir John Lubbock, F.R.S.', *Notes and Records of the Royal Society of London*, vol. 13, no. 1, June 1958, pp. 49–58

Rappaport, Erika D., '"The Halls of Temptation": Gender, Politics, and the Construction of the Department Store in Late Victorian London', *Journal of British Studies*, vol. 35, no. 1, January 1996

Rappaport, Erika, *Shopping for Pleasure: Women in the Making of London's West End*, Chichester: Princeton University Press, 2001

Reekie, Gail, *Temptations: Sex, Selling and the Department Store*, St Leonards, NSW: Allen & Unwin, 1993

Rendall, Jane, '"Industrious Females" and "Professional Beauties":

Or Fine Articles for Sale in the Burlington Arcade', in Iain Borden et al. (eds.), *Strangely Familiar: Narratives of Architecture in the City*, London: Routledge, 1996

Richardson, Sir William, *A Union of Many Trades: The History of USDAW*, Manchester: USDAW, 1979

Roberts, Elizabeth, *Women's Work 1840–1940*, Basingstoke: Macmillan, 1988

Robertson, Nicole, *The Co-operative Movement and Communities in Britain, 1914–1960: Minding Their Own Business*, Farnham: Ashgate, 2010

Robinson, Olive and Wallace, John, 'Part-time Employment and Low Pay in Retail Distribution in Britain', *Industrial Relations Journal*, vol. 5, issue 1, 1974

Roodhouse, Mark, *Black Market Britain, 1939–55*, Oxford: Oxford University Press, 2013

Sanders, Lise Shapiro, *Consuming Fantasies: Labor, Leisure, and the London Shopgirl, 1880–1920*, Columbus: Ohio State University Press, 2006

Scott, Gillian, *Feminism and the Politics of Working Women: The Women's Co-operative Guild, 1880s to the Second World War*, London: UCL Press, 1998

Scott, Peter and Walker, James, 'Advertising, Promotion, and the Competitive Advantage of Interwar British Department Stores', *Economic History Review*, vol. 63, issue 4, 2010, pp. 1105–28

Seaton, Paul, *A Sixpenny Romance: Celebrating a Century of Value at Woolworths*, London: 3D and 6D Pictures Ltd., 2009

Shaw, Jenny, *Shopping: Social and Cultural Perspectives*, London: Polity Press, 2010

Shonfield, Zuzanna, *The Precariously Privileged: A Professional Family in Victorian London*, Oxford: Oxford University Press, 1987

Storch, Robert D. (ed.), *Popular Culture and Custom in Nineteenth-Century England*, London: Croom Helm, 1982

Stratmann, Linda, *Whiteley's Folly: The Life and Death of a Salesman*, London: The History Press, 2004

Summerfield, Penny, *Women Workers in the Second World War: Production and Patriarchy in Conflict*, London: Routledge, 1989

Thom, Deborah, 'Women and Work in Wartime Britain', in Richard Wall and Jay Winter (eds.), *The Upheaval of War*, Cambridge: Cambridge University Press, 1988, pp. 297–326

Thom, Deborah, *Nice Girls and Rude Girls: Women Workers in World War One*, Cambridge: Cambrige University Press, 1998

Thompson, James, 'Political Economy, Labour and the Minimum Wage', in Ewen Green and Duncan Tanner (eds.), *The Strange Survival of Liberal England*, Cambridge: Cambridge University Press, 2007, pp. 62-88

Todd, Selina, *Young Women, Work, and Family in England 1918–1950*, Oxford: Oxford University Press, 2005

Toulmin, Vanessa, Popple, Simon and Russell, Patrick, *The Lost World of Mitchell and Kenyon: Edwardian Britain on Film*, London: BFI Publishing, 2004

Turner, Alwyn, *The Biba Experience*, Woodbridge: Antique Collectors Club, *c*.2004

Usdaw, *Usdaw's History*, www.usdaw.org.uk/aboutus/usdawshistory.aspx (accessed 20 March 2014)

Walkowitz, Judith, *Prostitution and Victorian Society*, Cambridge: Cambridge University Press, 1980

Walkowitz, Judith, *City of Dreadful Delight: Narratives of Sexual Danger in Late-Victorian London*, London: Virago, 1992

Wandor, Michelene, *Once a Feminist: Stories of a Generation*, London: Virago, 1990

Whitaker, Jan, *The Department Store: History, Design, Display*, London: Thames & Hudson, 2011

Whitaker, Wilfred, *Victorian and Edwardian Shopworkers*, Newton Abbot: David and Charles, 1973

Wilkinson, Amanda, 'Women and Occupations in the Census of England and Wales: 1851–1901', unpub. Ph.D thesis, University of Essex, 2012

Winstanley, Michael, *The Shopkeeper's World, 1830–1914*, Manchester: Manchester University Press, 1983

Winstanley, Michael (ed.), *A Traditional Grocer: T.D. Smith's of Lancaster 1858–1981*, Occasional Paper 21, Centre for North-West Regional Studies, Lancaster: University of Lancaster, 1991

Woodhead, Lindy, *Shopping, Seduction and Mr Selfridge*, London: Profile Books, 2007

Woodward, Joan, *The Saleswoman: A Study in Attitudes and Behaviour in Retail Distribution*, London: Isaac Pitman & Sons, 1960

Worley, Tom, *Witney in Old Photographs*, Gloucester: Alan Sutton, 1987

Worth, Rachel, *Fashion for the People: A History of Clothing at Marks & Spencer*, Oxford: Berg, 2007

Zweiniger-Bargielowska, Ina, *Austerity in Britain: Rationing, Controls and Consumption, 1939–1955*, Oxford: Oxford University Press, 2000

Zweiniger-Bargielowska, Ina (ed.), *Women in Twentieth-Century Britain*, Harlow: Pearson/Longman, 2001

INDEX